D0025379

WITHDRAWN
Von Riesen Library
MoCook Community College

The Psychology of Terrorism

The Psychology of Terrorism

$\blacklozenge$

Volume I
A Public Understanding

Edited by Chris E. Stout
Foreword by Klaus Schwab

Psychological Dimensions to War and Peace
Harvey Langholtz, Series Editor

PRAEGER

Westport, Connecticut
London

von Riesen Library
McCook Community College

Library of Congress Cataloging-in-Publication Data

The psychology of terrorism / edited by Chris E. Stout ; foreword by Klaus Schwab.
    p. cm.—(Psychological dimensions to war and peace, ISSN 1540–5265)
    Includes bibliographical references and index.
    ISBN 0–275–97771–4 (set)—ISBN 0–275–97865–6 (vol. I)—ISBN 0–275–97866–4
(vol. II)—ISBN 0–275–97867–2 (vol. III)—ISBN 0–275–97868–0 (vol. IV)
    1. Terrorism—Psychological aspects. 2. Terrorists—Psychology. 3.
Terrorism—Prevention. I. Stout, Chris E. II. Series.
HV6431 .P798 2002
303.6'25—dc21   2002072845

British Library Cataloguing in Publication Data is available.

Copyright © 2002 by Chris E. Stout

All rights reserved. No portion of this book may be
reproduced, by any process or technique, without the
express written consent of the publisher.

Library of Congress Catalog Card Number: 2002072845
ISBN: set: 0-275-97771-4
      v.I: 0-275-97865-6
      v.II: 0-275-97866-4
      v.III: 0-275-97867-2
      v.IV: 0-275-97868-0
ISSN: 1540-5265

First published in 2002

Praeger Publishers, 88 Post Road West, Westport, CT 06881
An imprint of Greenwood Publishing Group, Inc.
www.praeger.com

Printed in the United States of America

The paper used in this book complies with the
Permanent Paper Standard issued by the National
Information Standards Organization (Z39.48-1984).

10 9 8 7 6 5 4 3 2 1

To my parents, Carlos L. and Helen E. (Simmons) Stout,
to my wife and soulmate, Dr. Karen Beckstrand, and
to my children and heroes, Grayson Beckstrand Stout and
Annika Beckstrand Stout.

You all have taught and continue to teach me so very much.

Contents

Foreword

First of all, I want to note the impressive collection of academics, thinkers, activists, and clinicians congregated in this set of volumes. Through their active engagement, the result is a series of works that crosscut an immense range of related factors—historical contexts; group dynamics; social psychological aspects; behavioral, forensic, psychopathological, evolutionary theory, peace-building, and conflict resolution perspectives; as well as the political, clinical, and social aspects of prevention, intervention, and security issues. Global perspectives vis-à-vis understanding, empathy, bias, prejudice, racism, and hate are also represented.

This group of authors offers a unique combination of talents and viewpoints rarely seen in the worlds of academia or activism. Their work and voices move knowledge and understanding forward in a way that will serve as a framework and catalyst for readers to consider ways in which to respond to terrorism in its various displays. Dr. Stout has fostered a self-organizing environment that has enabled this work to be a collaboration of ideas that goes beyond the traditional and almost complacent; instead it is realistically erudite and even provocative in some instances.

I suspect that the readership will likewise be broad and crosscutting—including academics and departments of psychology, political science, religious studies, military sciences, law enforcement, public health, sociology, anthropology, social work, and law, as well as the lay public and the media, policy makers, elected government officials, leaders of nongovernmental organizations, ambassadors and diplomats, military leaders, law enforcement professionals, the intelligence community, and members of think tanks and private and public policy institutes and centers.

Such integration of diversity in thought and perspective parallels our "Forum Plus" strategy at the World Economic Forum. This strategy aims to advance critical issues on the global agenda through the creation of task forces and initiatives that integrate business, governments, international organizations, civil society, academics, and technical experts.

Similarly, Dr. Stout has been successful in gathering some of the greatest thinkers on this topic from around the world, including Fulbright scholars, a Kellogg International fellow, a Pulitzer Prize winner, a Beale fellow (Harvard), a *boursier de la Confédération Suisse*, a Medical Research Council fellow, American Psychological Association fellows, a Royal College of Physicians fellow, an American College of Psychiatrists fellow, American Psychiatric Association fellows, and a Regents scholar. Authors represent a wide array of academic institutions: the University of Pennsylvania; Harvard Medical School; Rutgers University; Princeton University; Northwestern University Medical School; Mount Sinai School of Medicine; Nelson Mandela School of Medicine, University of Natal, South Africa; George Mason University; University of Massachusetts; University of Michigan; Civitan International Research Center at the University of Alabama; Institute for Mental Health Initiatives at George Washington University; Marylhurst University; Portland State University; Southwest Texas State University; Al Aksa University in Gaza; University of Lagos, Akoka-Yaba, Lagos, Nigeria; University of Wisconsin; Northern Arizona University; Bryn Mawr College; Randolph-Macon College; Illinois State University; University of South Florida; Elmhurst College; Howard University; University of Texas Health Science Center; Texas A&M College of Medicine; University of California; Saybrook Graduate School and Research Center; New School University; and New York University. Authors also represent the United Nations (a Humanitarian Affairs Officer, an Assistant to the Under-Secretary-General for Peacekeeping, and an Assistant to the Special Representative of the Secretary-General to the former Yugoslavia and to NATO), the Disaster Mental Health Institute; the Comprehensive Medical Center in Dubai, United Arab Emirates; GGZ Den Bosch/Outpatient and Daytreatment Centre for Refugees in the Netherlands; the Human Sciences Research Council in South Africa; Delta Psychiatric Teaching Hospital in Poortugaal, the Netherlands; Maagalim–Institute of Psychotherapy and Counseling in Tel Aviv; the United Nations Development Program for Women; the USAID Rwanda Rule of Law Project; and the Christian Children's Fund.

Many of the authors are also current or past officers of a wide variety of professional associations and other organizations: the World Psychiatric Association on Urban Mental Health; the Commission on Global Psychiatry of the American Psychiatric Association; the South African Institute for Traumatic Stress; Solomon Asch's Center for Ethno-Political Conflict at the University of Pennsylvania; the American Psychological Association Committee on Global Violence and Security within Division 48; the Society for the Study of Peace, Conflict, and Violence; the Association for Humanistic Psychology; the Non Governmental Organizations Executive Committee on Mental Health—UN; Psychologists for Social Responsibility; the Conflict Resolution Action Committee; the Conflict Resolution Working Group (of Division 48 of the American Psychological Association); the Philadelphia Project for Global Security; the American Academy of Psychiatry and the Law; the National Council of State Medical Directors; the Board of Presidents of the Socialist Countries' Psychiatric Associations in Sofia, Bulgaria; the Society for the Study of Peace, Conflict and Violence: Peace Psychology Division of the American Psychological Association (APA); the International Society for Political Psychology; the Committee for International Liaisons for the Division of International Psychology (APA); and the Common Bond Institute.

Dr. Stout has also assembled some of the best and the brightest to serve as his Editorial Advisory Board: Terrance Koller, Dana Royce Baerger, Malini Patel, Ron Levant, and Stephen Kouris.

The rapid growth of global communications, information technology, and international business in the second half of the twentieth century increased the need for a common platform where the stakeholders of society could be brought together to consider and advance the key issues on the global agenda. The World Economic Forum's goal is to provide that platform, asking a mix of individuals to articulate the major problems facing the world and to find solutions. Works like this are catalytic to our thinking and dialogue.

It is our hope at the Forum to support the global public interest and to improve the state of the world. I believe this series adds to such a mission by its integration of thinking and facilitation of dialogue among different stakeholders and across different regions and intellectual disciplines. This series promotes progress by expanding common ground and developing new approaches.

Klaus Schwab
Founder and President
World Economic Forum

Acknowledgments

A project such as this one—with authors from all over the world covering a breadth and depth of examination of such a complex topic—can only happen as the result of a team effort. As such, I would like first of all to thank my family. Annika, Grayson, and I have sacrificed many a weekend of playing together; and I have also missed time with my very supportive partner and wife, Dr. Karen Beckstrand. Debora Carvalko, our editor at Greenwood, has been the crucial link in this project. She has worked with herculean effort to keep things organized and working. In fact, it is thanks to her that this project was even undertaken. The Editorial Advisory Board worked diligently, reading and commenting on many more manuscripts than those seen herein. The work of Terrence Koller, Malini Patel, Dana Royce Baerger, Steven P. Kouris, and Ronald F. Levant was impeccable and key to ensuring the quality of the chapters. I am also indebted to the council of Hedwin Naimark for invaluable help and thinking.

Professor Klaus Schwab has been a valued resource to me over the years and he was kind enough to provide the foreword. Harvey Langholtz has been an ongoing source of inspiration and mentorship to me. He is without a doubt the most diplomatic of all psychologists I know (it must have been all those years at the United Nations). And, this project would have been no more than an idea without the intellectual productivity of the contributing authors. We were fortunate to have more submissions than we could use in the end, but even those whose works were not used surely had an impact on my thinking and perspective, and I am very grateful. Finally, behind-the-scenes thanks to Ralph Musicant, Lawrence W. Osborn, Phillip Zimbardo, Patrick DeLeon, and Michael Horowitz.

I am markedly indebted to you all at a level that I shall never be able to repay. My sincere thanks to each of you.

Introduction

In thinking about the words to write here, I am struck with the vast array of ironies.

I had been writing and presenting talks on issues of terrorism for a while before September 11, 2001. In June 2001, I had submitted a proposal dealing with issues of terrorism for a clinical practice conference in November 2001, and I cannot help but suspect that the proposal could easily have been rejected because of a busy agenda and other competing topics that would have been considered more important to attendees. Instead, the proposal was accepted and it was the largest crowd I have ever addressed. Standing room only, and the only presentation over the course of a three-day conference that was videotaped. Sad, indeed, how some things change. I now often find myself reminding audiences that terrorism existed before September 11, 2001. In fact, that was what my talk was about. Terrorism in Japan, in Lebanon, in Ireland. In the world. In our world. For many of us who are U.S. citizens, the term "our world" now has a new and different meaning.

I have presented and written a fair amount on terrorism, and war, and trauma, and civilian casualties. I've worked with children who have been tortured, talked with traumatized refugees, broken bread with former political prisoners, and worked with a center offering pro bono clinical services to refugees who are victims of torture. I've seen the aftermath of atrocities—exhumed corpses, mass graves, and murdered infants. I have gone on medical missions to far-off places around the world. I have slides and statistics, bar graphs and citations; I can quote numerous facts and figures. But prior to September 11, 2001, all of that was done with a certain degree of clinical detachment. I would go somewhere else, and then come home. I have not ever been in an active war zone, nor have I been a victim of a terrorist attack. After September 11, I feel a bit different.

More people now know what is meant by a "dirty bomb," or what anthrax and Cipro are, than knew before September 11. I'm not sure if that is a good thing or not. I work in Chicago, the city that again has title to the tallest building in the United States. Who could have ever imagined such an odd occurrence? The reclaiming of such a title as the result of a kiloton of destructive force toppling the towers of the World Trade Center, all for the price of a plane ticket and a box cutter. Unbelievable.

I cannot help but wonder what might have been different if the West/North had dealt before September 11 with a brewing, yet largely ignored, issues—from an intelligence perspective, a psychological perspective (in all its varieties, forms, and flavors), a diplomacy and foreign policy perspective. I wonder what might have been achieved in tackling the larger dynamics of both the good and the bad that accompany globalization. All of this juxtaposed with issues of religious fundamentalism and politics. I'd like to believe things would have been better, but perhaps they would not.

Terrorism is a complex issue that does not respond well to reductionism. I apologize in advance if somehow this project looks as if it tries to simplify the complexities. My objective is not to teach the reader everything he or she ever wanted to know about terrorism in four easy lessons, but rather to offer a sampling of diverse and rich thought. Perhaps this can be the spark that starts a dialogue or a debate. That is OK by me. I have been amazed at the diversity, if not downright division, of some of the opinions and resultant debates following September 11. There are arguments regarding violent and aggressive responses versus forgiveness and passivism, evil versus good, behavioral reinforcement versus social psychology theories, isolationism versus globalism, "we are victims" versus "we brought this on ourselves," and my favorite dichotomy—"this is a start of the end" versus "this is the start of a new beginning." I think back to the horrible nature of the Oklahoma City bombing. That event was not at the same level as the New York and D.C. attacks in terms of the loss of life, damage, destruction and, frankly, vast media coverage. But the horror may also be mitigated by the fact that it was done by a McVeigh, not a bin Laden.

Everything is a political act, it simply cannot be escaped. A lack of political participation (such as not voting) or a lack of political activism (such as not supporting a cause) is still a political act (as in support of a status quo). As you will see, some of our authors are academics, some are clinicians, and some are activists. Try as we all do to check our political biases at the door, they surely squeak in, and most likely in ways that are difficult to see. I hope that an Editorial Advisory Board makes it more difficult to miss these biases, but I still suggest that readers, like all good academics, seek to understand by questioning assumptions and looking for empirical evidence wherever possible. Certainly this topic may often not comply with such methods, but we have all tried our best to present good scholarship herein.

This project started out as one book. It quickly grew to four volumes. Many more chapters went unused due to space limitations, duplication, or other technical reasons. There simply is no singular psychology of terrorism, no unified field theory if you will. None of the chapters is a stand-alone work; they are best understood in the greater context of the book, and then likewise in the wider context of the series. In some instances, the reader may see differences of perspectives or tensions between viewpoints. None of the books is a homogenized or sterile rendition of information. Personally, I find it difficult to talk about terrorism without also talking about war. And it's hard to discuss war without getting into issues of torture. Similarly, it's difficult to discuss torture without also discussing violence, and so forth. Thus, in this project on terrorism, readers will see discussions concerning such various related issues, because none of these issues can easily or correctly be dis-integrated from terrorism. Thus these four books emanated from an organic, self-organizing developmental process, resulting in:

I.   The Psychology of Terrorism: A Public Understanding

II. The Psychology of Terrorism: Clinical Aspects and Responses

III. The Psychology of Terrorism: Theoretical Understandings and Perspectives (with a special section on the Roles and Impacts of Religions)

IV. The Psychology of Terrorism: Programs and Practices in Response and Prevention

While there is no unifying perspective per se, I hope that these books may act as a unified source of perspectives. Also, they are incomplete. Individuals representing even more perspectives had hoped to contribute, but the realities prevented them from doing so. Certainly there will be continued interest, and I hope to see much more on these issues as we all become more aware and wise.

Volume I—A Public Understanding—provides an overview of issues in a way to help the public, in general, better understand the various issues involved. Volume II—Clinical Aspects and Responses—is an adequately telling title and offers much in the way of dealing with the emotional impacts of such traumas. Volume III—Theoretical Understandings and Perspectives—offers various perspectives of psychological understanding and theory intertwined with culture, context, politics, globalization, and social injustice as well as diplomatic processes. This volume also has a special section on the roles and impacts of religions that covers apocalyptic dreams, cults, religious archetypes, Islamic fundamentalism, and religious fanaticism.

Volume IV—Programs and Practices in Response and Prevention—provides a mix of preventative ideas and methods for youth and communities, as well as therapeutic aspects for those in trouble. For example, it includes articles on ethnopolitical warfare, family traumatic stress and refugee children; children's responses to traumatic events; aggression in adolescents; peace building; cooperative learning communities; antiviolence programming in school settings; and raising inclusively caring children. Granted, not all of these programs can be applied to a global set of venues, but they may offer much to those interested in developing their own variations on the theme.

What is my goal with this project? As noted earlier, I hope it provides readers with a mix of opinion and perspectives from which further thought and dialogue may occur. As you read these volumes, I would like you to keep in mind that through the work you do, no matter who you are, you can have an impact upon others that affects not only the individuals you encounter today, but potentially generations thereafter.

1

Controlling Political Terrorism: Practicality, Not Psychology

William H. Reid

Is there a terrorist psychology?

Mental health professionals are often asked, "What makes people become terrorists?" or "What's wrong with those people?" First, there are many kinds of terrorism and terror-violence.[1] The answers to these questions, to the extent that anyone knows them, vary from one type of terrorism to another and from event to event. Second, although everyone has a personality, and personality is important in behavior, the idea that there are archetypal terrorist personalities, or mental illnesses that predispose one to what most people call terrorism, is largely a myth. We *want* terrorists to have particular psychological characteristics, so that we might be able to "figure them out" and eliminate, mitigate, or at least define the foe. But wishing doesn't make it so. The real explanations are simpler than that, and the real solutions, unfortunately, are more complex.

Thus this chapter may not sound very "psychological" at times. It will more address what terrorism is *not* (vis-à-vis psychology and psychiatry) than what it *is*, in an effort to help readers understand that the mental health professions, for the most part, should not be expected to have many answers to this vexing sociopolitical problem. It is consistent with work done two decades ago by the American Psychiatric Association, which developed a task force that worked with government agencies and produced a small volume on terrorism and its victims (Eichelman, Soskis, & Reid, 1983). The consensus of the task force and the various agencies and organizations with which we worked was that (with some highly specialized exceptions in military, law enforcement, and diplomatic consultation) the roles for and expertise of the mental health professions lie primarily in victim care (and sometimes, when mental illness is a factor, perpetrator assessment or treatment). That view has been replicated many times, in both social study and practical application; many of the roles contemplated are addressed elsewhere in this book.

DEFINITION

It is important to define terrorism for purposes of this discussion. We will address those who practice a *pattern of sudden violent or fear-inducing action against civilians, not part of a national military action in a declared war between nations.* The chapter will refer to terror-violence aimed at groups rather than individuals (although particular events may have one physical victim). We will omit hostage taking during ordinary robberies, and isolated incidents spawned by delusion or paranoia.

That definition is limiting, but important if one is to avoid confusion and focus the topic. It omits wars, no matter how cruel. It does not include states' acts against their own citizens (which kill far more people than international and non-state actions [Rummel, 1994]) or torture of state-held prisoners, even though many readers would call torture terroristic (and virtually all would probably call it despicable). "Revolutionary" acts organized against military targets within the revolutionary's own country are excluded. We will try to avoid the conundrum that "one man's terrorist is another man's freedom fighter."[2]

LIMITED UTILITY OF PSYCHOLOGICAL MODELS

More than 25 years ago, Frederick Hacker presented in *Crusaders, Criminals, Crazies* a psychiatrist's view that terrorists could be divided into those categories. He viewed most events similar to U.S. embassy bombings and the September 11, 2001, attacks as having been carried out by "crusaders," or people working for a political or philosophical cause. He made them "psychological" by referring to things like "grandiose identification with a sacred cause and its representatives" and "giving up . . . individual responsibility, and individual interest, experience[ing] the 'high' of 'liberation' from his individual problems, guilts and anxiety" (Hacker, 1976). That seemed to make sense; it gave many scholars and defenders an impression (unfortunately impractical and probably erroneous) of knowing what they were doing. Hacker's principle of "the three Cs" survives to this day.

Hacker's categorization and the work of a few social scholars (such as the Rand Corporation's Brian Jenkins) have some utility, but it is important to realize that most terrorists, by our definition above in the first few paragraphs, aren't mentally ill, and they probably don't have any more psychological flaws than most criminals.

Their behavior is vexing and often inexcusable, but they should not be confused with people whose emotional status creates some legitimate rationalization for, much less exoneration of, their behavior. The long-term social influences on subordinate members within organizations, such as the exploitation of followers who are particularly dependent or emotionally needy, is well studied and described elsewhere in this book. Contrary to the wishes of some who would write about them, those influences rarely apply to organization leaders and decision makers. Instead, such leaders usually act from other, more practical motivations as discussed below.

Even so-called "suicide" terrorists, who seem foreign to our culture and make us feel helplessly vulnerable, are not difficult to explain on practical, rather than psychological, grounds. People die in the service of some personal or political goal for many reasons, including religious promise, cultural expectation instilled from early development, and patriotic fervor. Other sources of motivation include payments to the person's family if the mission succeeds, harm to the family if the mission fails, and a quick, "meaningful" death (or family payment) for perpetrators with terminal illness. Intoxication and acute psychological preparation (like hypnosis, simplistic "brainwashing," or operant conditioning), so popular in films and accounts of the Japanese kamikaze, are best left to the movies.

THE PRACTICALITY, AND FAILURES, OF TERRORIST BEHAVIOR

Terrorism has been with us for centuries; little about it is unique. Its utility overshadows social theory and journalistic wanderings, and tends to outstrip the psychological hypotheses that are now mostly consigned to academia, some think tanks, and opinion pieces. We have had to become more practical.

Terrorists and their organizations have *always* been practical. They use principles that are older than any government and that date to hundreds of years before Christ. If one views their goal as government overthrow or broad social change, they have almost always failed. If, however, one recognizes their goals as *disruption, deflection of purpose, drain of resources, attention gathering, and/or organization profit,* then their potential for success is substantial (Figure 1.1).

FIGURE 1.1: GOALS OF TERRORISM

- **Disruption.** Creating chaos, fear, and confusion in the target; making routine activity difficult.
- **Deflection of Purpose.** Causing the target group or population to curtail routine activities and focus on the terrorist act and related issues.
- **Drain of Resources.** Causing resources ordinarily used for other activities to be diverted to the purpose of dealing with the terrorist activity or its victims.

- **Attention Gathering.** Bringing attention, notoriety, and/or some level of validity or definition to the terrorist group, often implying a sort of "marketing" to achieve legitimacy or authority for the group (but not particularly for the espoused cause).
- **Organization Profit.** The very common practice of terrorists cloaking themselves in a "crusade" that is more accurately viewed as criminal behavior. Even groups that preach against capitalism spend much of their energy raising funds and using money from capitalist endeavors. State sponsorship is a primary source of large-organization terrorist funding and operating ability. The leader or group that speaks loudly of a social or religious purpose is often actually performing a task for hire (and perhaps rationalizing its criminality and entrepreneurism with pious rhetoric). Terrorism, like organized crime, is often big business.

CONTROLLING TERRORISM AND ITS DAMAGE

Control of terrorist behavior and related damage lies largely in weakening or eliminating the individual terrorist; controlling, "hardening," or eliminating routes of terrorist attack; decreasing terrorist funding and sponsorship; and/or making the terrorist's goal too expensive to pursue.

Eliminating the Terrorist

Eliminating the terrorist organization is difficult, but not always impossible. One strategy favors "cutting off the head of the viper," with the expectation that the organization will be weakened or die. Although some organizations, particularly smaller ones, do depend on a particular leader, older and better-developed ones are more like Hydra (the mythological monster who, when its head was cut off, simply grew two more) than a viper. Target states also consider complex issues of martyrdom and the usefulness of information that may be gleaned from leaders after their capture, and thus may try not to kill them.

The "cell" structure of many terrorist organizations, a simple but effective group format used by covert groups for centuries, makes it difficult to penetrate or weaken them. Such organizations are made up of many very small groups ("cells," sometimes as few as three people each) that know little about the other cells, have contact with only one or two other cells, and communicate with other cells through only one primary channel. (An example is the interlocking cells of 1950s U.S. communism and World War II underground organizations). The structure creates many layers of organization, but the administration can operate with some efficiency. It also has great advantages of relative impenetrability and diffusion of important tasks. There are almost no truly vital points for attack or infiltration; destruction of one cell does not irreparably damage the whole. Unlike biological cells, in which the DNA is a mirror of the entire organism, capture or infiltration of a terrorist cell usually cannot yield comprehensive information about the overall organization.

Hardening Targets and Routes of Attack

The most common approach to controlling terrorist behavior includes decreasing terrorist effectiveness by such measures as predicting targets, making targets more difficult to damage or reach ("hardening" them), lowering their value to the terrorist, and keeping effective weapons out of terrorist hands.

Predicting targets involves determining what things or events (for instance, those with popular or patriotic significance), dates (such as national holidays), or schedules (times of particular opportunity) have the most potential value to the terrorist purpose, and then taking appropriate action. Target-hardening methods may be as simple as erecting barricades or installing local security measures, but also may include complex means of broadly limiting access and information (for example, through hiding a target, creating sham targets, or using encryption), restricting geographic routes (for example, by limiting or monitoring airspace), and creating comprehensive local or national defense systems.

Lowering target value implies making the target less interesting to terrorists by, for example, duplicating or diluting the valuable items or information. Thus, disrupting or destroying one target would have little effect on overall operations. Having multiple power plants, communication centers, and water supplies, as well as matrix power and communication networks that do not depend on single or linear routing, means that one or two strikes will not cripple those services. The Internet, for example, is relatively invulnerable to the loss of several hubs. Diluting and distributing valuable stockpiles (for example of food, weapons, gold, and even technology and people) decreases the target value of each. The well-known customs of separating the president and vice president in time of danger and keeping one cabinet member at a distant location during the State of the Union address are examples of this strategy.

Decreasing terrorists' access to weapons is a Sisyphean task. Small arms are ubiquitous in most parts of the world, although local control is feasible in some places and large shipments can be interdicted. It is arguably more important, at least on a national and international scale, to interdict and/or monitor highly destructive weapon *systems*, including (but not limited to) so-called weapons of mass destruction (including nuclear and other radiologic devices, chemical and biological weapon stockpiles and related materials, and ballistic [missile] delivery systems).

Decreasing Funding and Sponsorship

Funding and sponsorship are very important to terrorist groups, especially large-scale groups. It is easy to see that money is required for all levels of operations, but one often forgets that organizations with dozens, hundreds, or thousands of members cannot exist for very long without considerable help from sponsoring communities or countries. Sometimes, just as in the case of some oppressive governments and their citizens, the community help is involuntary, the result of intimidation or extortion. Larger, nongovernmental terrorist groups, however, routinely enjoy the willing support of at least some local people, or even of entire nations. That support may arise from pragmatic issues (such as to protect a local coca or opium poppy economy), popular or religious preferences (for example some environmental groups and some Islamic, Jewish, or Christian fundamentalists), or political expediency (for example, in state-sponsored transnational[3] terrorism).

Economic measures, such as interrupting cash flow and curtailing funding and banking mechanisms, are being highlighted in the current U.S.-led "war on terrorism." Decreasing local and popular sponsorship (for example through education or propaganda, providing humanitarian aid, rewarding those who fight against the perpetrators, or punishing those who support or shelter them) is often effective.

Increasing Terrorist Costs

The approach of making terrorist action more and more expensive incorporates elements of the first three broad strategies described above, but it deserves separate mention. Some acts of terror-violence (such as a simple bombing or kidnapping) cost the attacking organization little at first, but if diligent law enforcement leads to perpetrator imprisonment, loss of organization funding, or ostracism by the sheltering group or country, simple acts become much more expensive to carry out.

In another example of this approach, also mentioned in the chapter titled "Bioterrorism: Separating Fact, Fiction, and Hysteria," larger countries (such as the United States) finance substantial purchases of expensive and sophisticated weapons and weapon systems (often at inflated prices) when they become available on the "black market" and then (usually) destroy them. This strategy eliminates some weapons immediately and drives up the price for those that remain.

WHAT DOESN'T WORK

Controlling terrorism does not lie in meeting terrorists' demands (for example, by paying them or by promising social or political change), in attempting to otherwise mollify the terrorist organization, or in being fearful of angering the perpetrators (Figure 1.2). Well-organized terrorist activity is not carried out in anger (although some of the participants may, of course, be driven by anger); it is carefully planned and executed for specific value and effect, at specific times and points of opportunity. Strategies of mollification or placation, occasionally suggested by potential victims, certain commentators, or shortsighted theorists, are notoriously unreliable and virtually always lead to more (or further threats of) terror-violence. They reinforce terrorist behavior and strengthen the terrorist organization's reputation and political position.

The idea that target groups should somehow be careful not to anger terrorist perpetrators is particularly interesting, and reminiscent of frightened primitive villagers sacrificing food (or more) to appease some god about whom their entire "knowledge" is based on myth or coincidence. While there is certainly reason to be cautious in the face of acute danger, some people view almost any aggressive antiterrorist action as likely to make matters worse by further inciting people who are already mad at their victims. A minority of Americans believe the United States should stop its current rhetoric and international deployment lest they ignite reprisals. Many more *fear* reprisal, but accept the need to act decisively for long-term success.

Those who express strong opposition to taking legitimate, aggressive (and sometimes violent) action in an effort to decrease future terrorism are generally either ill-informed or acting out of personal or self-serving impulse. Neither history nor experience suggests that mollifying aggressors decreases their dangerous behavior. Whether one examines the unfortunately benign British and U.S. reactions to Hitler's expansion during the 1930s or the microcosm of dealing with an abusive parent or spouse, it is clear that recognizing the need for definitive action, and rapidly carrying out that action, is critical to decreasing ultimate violence and minimizing ultimate damage.

While one can understand *feelings* of fear or hopelessness (including, for example, concerns about one's children being in the military and sent into harm's way), it is a mistake to act on those feelings if such actions run counter to the need to stop a serious threat. Immediate impulses to stave off pain or danger are often far less important than the longer-term consequences of running from the fray. Hoping "the crocodile will eat me last" is a poor (and rather unethical) defense.

FIGURE 1.2: FEAR OF ANGERING PERPETRATORS

- Anger is not their point; group terrorist action is generally practical, not emotional.
- Neither history nor experience suggests that mollifying aggressors is helpful.
- Hoping "the crocodile will eat me last" is a poor survival plan, and a worse code for living.
- "Violence doesn't solve anything" is an overly simplistic generalization.
- Although never to be entered into lightly, the adage that "violence never solved anything" is just not true.

REFERENCES

Eichelman, B., Soskis, D. A., & Reid, W. H. (1983). *Terrorism: Multidisciplinary perspectives.* Washington, DC: American Psychiatric Press.

Hacker, F. J. (1976). *Crusaders, criminals, crazies: Terror and terrorism in our time.* New York: W. W. Norton.

Rummel, R. J. (1994). *Death by government.* New Brunswick, NJ: Transaction Press.

NOTES

1.   A term coined, or at least popularized in the field, by Professor M. Cherif Bassiouni of Loyola School of Law, Chicago.

2.   As expressed to the author decades ago by Professor J. K. Zawodny, a terrorism expert and former Polish freedom fighter.

3.   As contrasted with a state's oppressive or terroristic actions against its own citizens.

2

The Psychology of the Terrorist: Behavioral Perspectives

Rubén Ardila

The psychological study of terrorism is a relatively new field of scientific investigation, but it does not start with the attacks of September 11, 2001, on the World Trade Center and the Pentagon. Extensive studies have been carried out in the past two or three decades on such topics as the psychological profile of the terrorist, the impact of terrorist attacks on the public, structural violence and terrorism, and the mass media and terrorism.

The reference framework of these studies is social psychology, and more specifically, the psychology of peace. The fundamental precedents are the works of Milgram (1974) on obedience, Bandura (1973, 1986) on social learning, and Zimbardo (1973) on the terror in prisons.

Let's remember that *terrorism* comes from *terror* and that the goal of the terrorists' attacks is to generate panic, fear, paranoia, unrest, uncertainty, and other paralyzing, psychological emotions.

Terrorism implies using violence, or the threat of it, with political ends, and it is targeted against groups and not against specific individuals. It is utilized by lawless political groups that lack sufficient strength to face the enemy directly. Euzkadi Ta Azkatasuna (Basque Nation and Liberty; ETA) in Spain, the Irish Republican Army (IRA) in Ireland, and other political groups don't think they have enough force to defeat the state, but they do have the courage to instill terror by means of terrorist attacks. Such attacks undermine public confidence in the invulnerability of the state and thus affect all aspects of daily life.

Psychology has shown that terrorists have been carefully shaped (programmed) to destroy the enemy at any expense, even with their own lives. They practice blind obedience to authority (as Milgram has studied) and are completely involved in a political or religious ideology. They are fatalistic and educated, have few material possessions, and the certainty that they have nothing to lose except their lives for the achievement of a superior and very important cause. They can destroy, damage, kill, or harm themselves. Psychologists assert that terrorists introduce "creative evil" in its extreme form.

A terrorist act is not impulsive, without premeditation, or the fruit of an instant rage. It usually implies planning, premeditation, a careful study for months or even years, specific skills and training, and economic and human resources. In the case of the attacks of September 11, 2001, terrorists trained for a long time to pilot aircraft, spent a lot of money, participated in international networks, and planned each detail carefully. They directed their attacks against the economic, military, and political symbols of Western power.

Terrorism, therefore, is not senseless violence but rather the fruit of the resentment and lack of empowerment that lead to acts against the civilian population— men, women, and children. It is a sign of weakness attributable to the fact that the strength of the terrorists is inferior to that of the "enemy." The terrorists believe that through their acts they can undermine the strength of the "enemy" by spreading terror and paranoia.

The circle of revenge and retaliation is one of the most noticeable elements in terrorism. In many cases, the terrorists want to retaliate against real or imaginary enemies who did something bad to their people, to their culture, to their religion, or to their social group. If terrorists are destroyed without destroying the causes of resentment, the circle of violence is perpetuated, which is what has happened in many contexts.

It is likely that psychological study of the motivations of the terrorists, and of their complex personal and social dynamics, will shed light on these important issues of political life at the beginning of the twenty-first century.

THE BEHAVIORAL APPROACH

This chapter concentrates on the psychology of individuals who commit terrorist acts. This is done from the point of view of behavioral psychology, in particular of the experimental analysis of behavior, and post-Skinnerian developments. The field of work is the social context, the cultural contingencies, and in general the behavioral analysis of social issues (see Mattaini & Thyer, 1996).

We base our work on social language theory, on the behavioral analysis of cognition and language (Hayes, Hayes, Sato, & Ono, 1994), on rule-government behavior, and on the experimental synthesis of behavior (Ardila, 1992, 1993).

TERRORISM AND TERRORISTS

For many years, small groups of people willing to die for a cause have managed to sow terror in the hearts of thousands, even millions. Terrorism has existed for a long time, and it arises not only out of the Middle East. Nor does it attack only the great cities of Europe. Terrorism is a plague that has struck many countries for many decades, in periods of war and in periods of peace, in Israel and in Palestine, in Northern Ireland, in Spain, in Colombia, in the Philippines and in Africa and the Far East.

There are hundreds of definitions of terrorism. They have in common the affirmation that terrorism is an act of violence, or a threat of one, that is directed against noncombatants with the end of causing intimidation, seeking vengeance, or influencing public opinion. In many cases there are political, religious, social, or economic determinants of one kind or another. The psychological component is one of the most important.

Terrorists are usually young men (in very few cases women)[1]—faceless people carefully programmed to destroy their enemy at all costs. They are well trained, educated, blindly obedient to authority, living in a time zone of fatalism, and totally dedicated to a religious-cultural ideology. Their attacks are not senseless violence; they require extensive planning, training, professional expertise, financial resources, and networks of co-conspirators.

The *who* question (Who are the terrorists?) is closely related to the *why* questions (Why do they behave as they do? Why do they hate the United States, or any other country?) The personal, social, cultural, and religious motivations of the terrorists are a complex field of psychological work.

Terrorists use many symbols, they attack symbols, and they have symbolic functions. The attacks of September 11, 2001, were directed against the symbols of the economic, military, and political power of the United States. The terrorists were able to demonstrate that the "empire," the "giant," is vulnerable, fragile, and can be terrorized by a band of men armed with box cutters. It is the game of David against Goliath, or Samson against the Philistines.

In this symbolism, the terrorists personify evil. Evil has always existed in many forms, and there are individuals whom we consider as embodying evil, such as Satan, Hitler, and now Osama bin Laden.

Human beings have a tendency to center on dispositional evil as a particular property or characteristic of particular individuals. Nevertheless, it is important for us to focus on *dispositional determinants of evil* in order to recognize the generic forces of evil, to identify the breeding grounds that can seduce even good people to become perpetrators of evil.

We should not demonize the terrorists as an alien breed. Instead we should focus on their motivations and the dispositional determinants of their behavior. If we destroy the terrorists' leaders, they will become "martyrs" and will serve as models for new generations of terrorists.

A FUNCTIONAL ANALYSIS

Terrorists are born in many cases in marginalized cultures or social groups. They learn that they are "different," not part of the mainstream, and that they have nothing to lose. They are almost always indoctrinated with a political ideology of revenge—of hate and accumulated resentment. They are socialized as people with no power and no hope, whose lives probably will be as frustrating as the lives of their ancestors.

In this context, violence, destruction, and death are the stuff of everyday life. The terrorists have seen terror and massive murders of innocent people (civilians who are not involved in the confrontation). They consider these a natural consequence of war. They have learned that being violent produces satisfactory consequences, and that people who place bombs or shoot at innocent individuals almost never receive a punishment. Impunity, the lack of justice, and minimal control from organized society combine to make them feel strong and powerful. It is in this context of marginality and lack of power that they operate.

Terrorists divide the world into black and white, good and bad. The bad people are powerful and strong, but it is possible to hurt them and undermine their power. In many cases, the sociopolitical context helps: the rich are bad, exploitative, and cruel; the poor are good and suffer from the exploitation and cruelty of the rich. On a religious level, a terrorist might argue, "Christians want to impose their ideology on the other communities; Muslims must refuse to go along with these attempts and undermine the power of the Christians." In general, the enemy is the devil; it is Satan. This term is used indiscriminately by both Arab leaders and Western leaders to refer to the enemy.

Verbal contingencies play a crucial role in forming a terrorist. Instructions are repeated innumerable times, as is the context that gives support and social reinforcement. The terrorist learns the necessity to leave a mark, to have an impact on the world, and thereby to gain respect for his community.

When a person elects, or is elected, to execute a terrorist act that will cost him his life, he begins to occupy a different place in society (as a martyr, a living dead man, a hero who will carry out a vital task for the community). His sense of helplessness disappears. He acquires power, prestige and respectability.

Terrorists live in a world of verbal fantasies, of verbal illusions with strong stimulus functions. Terrorists see themselves as sacrifices for their deities, and they count on the approval and the backing of their culture. These beliefs give sense to their lives, symbolic forms to achieve immortality through their own deaths.

The learning of these conducts is accomplished through social learning. They are rule-governed behaviors. The future terrorist has had vicarious experiences with suicidal acts, but no personal experience due to the fact that the act leads to death; in other words, it is only executed once.

ARE THERE DIFFERENT TYPES OF TERRORISTS?

The behavioral analysis of terrorists leads us to ask ourselves whether the psychological determinants are the same in all contexts—in the Middle East, in Colombia, in Japan. Not all terrorists are willing to sacrifice their lives. Those who do so are almost always influenced by religious ideologies that promise them a future full of happiness in exchange for their sacrifice.

A youth on the West Bank of Palestine who explodes a bomb attached to his body knowing he is going to die in the attempt may not have the same psychological characteristics as another youth who places a bomb to destroy an electric energy tower in a rural zone of Colombia and sets it off at a distance. Both youths are terrorists who supposedly fight for ideologies that cannot be implemented and that cannot triumph by means of fair competition. The "enemy," the opposite ideology, is too strong and cannot be defeated openly but has to be weakened through terror and terrorism.

The first terrorist knows he is going to die. The second, on the other hand, strives to escape and nearly always does. The contingencies of reinforcement are exactly the same in the two cases.

Many terrorist aggressions are viewed by the people who commit them as an attack against the strong and powerful (for example, against capitalism, the United States, France, the dominant classes, the rich, and the politicians). In the developing world, a certain number of people consider the terrorist attacks as a revenge against the Empire, the globalization and the capitalism that is doing them wrong, that is impoverishing them, and so forth. These stereotypes are deeply rooted in certain contexts of the developing world and, in spite of being false, they affect the conduct and the attitude of the people. Supposedly, they are charging the Empire for the errors committed in the past.

In several Latin American countries there was—and in some cases there still is—terrorism from the left and from the right, state-supported terrorism, counterculture terrorism, and so forth. During the 1970s, Argentina and Chile suffered terrible situations. Today, Colombia has terrorist groups that strive to undermine the establishment and harm the upper classes, the politicians, and the rich (who, according to the terrorists, are the perpetrators of the poverty that devastates the nation). Instead, the terrorist attacks destroy the national wealth and augment poverty. This is the vicious circle of terrorism.

The reinforcements for terrorist behavior are very different, ranging from the money obtained from kidnapping, blackmail, and robberies to the hope of a future life in a nirvana beyond death. However, it appears that in all cases the support of the group, conformance to the norms of the culture, and the desire for revenge and vengeance seem to have a decisive importance as motivations for the terrorist behavior. Culture has norms and regulations, rewards and punishments for certain behaviors, and a complex network of contingencies and consequences.

CONCLUSION

Policymakers, journalists, and laypersons often ask psychologists to answer such questions as: What developmental factors make a person a terrorist? Why does he hate his victim so much that he will sacrifice his own life in order to kill him?

Psychology possesses knowledge that can be applied to the study of terrorism and terrorists, to the relationships between groups, and to biases, stereotypes, the prevention of new attacks, and so forth. Nevertheless, much more scientific investigation is required before we can provide immediate answers.

Psychologists know that the terrorist's behavior has been shaped for many years, and his response is a final generalization of this conditioning process. It is also known that social obedience, moral development, individual differences, and religious fanaticism play important roles. Powerlessness, resentment, and learned helplessness are also part of the process.

In relation to religious fanaticism, José Saramago, the Nobel Prize winner, says:

> On account of and in the name of God is why everything is permitted
> and justified, principally the worst, the most horrendous and cruel.
> For centuries the Inquisition was also, like the Taliban today, a terror-
> ist organization dedicated to perversely interpret sacred texts.

The religious fanaticism of previous centuries (for example, the struggles between Catholics and Protestants) has been rekindled in our time, with political arrays of great complexity.

Considering the psychology of the terrorist from a behavioral perspective allows us to present a coherent picture—even though it is neither a complete nor sufficiently integrated picture—of the cycle of terrorism. We cannot allow that transfer of hostility to develop, because it fuels the cycle of violence started by the terrorist. Terrorists create terror, and terror creates fear and anger. Fear and anger create aggression, and aggression against people of different culture and religion creates discrimination; this in turn leads to new forms of terrorism.

This is the vicious circle that social psychological research should try to understand and to break.

REFERENCES

Ardila, R. (1992). Toward unity in psychology: The experimental synthesis of behavior. *International Journal of Psychology, 27,* 299–310.

Ardila, R. (1993). *Síntesis experimental del comportamiento* (Experimental synthesis of behavior). Bogotá, Colombia: Editorial Planeta.

Bandura, A. (1973). *Aggression: A social learning analysis.* Englewood Cliffs, NJ: Prentice-Hall.

Bandura, A. (1986). *Social foundations of thought and action.* Englewood Cliffs, NJ: Prentice-Hall.

Hayes, S. C., Hayes L. J., Sato, M., & Ono, K. (1994). *Behavior analysis of language and cognition.* Reno, NV: Context Press.

Mattaini, M. A., & Thyer, B. A. (Eds.) (1996). *Finding solutions to social problems: Behavioral strategies for change.* Washington, DC: American Psychological Association.

Milgram, S. (1974). *Obedience to authority.* New York: Harper.

Zimbardo, P. G. (1973, April 8). The mind is a formidable jailer: A Pirandellian prison. *New York Times,* p. 38.

NOTE

1. In this chapter, when "he" and "his" are presented in an unspecified way, one should also read "she" and "her."

3

Intersubjective Dimensions of Terrorism and Its Transcendence

Diane Perlman

THINKING OUTSIDE THE BOX—THE NEW PARADIGM

So far, we[1] have not succeeded in preventing the escalation of the cycle of terrorism and retaliation. With increasing access to weapons of mass destruction, the stakes are higher than ever. Even the viability of life on earth is threatened.

As I complete this chapter in March of 2002, I can't help but wonder what will have happened in the world by the time that you read it. Will we have learned to act wisely to reduce terrorism, or will we have continued on a simplistic, short-sighted, one-sided, "common sense" path? In our commitment to fight terrorism, will we have provoked more, unwittingly fueling the cycle of retaliation and other unintended consequences? Will weapons of mass destruction be used? How many more lives, or even cities, might be destroyed? How much farther will we expand this war? How will U.S. actions be regarded in the world community?

A deep understanding of the extremes of human experience can be useful in designing practical strategies to make us all safer in the near and distant future. Whatever happens will have everything to do with whether we *act consciously* with forethought, insight, and intuition, or whether we *re*act instinctively, impulsively, and righteously. If we use a paradigm that splits the world into right and wrong, good and evil, us against them, and winning or losing in a zero sum game, everyone will eventually lose.

We may be right, we may be good, and we may be gripped by our need to take justified action, but there will be no way out. Acting in this right-wrong paradigm will magnify these same attitudes and feelings in our enemies, who will continue to find new ways of using our power against us, deepening the cycle of retaliation.

When we are outraged by a sense of injury, injustice, and moral violation, retaliation and the desire for revenge are completely natural and understandable. Acting naturally and instinctively, however, can be quite dangerous. It is inside the box. Eliminating terrorism is a tremendous psychological challenge, an uphill struggle that requires consciousness. Carl Jung, the founder of analytical psychology, described consciousness as a work against nature, an *opus contra naturum.* It is negative entropy—a deliberate effort toward development and organization. We have the possibility, though not the probability, of rising above our instinctual impulses. That process requires going outside the box.[2]

The course of history depends on whether we focus only on superficial eradication of *terrorists* or deep eradication of *terrorism*—the psychological, political, economic, social, and spiritual conditions that clearly foster terror.

WHAT TERRORISM TEACHES US ABOUT BEING HUMAN

Albert Einstein said, "The most incomprehensible thing about the universe is that it is comprehensible." We can say that the most incomprehensible thing about terrorism is that it is comprehensible. As long as we say that terrorism defies comprehension and as long as we reduce it to pure "evil," we will not even try to understand it and we will falsely believe that it is impossible to resolve.

People refer to terrorists as subhuman monsters. This attitude forecloses deeper thinking and wiser actions. In *The Interpersonal Theory of Psychiatry* (1953), psychiatrist and psychoanalyst Harry Stack Sullivan said, "everyone is much more simply human than otherwise" (p. 32). What does terrorism teach us about what it means to be human? For those who abhor attempts to understand terrorists because they are evil, subhuman, and don't deserve it, refusing to consider causes of suffering and just grievances, I contend we must do this for our own safety.

The following theses, including definitions of concepts, will be explored in this chapter:

- In order to reduce, eliminate, or transcend terrorism we must first penetrate its true nature. We can even discern a formula of the ingredients that combine to produce terrorism. A multilayered approach, using insights from depth psychology, trauma theory, and systems theory helps us understand the coexisting inner, outer, and intersubjective worlds of terror and thus design effective treatments.
- Terrorism teaches us something about the extremes of human experience and what happens when humans are pushed beyond the limits of what we are designed to tolerate. This kind of analysis offers promising guidance that can provide a way out of cycles of violence
- The first stage in the development of terrorism begins when intolerable life conditions cause suffering that produces internal psycho-

logical changes in people. These changes can be understood as a *psychological mutation,* a malignant alteration in the personality, caused by the repeated failure to respond to overwhelming trauma. Intolerable affects that are not treated cannot be endured. Failure to respond to repeated trauma, humiliation, and suffering produces utter hopelessness. When cries for help are not heeded, people are plunged into the depths of despair—an abyss that creates a change in personality. When appropriate methods of trying to get help do not work, people resort to deviant, destructive measures to receive attention, relief of suffering, and justice.

- The next step occurs when the intrapsychic (internal) psychological transformation moves out into the interpersonal, social, and political spheres. With trauma, intolerable affects are evacuated from the self and deposited into another through an unconscious mechanism called *projective identification.* This transforms the subjective experience of the recipient. Terrorism can be considered an act of projective identification. It can be a primitive form of communication about "early forms of mother-infant communication. Projective identification can be healthy or pathological. and can be a way of unconsciously influencing and controlling another.

- This projective identification constitutes a *traumatic reenactment,* a form of communication that draws the recipients into the drama, altering their subjective experience, drawing them into an intersubjective relationship with the terrorists. In the reenactment, the terrorists reverse their roles as victims to become masters of their fate. Traumatic reenactment, as used in psychoanalysis, is the phenomenon of recreating the dynamics of early experience in later life, and inducing old patterns in current relationships. Sigmund Freud referred to this as the "repetition compulsion." From birth we develop a personality organization to survive and adapt to our families and circumstances. We reenact early patterns in psychoanalysis, in work relationships, and in marriage, by provoking others to participate in our drama. This can either be an opportunity for unhealthy repetition or for a healing transformation if others can receive it as communication and do not play into the reenactment.

- The victims of terror are traumatized and are drawn into the process whereby they are provoked to expel their intolerable affects through acts of retaliation. The process escalates if recipients of terrorism act automatically, unconsciously, and self-righteously (which is "natural") through retaliation, thus deepening the cycle of violence. Inner and outer worlds interplay, forming a dynamic system. According to systems theory, this escalation can be considered a *positive feedback spiral,* as actions provoke greater reactions. A positive feedback spiral describes a process of change in living systems where feedback reinforces change, for better or worse, as in escalation of violence.

von Riesen Library
McCook Community College

- *Dehumanization of the "other"*—Trauma alters the quality of human relatedness, resulting in an archetypal emotionally charged image of members of the "other" ethnic group, race, country, experienced as not being in the same category of humanity. The "other" is feared, dreaded, dehumanized, experienced as more powerful and less human, and therefore can be killed without guilt.

- Terrorism is a form of *asymmetrical warfare.* A power imbalance, characterized by feelings of domination and humiliation, is part of the system. We can imagine a "terror system" as a volatile field generated by inequality between a dominant power and a weak power, compounded by great suffering with no hope of relief. This creates an unstable, intense dynamic that sets the stage for the emergence of leaders, recruits, sympathizers, supporters, and targets.

- Our response to terrorism once it erupts is an essential dimension in an unfolding drama—the "dance of terror." How we decipher the messages encoded in acts of terror, how we behave and how we engage with the "terror community" and the world community, will determine the course of escalation or de-escalation. Our contribution to escalation of violence may not be immediately obvious in the realm of "common sense," but is evident upon deep reflection.

- Direct, superficial, commonsense strategies are not effective in increasing global security and can actually make things worse by provoking unintended consequences (blowback). *First order change* focuses concretely on the content, problems, and trying to get rid of symptoms, according to systems and family theory; it does not address the sources of the problem and is generally ineffective in the long term (Watzlawick, Weakland, & Fish, 1974). Unidimensional focus on military strategies and counterterrorism is insufficient and eclipses thinking about other kinds of approaches that can be more powerful.

- *Second order change* addresses the level of process and deep structure of the system. Psychologically informed strategies that address root causes and powerful underlying emotional forces that fuel terrorism have far greater promise in increasing global security. These valuable resources are not being tapped. Working on this level, outside the box, allows the system to be transformed (Bandler, Grinder, & Satir, 1976, p. 138; Watzlawick et al., 1974).

- A severe global imbalance between investment in life-affirming and life-protecting resources and those directed toward death, destruction, domination, and punishment provides a larger context for allowing human suffering and the breeding of terrorism.

THE FORMULAS

A simple formula has been deciphered for the emergence of terrorism and its transcendence (Perlman, 1997). The key fact that terrorism simultaneously stems from and causes human suffering is ironically obvious and ignored.

The steps in the formula are:

Suffering → Desire for Compassion and Help → Reaching for Help → Help Fails → Dejection, Humiliation, Despair, and Rage → Transformation from Victim to Master of Fate → Compensation for Helplessness by Identification with Powerful Leader Who Stands Up to the Enemy → Evacuation of Suffering into Other Through Acts of Terrorism → Retaliation → More Suffering → Repeat Cycle

If we understand this pattern, we can intervene to break it to reach a different outcome, using this formula to transcend terrorism and reverse the cycle:

Suffering → Desire for Compassion and Help → Reaching for Help → Help Responds → People Are Calmed, Non-Negotiable Human Needs Are Met → Conflict Is Contained → Repair and Healing → Progress → Cycle Reversed

The critical component is intervening to alleviate suffering as early as possible. Even when it seems too late, everything must be done to address and contain trauma. What is needed is visionary, effective leadership with a strong moral imagination that emphasizes adequate responsiveness to human suffering.

HUMAN SUFFERING, TRAUMA, AND HEALING

The most salient feature of terrorism concerns the gross and repeated failure to respond to human suffering in its early stages and the systematic compounding of consequences.

We are designed with the provision to recover from "normal" trauma such as the loss of a parent or a natural catastrophe when the community responds in a healing manner with recognition, compassion, empathy, rituals, memorials, and so forth. Failure to provide these responses results in complicated mourning and exacerbation of the trauma.

Religious rituals as well as spontaneous outpourings contain elements of healing. Consider the response to the September 11 terrorist attacks—memorials, rituals, concerts, prayer services, and the gatherings at Union Square, which became a public space for healing filled with candles, flowers, activities, and so forth. All of these phenomena demonstrate the archetypal need for healing experiences.

Malicious, repetitive, or continuous inescapable trauma, such as abuse or war, is complicated by psychological factors including humiliation, domination, fear, terror, hate, rage, despair, and grief and by inadequate responses to these. Recognition, protection, support, love, truth, and justice help wounded people heal, find meaning, recover, and even emerge stronger in the best-case scenarios. Repeated trauma without a healing response can push people with fragile egos beyond the breaking point. Those with positive early life experiences, which form a solid core, can draw upon reserves that can enable them to better endure trauma.[3]

It is especially crushing when hope is elevated and then dashed. Palestinians, who were hopeful and jubilant at the signing of the Oslo accords, saw a serious decline in their economy and the rapid expansion of settlements. The *mujahideen* of Afghanistan who were elated after defeating the Soviets were abandoned to live in harsh misery.

Dashed hope produces a keen sense of rage, futurelessness, and deep despair. Having nothing left to live for can inspire fundamentalism and suicidality. It transforms victimhood to martyrdom, with compensatory mastery, pride, and justification.

Living under slavery, occupation, oppression, and other collective trauma can render traumatized adults incapable of responding adequately to their children. Collective trauma affects the whole society and is transmitted from generation to generation. Worsening conditions over time magnify frustration and despair. The loss of a glorious past and feeling the acute yearnings of one's parents with no hope in sight pervades the experience of growing up in misery while feeling envy and humiliation associated with those who have privilege and power.

A healing process needs to be physical, psychological, social, political, economic, and spiritual.[4] Failure to receive soothing is intolerable and experienced as a re-traumatization. Bystanders who fail to stop the pain are also targets of anger, terror, and hostage taking.

Trauma renders people susceptible to manipulation by powerful leaders who use symbols and language in ways that provide hope and dignity, as we see with Hitler, Milosovic, bin Laden, and others. Punishment also makes people hypnotically susceptible and obedient to authority.

Oppressive, authoritarian, patriarchal, gender-split cultures in war-torn countries are fertile breeding grounds for terrorism, with internal and external sources of oppression. Massive collective trauma generates fear, which intensifies oppression within a society. Individual trauma converges with mass psychology, as people get swept up in the group mind.

These cultures demand fierce group loyalty and idealization. Suppression of criticism of one's own group makes outside scapegoats appealing targets for blame, outlets for discharge of tension generated in one's group. There may be legitimate grievances, but the intensity and direction of the rage are overdetermined.

Continuous unresolved suffering in the context of a power imbalance creates an unstable psychological and political condition in which intolerable affects are unconsciously evacuated from the self or the group, and projected into the "other" through projective identification. This expands the cycle of terror.

A sign of collective wisdom is the emergence of new political rituals, such as truth and reconciliation processes, war crimes tribunals, and reintegration of child soldiers into communities, akin to many ancient religious practices. These processes acknowledge suffering, prevent transmission of trauma, end cycles of violence, and assist the society in healing.

PSYCHE AND SYSTEM

Psychoanalytic treatment of trauma sheds light on the dynamics of terrorism. It is based on people who have suffered abuse and entered into psychoanalytic treatment, primarily educated people who can afford psychoanalysis. Sophisticated techniques developed over decades demonstrate how the effects of trauma can be contained, healed, and transcended. We can apply a therapeutic posture to politics.

Even people without trauma can be swept up by powerful social forces. Social psychology experiments have demonstrated that even well-educated, privileged American youth can behave cruelly, as revealed in the work of Philip Zimbardo (2002), social psychologist and president of the American Psychological Association. In his well-known Stanford prison experiment, students assigned in a simulation to roles of either prisoners or guards became so intensely absorbed in playing their roles destructively that the two-week experiment had to be terminated after six days. If experimental conditions can drive college students to be abusive in a few days, we can imagine the effects of real, prolonged physical and psychological suffering.

REPEATED TRAUMA AND PSYCHOLOGICAL MUTATION

According to self-psychologist Robert Stolerow (1991), trauma generates pathology by a two-stage process. The experience of trauma itself need not cause pathology. After trauma, people naturally reach out for care, comfort, validation, and support. When this reaching out is met with silence, disbelief, rebuff, or collusion, a pathogenic process ensues. Rejection deepens the trauma, literally adding insult to injury.

When attempts to secure help are met, recovery and healing take place, preventing pathology and/or later violence. Thus bystanders bear a significant responsibility.

If the pattern of trauma and rebuff is repeated, people can be radically plunged into an intolerable abyss, causing a psychological mutation. Harry Stack Sullivan described his conceptualization of *malevolent transformation,* "calculated to get around the idea that man is essentially evil." In *The Interpersonal Theory of Psychiatry* (1953), Sullivan observed that children who had certain kinds of early experiences became malevolent. People were denied tenderness and were met with reactions that led "frequently to . . . being disadvantaged, made anxious, being made fun of. . . . Under these circumstances, the developmental course changes to the point that the perceived need for tenderness brings a foresight of anxiety or pain"

(p. 213). Instead of showing a need for tenderness, "the child shows something else, and that something else is the basic, malevolent attitude, the attitude that one lives among enemies . . ." (p. 214).

In people fortunate enough to be raised by loving adults, vulnerable feelings carry the expectation of comfort, while in these children, mere feelings of vulnerability signal the expectation of harshness. Tender feelings in themselves become terrifying.

In *The Primitive Edge of Experience* (1989), psychoanalyst Thomas Ogden describes *autistic-contiguous position*, a primitive, raw, sensation-dominated dimension of human experience. In a nurturing environment, we are provided with "a feeling of softness that we later associate with ideas like security, safety, relaxation, warmth, and affection." When there is instead the presence of harshness, it leads to "autistic-contiguous anxiety," characterized by "feelings of disconnectedness, fragmentation, 'impending disintegration of one's surface' and terrifying feelings" (pp. 67–68). To defend against these intolerable feelings, one forms a hard, protective shell. Relationships are characterized by superficial imitation. "Imitation serves not only as a form of perception, a defense, and a way of 'holding onto' (being shaped by) the other, it serves as . . ." (pp. 74–75) a way of relating to people.

The harsh early experience of the young recruits described in Ahmed Rashid's *The Taliban* (2000) are consistent with the forms of psychological damage described above. Trauma is evident in the later actions of these youth, aged fourteen to twenty-four, who joined Mullah Omar.

> These boys were a world apart from the Mujaheddin whom I had got to know in the 1980s . . . These boys were from a generation who had never seen their country at peace. . . . They had no memories of their tribes, their elders, their neighbors, nor the complex mix of ethnic peoples that make up their villages and their homeland. These boys were what the war had thrown up like the sea's surrender on the beach of history.

> They had no memories from the past, no plans for the future, while the present was everything. They were literally the orphans of the war, the rootless and the restless, the jobless and the economically deprived with little self-knowledge. They admired war because it was the only occupation they could possibly adapt to. Their simple belief in a messianic, puritan Islam which had been drummed into them by simple village mullahs was the only prop they could hold onto and which gave their lives some meaning.

> Many in fact were orphans who had grown up without women— mothers, sisters or cousins. Others were *madrassa* students who had grown up in strict confines of segregated refugee camp life where the comings and goings of female relatives were curtailed. . . . these boys had lived rough, tough lives. They had simply never known the company of women. (pp. 32–33)

Inner trauma, unresolved grief, the absence of softness and holding, the severing from females and qualities referred to as "the feminine," the loss of childhood experiences of joy, play, tenderness, freedom, and love are played out locally and globally. The suppression of women, the suppression of manifestations of Eros, the life force—females, music, and kite flying—are a projection of an inner drama. Those qualities that have been killed off on the inside are now killed off on the outside through representatives who embody those killed-off qualities.

This bereft generation is also vulnerable to "trauma bonding," described in *Bearing Witness* (Bloom & Reichert, 1998).

> Even more ominous for repeatedly traumatized people is their pronounced tendency to use highly abnormal and dangerous relationships as their normal idea of what relationships are supposed to be (Herman, 1992; James, 1994; Van der Kolk, 1989). Trauma-bonding is a relationship based on terror and twisting of normal attachment behavior into something perverse and cruel. (p. 139)

So these traumatized, war-orphaned, refugee boys formed a powerful, pathological attachment to their authoritarian substitute parental figures, who exploited their vulnerability.

THE DYNAMICS OF LEADERS AND RECRUITS

Across cultures, young adult males tend to join in groups—military, athletic, or religious groups—in which they are intensely trained by powerful authority figures (officers, coaches, or clergy). An archetypal energy attracts young males to such experiences, which provide identity, community, security, and perhaps a sense of superiority.

Terrorist cultures contain an aberrant, traumatized, exaggerated, pathological variation of these elements. The damaged boys described in *The Taliban* (2000) were vulnerable to enchantment by powerful leaders, who provided a sense of coherence. Trauma rendered them vulnerable to manipulative leaders who used fundamentalist beliefs to extend their power and offer appeal of an afterlife when this life is intolerable.

Terrorist leaders have been described as malignant narcissists in *Bloodlines* (Volkan, 1997), and paranoid in *Political Paranoia* (Robins & Post, 1997) with delusions of persecution and grandeur, "intended to overcome the sense of inferiority, unworthiness, and unlovability" (p. 16).

According to Volkan (1997), "Terrorist leaders, however, are rarely mentally ill. Many are highly intelligent with the ability for strategic planning, even if personal identity problems are common among them . . . terrorist leaders tend to shore up their internal sense of self by seeking the power to hurt and by expressing their sense of entitlement to power" (p. 161).

Interviews reveal that terrorist leaders experienced beatings, incest, violations of boundaries, victimization, rejection, abandonment, and severe humiliation in childhood, often by their enemies. Terrorist leaders recreate an oppressive environment within their own communities in a traumatic reenactment.

> So strong is the terrorist cell's perceived need to silence opposition and establish unassailable authority within its own ethnic group, that a campaign of internally directed terror—toward people of its own ethnicity—is often considered essential to an effective campaign against the other dominant large group. . . . Fear is generated both to crush internal opposition and to disrupt the enemy. (Volkan, 1997, p. 159)

Inducing fear is a technique used by terrorist leaders to intensify identification with the leader and a sense of security with his power. When the dominant group retaliates

> the fear and anxiety of young people in the terrorist's ethnic group increase. This escalation of violence, combined with the rage toward the enemy group, propels members of the terrorist's ethnic group to rally around the terrorist leader. . . . Retaliation by the dominant group may only intensify the terrorist followers' identification with their own leaders. (Volkan, 1997, p. 164)

We can clearly see the ripple effects of terror and trauma, where individual trauma is played out within the group and then projected onto external targets, who may behave in ways that make them good hooks for these projections, thus unwittingly playing into the dance of terror. Recruits cannot challenge their own leaders, and may not even be aware of being dominated and oppressed by them. They are confused by feelings of loyalty, dependence, and traumatic bonding. It is easy to focus their rage on an outer enemy, who may or may not have contributed to their suffering but is nonetheless a permissible target. Family therapist and theorist Murray Bowen's theory of triangulation states that when there is tension in a two-party system, the parties will seek out a third focus to reduce the tension between them. This is a dynamic in scapegoating (Bowen, 1978).

Volkan states that terrorist leaders with a diagnosis of malignant narcissism are similar to serial killers. Christopher Bollas's study of serial killers in his chapter "The Structure of Evil" gives us insights into the psyche of the masterminds of terror (Bollas, 1995).

"The Structure of Evil" is exemplified by the story of temptation in the Garden of Eden, where "the 'Evil one' presents himself as good and earns the other's trust." The structure contains a link between the "power of the tempter and the weakness of the subject's resolve" and the "power of the charmer was seen as proportionate to the recipient's need" (pp. 182–183).

Bollas's brilliant description of how serial killers reenact their own experience of annihilation of the self may shed light on understanding people such as bin Laden, Hitler, Saddam Hussein, and Milosevic. The innocence of the victim is part of the dynamic of the structure of evil, as the killer reenacts the soul murder of his own innocence. Following the 2002 murder of *Wall Street Journal* reporter Daniel Pearl, his family said in a public statement that they could not imagine anyone murdering someone with such a "gentle soul." Bollas's observations tragically explain how the victim's innocence is part of the dynamic.

The malignant narcissism of these killers can be understood through the story of Satan's fall. Bollas refers to Milton's *Paradise Lost*:

> illuminating how loss of love and catastrophic displacement can foster an envious hatred of life mutating into an identification with the anti-life, Milton reaches the nature and effect of trauma. The prince of darkness is a traumatized soul who feels condemned to work his trauma upon the human race, trying to bring others to an equivalent fall. It is impossible to exclude from our consideration of Milton's Satan the overwhelming power and structural malevolence of God's authority, which seems grotesquely harmonized with the lust for power to which Satan succumbs. (p. 184)

Bollas found that serial killers had experiences that could be described as soul murder, or annihilation of the self, in childhood. Like the vampire myth, the serial killer is a killed self, condemned to remain in a state of living death. He reenacts his own psychic death by replaying it with innocent victims who represent his killed innocent self. Killing is an attempt at transformation from victim to master. Bollas urges us to consider the complexity of murder rather than reducing it to pure evil:

> Evil, considered as a structure, points to a complex reorganization of trauma in which the subject recollects the loss of love and the birth of hate by putting subsequent others through the unconscious terms of a malevolent extinction of the self. (pp. 219–220)

Applying the metaphor of Satan's fall from the serial killer to the terrorist leader, we can get a sense of a psychological drama embedded within a political drama. A narcissistic person with intelligence, charm, and talent, having endured malevolent trauma and wrenching humiliation, is driven by the compulsion to restore his esteem, gain mastery, and redress past injustices. Unlike the serial killer, the terrorist leader is drawn into a larger, mythical story, flooded with archetypal energies. In this volatile field, a person with the right qualities can fill the leading role, both manipulating and being manipulated by the powerful forces in the system.

THE POLITICS OF ENVY AND HUMILIATION

Envy and humiliation are significant in histories of individuals and groups who become violent. We became aware of humiliation caused by bullying in the Columbine school shootings. We also see murders after someone is fired from a job or gets a poor grade. Education about bullying focuses on the interpersonal level, with little application to global bullying and humiliation.

The power of humiliation cannot be underestimated. Humiliation and envy, which go together, are exceedingly destructive emotions. Being humiliated is like being filled with poison that has to be expelled in order to regain composure. Humiliation carries a narcissistic wound that contains an implicit demand for rectification, often by taking down the humiliator.

In a videotaped message by Osama bin Laden that aired in October 2001, he emphasized the relationship between the attacks and the fact that his people had been humiliated for eighty years. Regardless of what people think of bin Laden, it behooves us to take the issue of humiliation seriously for our own security.

Shibley Telhami, Anwar Sadat professor for peace and development at the University of Maryland, in referring to the Palestinian-Israeli conflict, said on CNN in November 2001 that humiliation is more important than poverty as a cause of violence and terrorism. During the Cuban missile crisis of 1962, John and Bobby Kennedy recognized that they had to find a way to let Khrushchev save face in order to end the threat of nuclear attack. Intelligent political maneuvers are designed to consider face-saving strategies.

TERRORISM AS A TRAUMATIC REENACTMENT

People often engage in behaviors that bring them unhappiness and pain. Freud called this the "repetition compulsion." He said that even more powerful than the drive for pleasure is the drive to repeat, even if what we repeat is painful. Terrorist leaders and recruits play out their traumas inside and outside their groups.

From an evolutionary perspective, we would imagine that this pervasive pattern must have some survival value. It seems cosmically unfair that people who have had the great misfortune of suffering trauma are doomed to reenact it and hurt others. Reenactment is a way the psyche speaks.

Overwhelming experiences "frozen" in the psyche continue to exert effects by constricting psychic freedom in ways that are detrimental to quality of life and relationships. As a matter of adaptation and survival, we would hypothesize that these unassimilated elements in the psyche could find a way to be recognized and processed so that a person could develop and improve his or her quality of life.

An example of a healthy expression of this survival mechanism is a baby's cry to signal pain. Adults who hear the cry are affected by the emotion. They cannot tolerate the cry and wish to make it better. They respond with empathy, address the need, and provide satisfaction, security, and trust. This idea is applied to trauma in *Bearing Witness* (Bloom & Reichert, 1998):

> Children who have been traumatized cannot heal themselves alone. It is one of the tragedies of human existence that what begins as life-saving coping skills, ends up delivering us into the hands of compulsive repetition. We are destined to reenact what we cannot remember. Freud called it the *repetition compulsion* and he said, "He produces it not as a memory, but as an action; he repeats it, without, of course, knowing that he is repeating. . . . He cannot escape from this compulsion to repeat; and in the end we understand that this is his way of remembering." (Van der Kolk & Ducey, 1989, p. 271) (p. 141)

It is both a way of remembering and of communicating the memory to others. In an unconscious process of traumatic reenactment, one provokes other people to recreate experiences similar to the original trauma. In the reenactment, a person may alternate playing both sides of their experience, becoming a victim again or attempting to master the situation by enacting the part of the perpetrator with someone more helpless who represents their traumatized self.

REENACTMENT THROUGH PROJECTIVE IDENTIFICATION

Reenactment can either set the stage for retraumatization or it can contain the seeds for healing. Through an intersubjective experience, unconsciously motivated, psychoanalysts are drawn into the roles of abuser and abused at different moments. When an individual or group reenacts early trauma, others are induced to retaliate, and are unconsciously drawn into the repetition. The pull to reenact is strong. Resisting reenactment is a conscious, deliberate effort, a "work against nature," required to contain this process.

Projective identification was introduced by psychoanalyst Melanie Klein and developed further by others (Ogden, 1989). It is a common aspect of intersubjective experience, a form of unconscious communication in which one transmits one's own internal experience to another, like a psychic infection. It can be euphoric or it can be frightening or enraging.

With trauma, projective identification is an unconscious mechanism by which one evacuates intolerable affects and *deposits* them into the "other." The "other" may feel possessed by alien psychic contents, and may be pulled into the reenactment. This way a person may influence and control others through this unconscious process.

In therapy, the analyst may be provoked by the client's toxic, unassimilated affects, and be pulled to retaliate through rejection or hostile interpretation. Intersubjective psychoanalysts are trained to resist the pull to reenact and retaliate. The analyst provides a "container," a safe "holding environment," in the words of pediatrician and psychoanalyst Donald Winnicott (Greenberg & Mitchell, 1983), and can receive this as a communication about preverbal experience. At the most difficult moment, the analyst can sense what the client must have felt like as a child. The analyst uses this awareness for empathy, which has a healing effect and helps metabolize the negative affect. It makes the unconscious conscious, remembers the forgotten, and empowers one to master affects that previously gripped the person. One no longer need reenact the drama, and is freer to have more satisfying relationships. The goal is consciousness and liberation from the cycle of suffering.

Knowledge from this "laboratory" for processing trauma has applications to terrorism, but requires institutional and political support. Retaliation draws us into the reenactment, plays into the projections, escalates cycles of violence, and prevents consciousness.

INTERSUBJECTIVITY, ROLE REVERSAL, AND PERVERSE EMPATHY

Terrorism is an intersubjective experience. The intolerable affects of the terrorists are projected into the recipients of terror—the powerful, the envied, the humiliating, the privileged ones. Terrorism, as a form of projective identification and a form of communication, involuntarily draws its victims into its drama. The victims experience a transformation of their subjectivity, as they are now possessed by terror. They now feel the powerlessness, frustration, grief, and terror previously carried by the terrorist.

The victims are now engaged in an intense psychic relationship with the terrorists, and are filled with a new, unfamiliar, alien set of emotions. Roles are reversed.

HELPLESS	POWERFUL
VICTIM	MASTER OF FATE
DOMINATED	IN CONTROL
INFERIOR	SUPERIOR
ENVIOUS	ENTITLED
HUMILIATED	PROUD
TERRORIZED	OBLIVIOUS

Terrorism can be thought of as a perversion of the desire for empathy. After September 11, 2001, everyone from bin Laden to America's allies said in one form or another, "Now you know how we feel" with a sense of grim satisfaction. It is a universal human experience to want others to know how we feel when we are suffering. Perhaps the desire for empathy is an unrelenting nonnegotiable requirement. Again, according to needs theory, if empathy is not naturally forthcoming it will be extracted in a pathological manner.

TERRORISM AS A PERVERSION OF THE DESIRE FOR TRUTH, FREEDOM, AND JUSTICE

Like empathy, we also have a universal urge for life, truth, justice, equality, dignity, and freedom. When empathy, truth, and justice are not available, they will be secured by any means. As Freud said, if sexuality is thwarted, it will seek expression by devious means. There is an instinctual drive for truth and justice that I have coined as *verido*, like the drive for sex, libido. As with libido, if the drive for truth and justice is blocked, verido will seek perverse means for realization.

When one is suffering, one wants recognition of truth and redress. When there is inequality, one yearns for equality. If these are not forthcoming, an act of terrorism, unconsciously designed, attempts to secure these needs at any cost. Attention is gained. Perverse empathy is achieved when the other feels pain and loss, too. By making the powerful helpless, equality is achieved. It would have been preferable by far to achieve equality in a healthier way.

PUNIMANIA AND THE URGE TO RETALIATE

Intolerable affects projected onto the privileged ones feel alien and unfamiliar. Many of the recipients, in shock, grief-stricken and enraged, may desire to expel their feelings through revenge, thus deepening the cycle of violence. However, the privileged ones have more psychic freedom, capacity for reflection, flexibility, and creativity. They may be less driven by an enduring sense of historical grievance. Like the psychoanalyst, they have the potential to resist the pull to retaliate. In fact, many family members of people who died in the September 11 attacks started a group called "Not in My Name" and advocated against retaliation, because they did not want others to suffer as they had.

Nonetheless, urges to retaliate feel justified. Citizens who question this are considered unpatriotic, anti-American, or naïve. Punishment, or revenge, is intensely felt to be required because "they" deserve it. It is uncritically accepted as necessary, even if it makes things worse for the punisher. Punishment is deemed more important than its consequences, and it often leads to unintended consequences, now popularly known as "blowback."

I have coined the term *punimania* to describe the overwhelming urge to punish, which may or may not be justified, when punishment: 1) does not address or resolve the root causes of the problem, 2) generates more suffering for innocent people in widening circles over time and space, and 3) has the probability of making things worse, even for the punisher. There are many examples of this, but an obvious one is the escalation of violence between the Israelis and Palestinians.

What if we paused to imagine that the feelings of the terrorists' people have been deposited into us? This by no means condones the terrorist. Is there a way to do global therapy to contain and transmute the trauma, to use it for knowledge, empathy, and consciousness? It is in our interest because we don't want to generate more suffering that will surely come back at us. Can we differentiate the few terrorist leaders from the masses, decent leaders, and governments whose grievances they express, and regard them in a less polarizing, provocative manner? Can we reduce hatred toward us? The response would not be to gratify the terrorists, but to consider the suffering of the masses that led to the terrorist acts, and to be careful not to engage in policies that increase suffering anywhere. This is enlightened self-interest.

FROM VICTIM TO MASTER OF ONE'S FATE

When there seems to be no way out, terrorism is a way of transforming victimhood to mastery. Being weak and feeling victimized are intolerable psychological states. Object relations theorist and psychoanalyst W. R. D. Fairbairn observed that people would rather be bad than weak[5] (Greenberg & Mitchell, 1983). Vamik Volkan, psychoanalyst and former president of the International Society of Political Psychology, observed that people would rather die physically than psychologically (1985), giving the example of Armenians' refusal to accept Azerbaijani blood after the Armenian earthquake. There are many other examples.

In "Searching for Answers to Gaza's Suicide Bombings" (1997), Andoni observed that "The intifada seemed to turn Palestinians from victims to masters of their fate." Likewise, Oliver and Steinberg (1997), in a study of suicide bombers, describe suicide bombing as "a preemptive strike." Rather than let the enemy kill them, they kill themselves to deprive enemy of the experience, "attaining some kind of mastery over the inevitable," over the destruction of the self. In a CNN interview in March 2002, a potential suicide bomber said, "They kill me if I go here, they kill me if I go there. I might as well kill myself and take some of them with me." Ironically, it is psychologically similar to the Masada phenomenon of "Kiddush HaShem," the sanctification of God's name, whereby it is a holy act to take one's life rather than allow the enemy to do so.

This helps us understand martyrdom, which in 2002 had been elevated to the level of cultural heroism, with more willing volunteers than when the above statements were made.

SYSTEMS THEORY AND TERRORISM AS ASYMMETRICAL WARFARE

We refer to terrorism as the warfare of the weak, although certain actions of powerful states fit the original definitions of terror. Thus, a primary aspect in the drama of terrorism is the desire of the powerless to bring down the powerful. This is a universal mythological motif that we see in stories like David and Goliath and Jack and the Beanstalk.

Terrorism is a form of asymmetrical warfare. It is a recourse for people who are oppressed, occupied, or dominated. According to needs theory (Fogg, 2001), people prefer to have their needs met by decent means, and attempt to do so at first. If reasonable attempts fail, they will resort to more devious, extreme methods. If needs could be met decently, then cruel, manipulative, dangerous leaders would lose public support.

No one is satisfied to remain in a position of inequality and deprivation of basic physical and psychological needs. Power imbalances are inherently unstable in the long term, as we have seen with the civil rights, women's rights, gay rights, and other movements. In a world with increasing access to weapons of mass destruction, this fact is very worrisome. As long as people feel weak, inferior, dominated, and deprived, they will be naturally driven to even the score, just as water seeks its own level. This is a law of nature. When a team of healthy, secure, privileged youth loses a basketball game, its members are in a psychological state of being intensely preoccupied with winning the next time to restore their position. Such a desire is all the more intense in the case of true and prolonged humiliation and suffering.

Processes of asymmetrical warfare and cycles of retaliation follow patterns that can be understood in terms of systems theories. Davidson (1983) says, ". . . because life is governed by the natural laws of systems, a successful participant must learn the rules" (p. 95).

Family systems therapists apply concepts from general systems theory to family dynamics. When progress in individual therapy was undermined in the family, they discovered that family systems attempt to maintain homeostatic balance through negative feedback loops, self-correcting processes, acting like thermostats. Lynn Hoffman refers to these as the "the first cybernetics" (1971).

Hoffman (1971) quotes Magoroh Maruyama, who emphasizes the greater importance of "the second cybernetics," "which he sees as an essential agency for change in living forms" (p. 285). These processes are called positive feedback loops, deviation amplifying mutual causal processes, positive feedback spirals (Napier & Whitaker, 1978, p. 82), and schizmogenesis (Bateson, 1972, p. 324), and they can have the effect of changing systems, for better or worse.

> Such systems are ubiquitous: accumulation of capital in industry, evolution of living organisms, the rise of cultures of various types, interpersonal processes which produce mental illness, international conflicts, and the processes which are loosely termed as "vicious circles" and "compound interests"; in short, all processes of mutual causal relationships that amplify an insignificant or accidental kick, build up deviation, and diverge form the initial condition. (Maruyama in Hoffman, 1971, p. 285)

Deviation amplifying mutual causal processes reinforce change in either direction, as "when a child's behavior steadily improves with praise or deteriorates with blame" (Davidson, 1983, p. 203). Davidson also describes how a viable system can be destroyed by feeding back inaccurate and misinformation, as in biased journalism. The nuclear arms race and the escalation of terrorism are examples of destructive positive feedback spirals.

It is easy to see the tragic escalation of retaliation between the Israelis and the Palestinians, which shifted from a negative feedback loop to a positive feedback spiral in the fall of 2000. The spiral continued, even while knowing that each "justified" action would provoke another, worse "justified" reaction. If we applied this knowledge of feedback loops consciously, we could avoid escalation and design strategies and policies that would reduce violence.

An example of a conscious, creative positive feedback spiral is described by Charles Osgood (1981), who developed the approach to de-escalation called "graduated and reciprocated initiatives in tension-reduction," or GRIT. GRIT aims "to reduce and control international tension levels and to create an atmosphere of mutual trust within which negotiations on critical military and political issues can have a better chance of succeeding." There have been some historical cases where this has been applied successfully as part of a complex strategy in tension reduction and violence prevention.

Let's return to the quote from Bollas (1995) in light of positive feedback loops. "It is impossible to exclude from our consideration of Milton's Satan the overwhelming power and structural malevolence of God's authority, which seems grotesquely harmonized with the lust for power to which Satan succumbs" (p. 184). God and Satan are bound to each other in this dynamic tension. The position of God sounds like the position of the United States, having "overwhelming power" and what is sometimes perceived as "malevolent authority" by our enemies. The enemy's "lust for power" is provoked by the United States' monopolistic possession of power. It is telling that the enemy calls the United States "the Great Satan." The greater the United States' exercise of power, the greater the enemy's reaction, thus illustrating the dynamics of this dance of terror.

There is no amount of power a nation can exercise that won't eventually evoke an asymmetrical response. Domination and control might have worked for millennia, but in a world with weapons of mass destruction there is no endgame to the dance of domination. Leaders, recruits, sympathizers, and supporters will arise to seek justice and dignity. They may believe the only way they can be uplifted is to take the dominant power down. Let us avoid playing into this.

The only endgame to the dance of power imbalance is the restoration of balance and equality. This is as much a matter of survival as it is of justice. According to the law of opposites, as the maxim goes, "you create what you resist." The United States has yet to discover the paradox that offers a way out of the dance of terror, that it can gain power (and security) by giving power.

PARADOX AND THE LIMITATIONS OF COUNTERTERRORISM

On September 11, the U.S.-led coalition became committed to an all-out "war on terrorism." While preparing to attack in Afghanistan, members of the Bush administration stated that the likelihood of retaliation against the United States was 100 percent, expecting more casualties at home than among the military abroad. There was widespread acceptance of the idea that the United States had no choice but to attack, even though it would provoke reprisals. There was virtually no challenge to the inevitability of escalation and the risk of innocent lives, and little imagination for outside-the-box strategies that might reduce terrorism. It seemed to be implicitly assumed that no other options existed.

We imagine terrorism as a permanent presence, hovering "out there" independent of our actions, waiting to get us no matter what we do. All we can possibly do is to wipe it out ourselves, not admitting that we know that such a thing is impossible. We have committed to counterterrorist experts and activities. While police action and surveillance are important components of a sound, complex strategy for eliminating terrorism, the singular emphasis on counterterrorism is limited. Moreover, military attacks and rejection of recourse to international justice are likely to provoke more hatred and resentment, leading to unintended consequences that ultimately make the United States more vulnerable. Cooperation with international justice might make U.S. citizens a lesser target and reduce resentment against the United States.

No amount of counterterrorism can make the United States secure, and may ultimately make it less secure. Efforts to suppress a symptom without addressing the cause will create more problems. Using common sense, being right, righteous, and reasonable usually makes things worse. If the United States succeeded in eliminating 99 percent of terrorism, it would still not be secure, for the remaining 1 percent could still do great damage. Counterterrorism approaches alone do not contain the seeds for ending terrorism and can never succeed completely because they do not penetrate the deeper nature of terrorism, only its superficial manifestation.

TRAUMA, GENDER, AND THE SPLITTING OF OPPOSITES

In optimal development, we achieve a healthy balance between the opposites— between self and other, male and female, us and them, life and death. With a traumatic upbringing, the opposites are split apart and out of balance.

Globally we have a severe imbalance in values, activities, and investments associated with life preservation and with destructive power. Life-sustaining qualities are falsely associated with "the feminine"—the earth, health, education, food, shelter, and so on. They are underfunded compared with military expenditures. We pay more to kill than to heal and protect. We pay more to punish than to prevent. We pay more to bomb than to build. In the United States, we spend more on building prisons than on schools. We get what we pay for.

Eros is defined here as the life force. It is sometimes mistakenly defined as "the feminine principle." In violent cultures, Eros activities are falsely assigned to the feminine, and denied to males, so both live a one-sided, unhealthy existence (Perlman, 1995). Gender-split cultures tend to be more violent, the Taliban being a prime example. Collective trauma causes a gender splitting that deprives males of life-affirming activities. They are required to deny essential elements of their personalities, which is a form of trauma. This generates the opposites of Eros, according to Jung; they are hate, fear (Phobos), and the will to power. "Where love reigns, there is no will to power; and where the will to power is paramount, love is lacking. The one is but the shadow of the other" (Jung, 1953, para. 78).

We have a global imbalance between life and death, us and them, the so-called masculine and feminine. While analyzing the dynamics of terrorism, we cannot ignore these imbalances that give rise to so much suffering. The Appendix features a chart by OS Earth, Inc. (www.osearth.com), an updated version from Buckminster Fuller's World Game Institute. It is a snapshot of the global imbalance between life and death, between love and fear. It is somehow easier to come up with money for destruction than for creation. As Jung said, consciousness is a work against nature. This is an image of our collective psyche. Out of fear, we act in ways that increase our fear, generating self-fulfilling prophecies and positive feedback spirals. This is a context that produces suffering, despair, fear, misery, humiliation, envy, and asymmetry—a context in which terrorism can arise. For a fraction of what the world spends on weapons, we could solve many of the root causes of violence.[6]

A WORK AGAINST NATURE

Albert Einstein said, "There's been a quantum leap technologically in our age, but unless there's another quantum leap in human relations, unless we learn to live in a new way towards one another, there will be a catastrophe."

Davidson (1983) uses the image of the Rubik's cube. If we focus on solving one facet of the problem, trying to get one side of the cube all red, for example, we actually set back the solution of the problem as a whole. Our intense approach to counterterrorism is like working on one facet of the Rubik's cube.

We know that it can't end terrorism, but we do not know what else to do. Uncommon sense is indicated here. This involves paradoxical thinking and psychological insight.

CONSCIOUS POLITICS AND POLITICAL EVOLUTION

Einstein also said, "The problems that we have created as a result of the level of thinking that we have done thus far cannot be solved at the same level of thinking at which we created them."

Living under the sword of Damocles, we Americans need to be exquisitely careful about our how we conduct ourselves in the world. The way we conduct ourselves can increase or decrease hatred and resentment against us. In pondering the questions of "why they hate us," we cannot afford to reduce self-examination to assertions of how good we really are. Accusations about being unpatriotic are inside the box and prevent us from acting in ways that make us safer. These "ego responses" are understandable, but not helpful.

The messages we send do make a difference. Saying that we are right and strong (even if this is true) and that we will dominate and defeat, will increase tension, fear, and resentment around the world. It can inspire and motivate desires to attack us. If we are highly conscious of the asymmetrical nature of warfare, we will use language and actions that do not emphasize the asymmetry, which is humiliating and dangerous. We might imagine ways of elevating others for our own safety. People are most dangerous when they are afraid, so we may want to be reassuring and be extra careful about provoking fear. We can be aware that we, too, are more dangerous when we are afraid.

We need a new approach, which I call "conscious politics." It comprises many concepts such as "political wisdom" or "political maturity." Like Daniel Goleman's groundbreaking concept, and bestseller, *Emotional Intelligence* (1995), we can envision a "political intelligence" that can be applied to reducing terrorism and transforming our posture in global politics. I use the term "transcendent politics," in which policies transcend particular interests, dualistic thinking, and consider optimal, win-win strategies with long-term benefit.

Einstein's comment about a new level of thinking suggests a "political evolution." Each century is bloodier than the last. A Chinese proverb states that "If we keep going in the same direction, we will end up where we are headed." Darwin's theory of natural selection, of "survival of the fittest," won't have the opportunity to play itself out if the politically maladaptive members of the species possess weapons of mass destruction.

This approach is not "political." It is not about right or left, liberal or conservative, Republican or Democrat, right or wrong. Dualistic, polarizing positions are inside the box and are part of the problem. This attitude deepens the conflict, makes it intractable, causes more trauma, and sets back progress. A therapeutic approach to politics is preoccupied with understanding all sides, the alleviation of suffering, healing from trauma, protection, problem solving, reversing positive feedback spirals, and ending the generational transmission of trauma.

"Conscious politics" is also "egoless politics," concerned with the welfare of the whole. It requires humility and giving up a dominating posture. Volkan's observation that "we would rather die physically than psychologically" applies to the United States as well; humility would be a kind of psychological death to the arrogant American ego. (Jung said that the death of the ego is a victory for the greater Self, for wholeness and consciousness.)

METAFORCE

The peace, antiwar, and disarmament movements have less credibility in the United States now than ever before. They have not articulated a plausible alternative strategy to military attack (Perlman, 2001). We have two main categories in our awareness—either attack or do nothing. Since doing nothing is untenable, we feel compelled to take military action. As a poor third alternative, negotiation and conflict resolution seem ineffective in dealing with brutal regimes.

Richard Wendell Fogg (2000) says that we don't need to abolish war, as "peaceniks" claim. We need to *replace* war. Fogg says we must use force—political force, economic force, social force, psychological, educational, physical, moral, intellectual, spiritual, emotional, and aesthetic forms of force—in combinations forming complex strategies (p. 179). He suggests systematic strategies, including reducing the opponent's fear, avoiding cornering the opponent, avoiding retaliating, satisfying just grievances, understanding the meaning of an attack, removing pressures, using mediators, designing win-win solutions, and so on, including some harsher nonviolent approaches when the more positive ones don't work. Fogg's ideas are consistent with some of the observations made by Martha Crenshaw (1999), Wesleyan professor and terrorism expert, at a special meeting at the United States Institute for Peace in April 1999, on "How Terrorism Ends." Some factors that serve to reduce terrorism are success or partial success, satisfying just grievances, organizational breakdown, drawing recruits away from leaders, economic loss, and providing new options and alternatives for political change.

Since we don't have a concept to describe bloodless forms of force, I have coined the term *metaforce*, which is not passive, and similar to the Indian terms *ahimsa* and *satyagraha*. Metaforce can be very effective in the long run. A PBS series and book, *A Force More Powerful* (2000), describe effective, powerful, nonviolent social movements.

There is a proposal now for a Global Nonviolent Peace Force (www.nonviolent peaceforce.org) that can be used to reduce tension and prevent violence so other strategies can be used to solve problems. A body of knowledge on violence prevention and conflict transformation already exists, although it is rarely mentioned in the media and the political arena. This means that many people are not aware of potentially successful strategies and lack imagination for creative, nonmilitary approaches.

TRANSCENDING TERRORISM, A QUANTUM LEAP

Maybe instead of the biggest superpower, the United States could be the biggest "super-empowerer." Awareness of the suffering in Afghanistan, realization of U.S. complicity in abandonment of the Afghan people after their war against the Soviet Union, and U.S. commitment to help rebuild the country are a good beginning shift in our consciousness. Ervin Staub (1989), past president of the International Society of Political Psychology, emphasizes how changing from passive bystanders to active ones, or rescuers, can turn the tide in preventing war and genocide.

Those in positions of greatest power and privilege bear responsibility for those in weaker positions. The difference between traumatic processes that lead to terrorism and those that lead to recovery lies in the power of the active bystander, revealed in the formula for terrorism. The key to transcending terrorism is intervening to alleviate suffering, as early as possible, wherever and whenever possible. This is a matter of national security, which is an oxymoron, as there is either universal security or no security in our global village.

There is no such thing as "neutrality." Those of us who are neither perpetrators nor victims are bystanders, witnesses. President Kennedy (1961, p. xiii) liked to quote Dante: "The hottest places in Hell are reserved for those who, in a time of great moral crisis, maintain their neutrality." In his acceptance speech for the Nobel Peace Prize in 1986, human rights activist Elie Wiesel said, "We must take sides. Neutrality helps the oppressor, never the victim. Silence encourages the tormentors, not the tormented."

LIBERATION FROM RETALIATION

"Men and nations behave wisely only after exhausting all other alternatives."

Abba Eban

"History, despite its wrenching pain
cannot be unlived, but if faced
With Courage, need not be lived again."

Maya Angelou, inaugural poem

September 11 provided a golden opportunity for us to transcend old patterns. Jung described neurosis as a one-sided conscious attitude. In elaborating the law of opposites, he used the term *enantiodromia* (Samuels, Shorter, & Plaut, 1986, p. 53), meaning when things go too far to one extreme, they turn into their opposite. The United States has been considered extremely arrogant, dominating, invulnerable, unilateral, and culturally immature. According to Jungian theory, if we are too one-sided, life events may confront us with our underdeveloped opposite aspects. Our hope lies in integrating our undeveloped opposite qualities—humility, a healthy awareness of our vulnerability, cooperation, maturity, and complexity. As Benjamin Barber, author of *Jihad vs. MacWorld,* said on C-Span Book TV in 2002, the United States needs to join the rest of the world.

Just as there is a two-part process in psychological mutation into violence (trauma followed by rejection), there may also be a two-part process in liberation from the cycle of violence. First the United States must liberate itself from the psychological effects of fifty years of intense engagement in the Cold War, followed by being the only superpower. Becoming free oneself is the first step. To complete the process of liberation, we must liberate others from suffering.

As a nation, we must face our history, "despite its wrenching pain," with courage—both the good we have done and the mistakes we have made out of fear, ignorance, and greed. We are not all good or all bad. A sign of psychological health is the capacity to live in the tension between the opposites. While appreciating the good we have done, we also need an accurate review of our history, including our support of brutal dictatorships and our collusion with acts of oppression.

The concept of "redemption" is not given its due in its potential for political evolution. It would help if we could be accountable for parts of our past, to reflect and atone for our mistakes, acknowledge our responsibility. There are ways in which we could redeem ourselves, even in the eyes of those who now resent us.

We are becoming more compassionate toward the suffering of others. The movement from victim to bystander to protector is a transformative process. People who live in comfort, freedom, and dignity with justice, tend not to be violent. Those who have suffered are soothed by acknowledgment of truth, address of injustice, and improvements in living conditions. Liberating others will increase our security and freedom.

As I am putting final touches on this chapter, my country is abrogating the Anti-Ballistic Missile Treaty (the cornerstone of stability for thirty years), threatening to develop a new class of "mininukes" (a more credible threat than our multi-megaton bombs), targeting non-nuclear states, still refusing to sign the No First Use treaty, posturing to attack Iraq, and angering its enemies and allies alike. I am terrified by our actions in the name of "security," by the psychologically flawed justifications for them, by the global responses to us, and above all to our dismissal of them. I am not optimistic that we are about to transcend the cycle of retaliation and escalation of violence. If we do, we will have undergone a profound transformation informed by knowledge of the inner and outer workings of the human psyche. It will require us to use our intersubjective experience of terrorism and all forms of violence, and to apply political wisdom, maturity, intelligence, consciousness, and metaforce in ways that will make us all safer. As a "possiblist" (a term coined by author Max Lerner when asked whether he was an optimist or a pessimist), I have described my best guess as to what might be required of us if we are to break destructive cycles.

REFERENCES

Andoni, L. (1997, Summer). Searching for answers to Gaza's suicide bombings. *Journal of Palestinian Studies, 26,* 33–45.

Bandler, R., Grinder, J., & Satir, V. (1976). *Changing with families: A book about further education for being human.* Palo Alto, CA: Science and Behavior Books.

Barber, B. R. (1995). *Jihad vs. McWorld.* New York: Times Books.

Bateson, G. (1972). *Steps to an ecology of mind.* New York: Ballantine Books.

Bloom, S. L., & Reichert, M. (1998). *Bearing witness: Violence and collective responsibility.* New York: Hayworth Maltreatment and Trauma Press.

Bollas, C. (1995). The structure of evil. In *Cracking up: The work of unconscious experience.* New York: Hill and Wang.

Bowen, M. (1978). *Family therapy in clinical practice.* New York: Jason Aronson.

Crenshaw, M. (1999). *How terrorism ends.* United States Institute of Peace, special report, http://www.usip.org/oc/sr/sr990525/sr990525.html.

Davidson, M. (1983). *Uncommon sense: The life and thought of Ludwig von Bertalanffy, father of general systems theory.* Los Angeles: J. P. Tarcher Inc.

Fogg, R. W. (2000). Nonmilitary responses to nuclear threat or attack. In J. Presler & S. J. Scholz, *Peacemaking: Lessons from the past, visions for the future.* Amsterdam, Netherlands: Rodopi.

Fogg, R. W. (October, 2001). Personal communication, "Deal with Moslem grievances."

Goleman, D. (1995). *Emotional intelligence: Why it can matter more than IQ.* New York: Bantam Books.

Greenberg, J., & Mitchell, S. (1983). *Object relations in psychoanalytic theory.* London: Cambridge University Press.

Hoffman, L. (1971). Deviation amplifying processes in natural groups. In J. Haley (Ed.), *Changing families: A family therapy reader.* New York: Grune & Stratton.

Jung, C. G. (1953). *Collected works,* Vol. 7. New York: Bollingen Foundation.

Kennedy, J. F. (1961). *Profiles in courage.* New York: Harper & Row.

Napier, A. Y., & Whitaker, C. (1978). *The family crucible.* New York: Bantam Books.

Ogden, T. (1989). *The primitive edge of experience.* New York: Jason Aronson.

Ogden, T. (1994) *Subjects of analysis.* Northvale, NJ: Jason Aronson.

Oliver, A. M., & Steinberg, P. (1997). National Public Radio interview.

Osgood, C. (1981). Disarmament demands GRIT. In E. Laslo & D. Keyes (Eds.), *Disarmament: The human factor.* Oxford, England: Pergamon Press.

Perlman, D. (1995). *Eros perverted: Analyzing violence through the lens of gender.* Slide Presentation, American Psychological Association, Division of Psychoanalysis, Spring Meeting, Santa Monica, April 1995; and the NGO Forum of the UN Fourth World Conference on Women, Beijing, China, August 1995.

Perlman, D. (1997, October 13–15). *The psychoanatomy of political terrorism.* Proceeding of the Gaza Community Mental Health Programme Third International Conference on Health and Human Rights, Gaza, Palestine.

Perlman, D. (2001). The fear of disarmament. In *Disarmament Times, 24,* 2.

Rashid, A. (2000). *The Taliban.* New Haven, CT: Yale University Press.

Robins, R. S., &. Post, J. M. (1997). *Political paranoia: The psychopolitics of hatred.* New Haven, CT: Yale University Press.

Samuels, A., Shorter, B., & Plaut, F. (1986). *A critical dictionary of Jungian analysis.* London: Routledge & Keagan Paul.

Staub, E. (1989). *The roots of evil: The origins of genocide and other group violence.* Cambridge: Cambridge University Press.

Stolerow, R. (1991, April). Address, American Psychological Association, Division of Psychoanalysis, Annual Spring Meeting, Philadelphia, PA.

Sullivan, H. S. (1953). *The interpersonal theory of psychiatry.* New York: W. W. Norton.

Telhami, S. CNN, November 2001

Volkan, V. (1985, July). Personal communication.

Volkan, V. (1997). *Bloodlines: From ethnic pride to ethnic terrorism.* New York: Farrar, Straus and Giroux.

Watzlawick, P., Weakland, J., & Fish, R. (1974). *Change: The principles of problem formation and problem resolution* New York: W. W. Norton.

Zimbardo, P. (2002). http://www.zimbardo.com.

NOTES

1. By "we" I mean the United States (or whoever has the most power) as the only superpower, acting primarily unilaterally on the world stage. There is much we can do to increase or decrease the cycle of violence.

2. The Nine-Dot Problem is an excellent example of how difficult it can be to think outside the box. The challenge is to connect the nine dots with four straight lines without lifting the pen from the paper.

Most people struggle with this for a long time, and after much frustration conclude that it is impossible. There is no solution. Many experience the same futility about war, the nuclear threat, terrorism, and ethnic conflicts. What prevents us from seeing a solution is that we limit ourselves by thinking in old ways that don't work. For a deeper explanation of this problem and the assumptions we tend to make in problem solving, visit http://www.consciouspolitics.com. For the solution to the problem, see the end of this chapter.

3. In the Transcending Trauma Project at the Penn Council on Relationships, our group found that Holocaust survivors who had strong positive family relationships before the war were better able to endure trauma and made better postwar adjustments.

4. "Spiritual" refers to a sense of upliftment, purpose, or meaning beyond one's material existence, and may or may not be religious in nature.

5. This appears to be more true for males than for females.

6. Thanks to Medard Gabel for permission to use his chart. For more information, check the Web site www.osearth.com.

APPENDIX

Figure 3.1 seeks to make the point that what the world needs to solve the major systemic problems confronting humanity is both available and affordable. Clearly, to deal with a problem as complex and large as, for example, the global food situation, with just a small part of a single graph is incomplete, at best. The following explanations of the chart's various components are not intended as complete or detailed plans, but rather as very broad brushstrokes intended to give the overall direction, scope, and strategy. The paper, "What the World Wants Project" goes into more detail. It is available from the World Game Institute at the address below. (References listed at bottom of page contain supporting documentation, further explication, and related information.)

Strategy 1. Eliminate Starvation and Malnourishment/Feeding Humanity: $19 billion per year for ten years, allocated as follows: $2 billion per year for an International Famine Relief Agency-spent on international grain reserve and emergency famine relief; $10 billion per year spent on farmer education through vastly expanded in-country extension services that teach/demonstrate sustainable agriculture, use of local fertilizer sources, pest and soil management techniques, post harvest preservation, and which provide clear market incentives for increased local production; $7 billion per year for indigenous fertilizer development. Educational resources of Strategy 10 coupled with this strategy. Closely linked with #'s 2, 3, 4, 9, 10. Cost: 55% of what US spends on weight loss per year.

Strategy 2A. Provide Health Care For All: $15 billion per year for ten years spent on providing primary health care through community health workers to all areas in the world that do not have access to health care. Closely linked with #'s 1, 3, 4, 5, 9.

Strategy 2B. Provide Special Child Health Care: $2.5 billion per year spent on: a) providing Vitamin A to children who lack it in their diet, thereby preventing blindness in 250,000 children/year; b) providing oral rehydration therapy for children with severe diarrhea; and c) immunizing 1 billion children in developing world against measles, tuberculosis, diphtheria, whooping cough, polio and tetanus, thereby preventing the death of 6-7 million children/year.

Strategy 2C. Iodine Deficiency Program: $40 million per year for iodine addition to table salt to eliminate iodine deficiency, thereby reducing the 566 million people who suffer from goiter and not adding to the 3 million who suffer from overt cretinism.

Strategy 2D. AIDS Prevention and Control Program: $6 billion per year allocated as follows: $3 billion per year for a global AIDS prevention education program; $2 billion per year for providing multiple drug therapy to AIDS patients in the developing world; $1 billion per year for research and development for an AIDS vaccine or cure.

Costs for all Health Care Strategies: 16% of what US spends on alcohol and tobacco per year.

Strategy 3. Eliminate Inadequate Housing and Homelessness: $21 billion per year for ten years spent on making available materials, tools and techniques to people without adequate housing. Closely linked with #'s 1, 4, 5, 9. Cost: amount US spends on golf every 16 months.

Strategy 4. Provide Clean and Abundant Water: $10 billion per year for ten years spent on making available materials, tools and training needed to build and maintain the needed wells, water and sewage pipes, sanitation facilities and water purifying systems. Closely related to #'s 1, 2, 3, 9. Cost: 1% of what the world spends on illegal drugs per year.

Strategy 5. Eliminate Illiteracy: $5 billion per year for ten years; $2 billion spent on a system of 10 to 12 communication satellites and their launching; $2 billion spent on ten million televisions, satellite dish receivers, and photovoltaic/battery units for power-all placed in village schools and other needed areas throughout high illiteracy areas; the rest (90% of funds), spent on culturally appropriate literacy programming and maintenance of system. Closely related to #'s 1, 2, 3, 4, 9, 10, 11. Cost: 5% of the cost of the Gulf War; 14 months of what the US spends on video games.

Strategy 6. Increase Energy Efficiency: $33 billion per year for ten years spent on increasing car fleet mileage to over 50 m.p.g., plus increasing appliance, industrial

FIGURE 3.1: WHAT THE WORLD WANTS
AND HOW TO PAY FOR IT

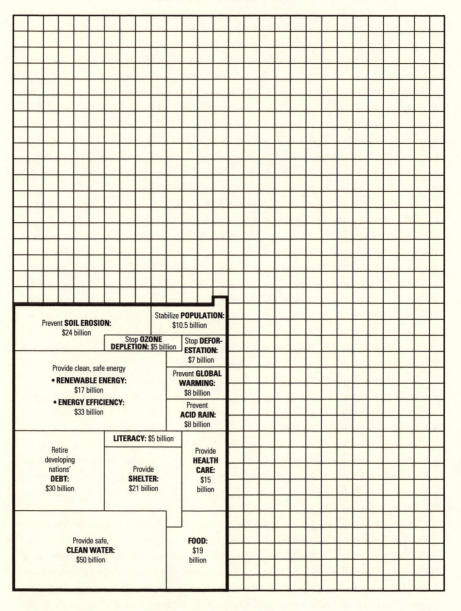

Prevent **SOIL EROSION:** $24 billion

Stabilize **POPULATION:** $10.5 billion

Stop **OZONE DEPLETION:** $5 billion

Stop **DEFOR-ESTATION:** $7 billion

Provide clean, safe energy
• **RENEWABLE ENERGY:** $17 billion
• **ENERGY EFFICIENCY:** $33 billion

Prevent **GLOBAL WARMING:** $8 billion

Prevent **ACID RAIN:** $8 billion

Retire developing nations' **DEBT:** $30 billion

LITERACY: $5 billion

Provide **SHELTER:** $21 billion

Provide **HEALTH CARE:** $15 billion

Provide safe, **CLEAN WATER:** $50 billion

FOOD: $19 billion

▦ = Total Chart = Total Annual World Military Expenditures ($1 trillion)

☐ = One-tenth of One Percent of Annual World Military Expenditures; or $1 billion processes, and household energy and materials use to state of the art. Closely linked with #'s 7, 8, 12, 13, 14. Cost: 13% of what US teenagers spend per year.

Strategy 7. Increase Renewable Energy. $20 billion per year for ten years spent on tax and other incentives for installation of renewable energy devices, graduated ten year phase-out of subsidies to fossil and nuclear fuels, research and development into more advanced renewable energy harnessing devices. Closely linked with #'s 6, 8, 11 12, 13, 14. Cost: 13% of current subsidies to electricity prices in the developing world.

Strategy 8. Debt Management. $30 billion per year for ten years spent on retiring $500 billion or more of current debt discounted to 50% face value. Not only helps developing countries get out of debt, but helps banks stay solvent and furthers international trade. Closely linked with #'s 1, 6, 7, 10, 11, 14. Cost: 3.8% of world's annual military expenditures.

Strategy 9. Stabilize Population. $10.5 billion per year for ten years spent on making birth control universally available. Closely linked with #'s 1, 2, 3, 4, 5. Cost: 1.3% of the world's annual military expenditures.

Strategy 10. Preserving Cropland. $24 billion per year for ten years spent on converting one-tenth of world's most vulnerable cropland that is simultaneously most susceptible to erosion, the location of most severe erosion, and the land that is no longer able to sustain agriculture, to pasture or woodland; and conserving and regenerating topsoil on remaining lands through sustainable farming techniques. Both accomplished through a combination of government regulation and incentive programs that remove the most vulnerable lands from crop production; and by farmer education through vastly expanded in-country extension services that teach/demonstrate sustainable agriculture and soil management techniques. Closely linked to # 1. Cost: $3 billion less than the annual cost of US farmland loss; half the amount of price subsidies given to US and European farmers.

Strategy 11. Reverse Deforestation. $7 billion per year for ten years spent on reforesting 150 million hectares needed to sustain ecological, fuelwood, and wood products needs. Planted by local villagers, costs would be $400 per hectare, including seedling costs. Additional costs for legislation, financial incentives, enforcement of rainforest protection. Closely linked with #'s 10, 11. Cost: 0.9% of world's annual military expenditures.

Strategy 12. Reverse Ozone Depletion. $5 billion per year for twenty years spent on phasing in substitutes for CF C-20, CFC taxes, incentives for further research and development. Closely linked with # 14. Cost: 3.7% of US government subsidies to energy, timber, construction, financial services and advertising industries.

Strategy 13. Stop Acid Rain. $8 billion per year for ten years spent on combination of tax incentive, government regulation and direct assistance programs that place pollution control devices (electrostatic precipitators, etc.) on all industrial users of coal, increase efficiency of industrial processes, cars, and appliances. Closely linked to #'s 6, 7, 11, 14. Cost: about 1% of world's annual military expenditures.

Strategy 14. Reverse Global Warming. $8 billion per year for twenty years spent on reducing carbon dioxide, methane and CFC release into atmosphere through combination of international accords, carbon taxes, increases in energy efficiency in industry, transportation, and household, decreases in fossil fuel use, increases in renewable energy use and reforestation. Closely linked with #'s 6, 7, 11, 13 . Cost: 17% of what the insurance industry paid out in the 1990s for weather related damage; 1% of world's annual military expenditures.

Strategy 15. Removal of Landmines: $2 billion per year for ten years spent on setting up cottage industries in each of the 64 countries that have landmines planted in their soils. Participants are intensively trained in the safe removal of landmines; compensation set at more than a days wage for each removed mine in each respective country. Closely linked with #'s 2, 16, 17, 18. Cost: less than the cost of a single B-2 bomber; less than one half what the US spends on perfume each year.

Strategy 16. Refugee Relief: $5 billion per year for ten years spent on an international Refugee Relief Agency that guarantees the safety of refugees and coordinates the delivery of food, shelter, health care and education. Closely linked with #'s 1, 2, 3, 4, 15, 18. Cost: 20% of the amount of arms sales to developing countries.

Strategy 17. Eliminating Nuclear Weapons: $7 billion per year for ten years spent on dismantling all the world's nuclear weapons and processing the plutonium and enriched uranium in nuclear reactors that produce power and render the radioactive materials into non-weapons grade material. Closely linked with #'s 15, 16, 18. Cost: 25% of what is spent each year on private "security"—private guards, weapons detectors, video surveillance, etc.

Strategy 18. Building Democracy: $2 billion per year for ten years spent on the following programs—an International Democratic Election Fund that would help finance voter education and multi-party elections in countries making the transition to democracy; a Global Polling Program that would ascertain what people from all over the world think and feel about key global issues; and a Global Problem Solving Simulation Tool that would enable anyone with access to the Internet to propose, develop and test strategies for solving real-world problems. Closely linked with #'s 5, 15, 16, 17. Cost for all three programs: less than one B-2 bomber; 0.025 % of the world's annual military expenditures.

Major References: UNDP, Human Development Report 1996 (New York: Oxford University Press, 1996); UNICEF, State of the World's Children 1996 1995, 1994; Giving children a future: The World Summit for Children, (New York: Oxford University Press, 1996, 1990); UNHCR Refugees II-95, Public Information Service UNHCR 1995; The World Bank, World Development Report 1996 (New York: Oxford University Press, 1996); World Resources Institute, World Resources 1995-96, 1992-93, World Watch Institute, Vital Signs 1996; State of the World 1988-96 (New York: W.W. Norton & Company, 1996); Ho-Ping: Food for Everyone; Energy, Earth and Everyone; World Game Institute, Doubleday, New York.

World Game Institute, 281 Bishop Hollow Road, Media, PA 19063
Phone: 610-566-0156   E-mail: medard@worldgame.org • www.worldgame.org
©2002 Medard Gabel

SOLUTION TO THE NINE-DOT PROBLEM

4

From the Northwest Imperative to Global Jihad: Social Psychological Aspects of the Construction of the Enemy, Political Violence, and Terror

Jonathan T. Drummond

> But now, with the hour of decision at hand, with the grim reality of racial extinction before us, some of us are beginning to understand the morality of survival is a higher morality than the morality of fairness. . . . It is time now for . . . saving our people and saving our civilization, no matter what it takes . . .
>
> Dr. William Pierce of the National Alliance, 2002

> It is now a dark and dismal time in the history of our race. All about us lie the green graves of our sires, yet, in a land once ours, we have become a people dispossessed . . . Our heroes and our culture have been insulted and degraded. The mongrel hordes clamor to sever us from our inheritance. . . . Our farms are being seized . . . The Capitalists and the Communists pick gleefully at our bones while the vile hook-nosed masters of usury orchestrate our destruction. What is to become of our children in a land such as this? . . . Do you hear the approaching thunder? It is that of the awakened Saxon. War is upon the land. The tyrant's blood will flow.
>
> Robert J. Mathews of the Order/Silent Brotherhood,[1] 1984, as cited in Flynn & Gerhardt, 1990, pp. 422–423

> . . . . sons and daughters of great Islam everywhere . . . Jihad is a Fard (compulsory duty) on each one of you to establish the rule of Allah on Earth and to liberate our countries and ourselves from occupiers, aggressors and tyrants. It

is a battle of life or death, victory or martyrdom; so live up to your pledge with
Allah . . .

Sheikh Ahmed Yassin of Hamas, 2001, p. 1

How is it that one comes to embrace religio- and ethnopolitical violence? Answer-
ing that question from an interdisciplinary perspective that prominently features
social psychology will be the focus of this chapter. Left at just that, however, we
would necessarily need to address killing done and intended by both state and sub-
state actors. Given space limitations and the rather conventional (though sometimes misleading) preference to characterize terrorists as non-state entities (Drummond & Darley, 2002), I will primarily focus upon sub-state actors. However, the
reader will see that, psychologically, there may be uncomfortably little to distinguish state and anti-state "terror."

The reader will immediately notice two themes in the opening quotes that will
be prominently expressed in this chapter. First, whether the quotes are taken from
the white separatist movement in the United States or Hamas (Harakat Muquwa-
ma Islamiyya, or Islamic Resistance Movement), there is clearly the expression of
some notion of self-defense or, more precisely, defense of a collective or extended
self. Most readers would readily admit that the option, even right, to defend oneself is universally held, and yet I suspect most will also approach this chapter from a
perspective in which they see themselves and their peers as those in need of defense,
not those quoted here. Pierce (who died of natural causes as I wrote this chapter)
clearly believed racial survival was threatened and in need of defense. On the other
hand, Stern (2001) labeled Pierce a "terrorist," and one who would apparently have
resorted to bioterrorism. Presumably then, by Stern's account, we need(ed) defense
from Pierce (and his National Alliance), and yet Stern provides no support for her
accusation, lest unpopular views, unsavory associations, and authorship of violent
novels make one a terrorist.[2] The matter of who is attacking, who is threatened,
and who is defending is contextually bound.

Because subjective context is important to understanding from "inside" a narrative, a phenomenological approach to interpretations of self-defense will be
employed. Similarly, Crenshaw (1988) has expressed the need to appreciate the
"subjective reality of the terrorist," and Snow, Rochford, Worden, and Benford
(1986) have called for greater attendance to grievance *interpretation* in the study of
social movements. It is not only academicians who recognize psychology's failure
to sufficiently apprehend "terrorism" phenomenologically, but "terrorists" as well.
Consider the following critique by Sheikh Fadlallah of Lebanese Hezbollah,
revered by some as the leading Islamist liberation theologian:[3]

> The problem with the discipline of psychology is that it attempts to
> study the phenomenon of martyrdom from the perspective of prag-
> matic vocabulary and laboratory results. They refuse to admit that cer-
> tain things can be understood only through labor and pain. You can
> never be capable of appreciating freedom if you do not come to grips
> with enslavement. You can appreciate the cries of the starved only

when you come to grips with the pangs of starvation. (cited in Abu-Rabi, 1996, p. 242)

While experimental psychology has its place, Fadlallah insightfully questions the generalizability of the discipline's findings to extreme conditions; accordingly, and where possible, I will rely upon primary sources and the words of those we seek to understand to better get inside the narrative.

Let me note that the reader should not mistake empathy or an intense attempt to understand phenomenologically with sympathy or excusal. This is all too easily done in evaluating phenomenological treatments, despite critics' best intentions. As it is often psychologically safer to distance state from anti-state terror or deem the terrorist mad or "evil," it is also comforting to deny the adversarial view is truly comprehensible, cognitively complex, and internally coherent; unfortunately, understanding is rarely found in comfort.

Second, we will be exploring religio- or ethnopolitical violence. This should not discourage the reader from applying the themes of this paper to the equally horrific violence generated in the name of "social justice," "equality," or "workers' rights"; socialism, for example, can reasonably be viewed as something of a religious movement in its emotional fervor and consequence (Le Bon, 1899/1982). Le Bon remarks:

> Behind all collective cruelty there is more often than not a belief, an idea of justice, a desire for moral satisfaction, a complete forgetfulness of personal interest, or readiness to sacrifice to the general interest . . . The crowd may become cruel, but it is above all altruistic, and is as easily led away to sacrifice itself as to destroy others. (Le Bon, 1899/1982, p. 101)

Collective violence may have the most admirable of motives, but the highest goals may lend themselves to efforts either noble or debauched. Notably, it was terrorism from the "left" that predominated in the latter decades of the twentieth century, and the two most murderous regimes over the century were *not* primarily nationalist or "religious," per se, but rather the communist states of the Soviet Union and the People's Republic of China (PRC) (Rummel, 1994).

Interestingly, Marxist, socialist, or communist movements, contrary to stated principles, often do express ethnic or nationalist motivations; this has been the case for both terrorists (Sprinzak, 1991) and governments. The cultural and literal genocide by the PRC that has claimed at least 1.2 million Tibetan lives has been primarily perpetrated by ethnic Han Chinese (Gyatso, 1990; Klein, 1990; personal communications with Tibetan refugees and activists, May 1996–June 2000),[4] and the Khmer Rouge were clearly racist in their slaughter, believing in the "racial superiority of the dark-skinned Khmer" (Rummel, 1994). State violence in the first decades of the Soviet Union was markedly Jewish (MacDonald, 1998, in press), leading Ginsberg (1993) to comment, ". . . the special contribution of the Jews to the Bolshevik state involved the organization of coercion" (p. 30); ironically, Jews would later be among those Stalin and his successors targeted and purged.[5] So, while our focus here will be on religio-political violence by sub-state actors, the concepts and processes explored may be widely applicable.

WHAT IS TERRORISM AND WHO IS A TERRORIST?

Before attempting to understand how terrorism is embraced, it is worthwhile to consider what is meant by "terrorism" or "terrorists." Better than 100 academic definitions compete for attention (Zulaika & Douglass, 1996). Even various agencies within a single government have conflicting definitions that may not match what is codified into law (Mahmood, 2001). "Terrorists" and "terrorism" may also change with policy and political relations. Many of those *mujahideen* hailed as the Afghani equivalent to the U.S. "founding fathers" by President Reagan in 1985 found themselves among President Clinton's "terrorists" in 1998 (Ahmad, 1998) and amidst President Bush's "evil ones" in 2001. From the *mujahideen* perspective, they were at all times engaged in the same effort—expelling the occupying infidel. The "terrorist" label shifts in the opposite direction as well; four men who were formerly despised terrorists (depending upon perspective) are also Nobel Peace Prize winners, and Gerry Adams may be a fifth in the making (Zulaika & Douglass, 1996).[6]

The "terrorist" label often privileges the state in ways that make it more a political category and less a useful designation for those wishing to better comprehend the actor and the act(s).[7] While there is broad agreement around the world that the events of September 11, 2001, constitute terrorism, presumably because they possess some set of clearly defining elements (see Drummond & Darley, 2002), we are left with cases that 1) appear to be terrorism but are not, 2) present organizations that are engaged in terror, and yet are something more, and 3) are not widely recognized as terrorism, but probably should be.[8]

In the first case, consider the previously mentioned accusations leveled at Pierce. More striking, the U.S. Department of Justice has for the past several years overstated its "terrorist" arrests and convictions, perhaps to support budget requests (Fazlollah & Nicholas, 2001). These "terrorists" include people who have been merely intoxicated on an airplane or were caught with a phony passport application.

Groups like Hamas fit the second case. While several hundred in the Izz a-din al-Qassam brigades are primarily responsible for suicide/martyrdom missions and other violence, various wings of Hamas provide for educational, medical, and other needs (Karon, 2001), sometimes with greater efficiency than the Palestinian Authority. Declaring such organizations terrorist groups is only partially correct. While some of their actions are appropriately viewed as egregious acts of indiscriminate violence, to the extent that Hamas militantly opposes an illegal Israeli occupation force (the Israeli Defense Force [IDF] and, perhaps, settlers) in violation of United Nations resolutions 242 and 338, it is plausibly in a struggle of liberation (Baghdadi, 2001).[9] Similar to states, organizations like Hamas may use violence in conjunction with socially acceptable media of non-violent change and improvement.

Lastly, there are cases that are not recognized as terrorism and probably should be. Usually, such cases involve state terrorism or sub-state actors supported by powerful states. The governments of Israel and Zimbabwe (or factions within them) are prime examples. In the first *intifada* (1987–1995) and the ongoing "al-Aqsa" *intifada* combined, more than 80 percent of the dead are Palestinians, and nearly as many Palestinian children have been killed (455) as have all Israelis combined (535); yet, there is a disturbing pattern in Western media in which Israelis are often presented as victims of "terrorism" while Palestinian innocents targeted by the IDF are not similarly characterized (Palestinian Central Bureau of Statistics, 2002; Zulaika & Douglass, 1996). Even sources that usually seek to be objective and equitable in their reporting, such as National Public Radio, can impart a partisan slant; over a recent six-month period, the killing of an Israeli under eighteen years of age was 4.5 times more likely to be reported than that of a Palestinian under eighteen (Ackerman, 2001). In addition to the illegal occupation, more than eighty thousand Israeli settlers moved into the occupied territories *during the Oslo peace process*, more than eighty Palestinian leaders have been systematically assassinated,[10] thousands of dwellings have been bulldozed, and the Palestinian people have been cantonized into more than two hundred discontinuous parcels of land (Barghouti, 2002; Said, 2001; Slater, 2001; Sontag, 2001).

In Zimbabwe, behind the rhetoric of land reform, President Robert Mugabe is attempting to extend his political life through both attacks on black political opposition (which he has called "puppets of the whites") and efforts most appropriately called ethnic cleansing (McGreal, 2001; Mutsaka, 2001; Swarns, 2001). Zimbabwe's vice president has declared, "Whites are not human beings" (McGreal, 2001, p. 2), and one of Mugabe's ministers has claimed Africa "for black people only" (Associated Press, 2001, p. 2). The word "terrorist" is not often chosen to characterize the administrations of Israel and Zimbabwe (at least not in the West), and yet, in common with many definitions of terrorism, they both employ violence and the threat of violence against noncombatants to generate fear, secure various ends, and coerce compliance or acquiescence. Zulaika and Douglass (1996) comment:

> It is not simply that, like "Communist" or "fascist," the word "terrorist" is being abused; rather the word itself is an abuse, a banality that disguises reality while impoverishing language and thought by obliterating distinctions. (p. 98)

"Terrorism," as traditionally used, fails not only scholar and policymaker, but also, more importantly, all the "invisible" victims of terror.

Terrorism too easily becomes only that violence done by a particular kind or category of perpetrator, asymmetric conflict that can be advantageously labeled by those with the power and/or interests to do so. It is a label ripe for enslavement by self-enhancement motives, advantageous comparison, and the self-serving bias:

"What *I* do, however unpleasant, is not terrorism; what *you* do is terrorism" (Cooper, 2001, p. 884). Terrorism becomes divorced from context; the phenomenon is stripped of its psychological grounds—the social construction of reality, perceptions, motivations, influences of others, and so on. Relevantly, President Musharraf of Pakistan recently asked, in regard to Kashmir, "Is Washington saying that all freedom struggles, everywhere, can be suppressed under the guise of the war on terrorism?" (Burns, 2002, p. A1). A Muslim struggle for self-determination or a response to the institutional failure of Indian democracy are two of perhaps a half dozen frames by which one might meaningfully interpret the conflict in Jammu-Kashmir. If all anti-state violence is to be rigidly constructed as terrorism, there can be little doubt that competing perspectives that might inform negotiations and agreements will be ignored to the loss of all invested parties.

There likely is a way to usefully define terrorism, and the differences between "freedom fighter" and "terrorist" may be more than euphemistic labeling or "pathetic attempts at making the contemptible respectable" (Bandura, 1990; Cooper, 2001, p. 892; Drummond & Darley, 2002); Ruby's (2002a) optimistic suggestion to escape prejudicial values by favoring behavioral perspectives over legal and moral perspectives has merit, but unfortunately suggests a monolithic approach to violence and dismisses cognition as well as its potential to inform solutions. The way out of this dilemma is to define terrorism in ways that fully appreciate the psychological, culturally contextualized construction of terrorism, as suggested in Drummond and Darley (2002). Granted, this creates multiple definitions of terrorism for any given conflict, but that is precisely the intention. The most important and widely attributed elements of "terrorism" in a given (sub)culture are empirically available. Once known, the varied definitions of terrorism wielded by conflicted and neutral parties may well reveal, by their prominent components, divergent or convergent positions and interests. Knowing how commonly held components of terrorism are at the same time differentially defined or constrained may also enhance communication. However, an approach that systematically values collections of culturally contextualized social constructions of terrorism is in its infancy. For that reason, from this point forward, I will largely use the more objective terms "religio-political," "ethnopolitical," or "political" to qualify violence; terror is but a single intended effect of political violence (and a narrowly affective one at that).

CASES AND SOURCES

Having suggested the ambiguity of "terror," let us now turn to the processes by which one (however judged) comes to religio-political killing. Let me first establish the four cases upon which I will draw. Most prominently, I will refer to 1) the white separatist movement in the United States and 2) the global Islamist resurgence (most notably Hamas, al-Qaeda, and those involved with the assassination of Egyptian President Anwar al-Sadat in October 1981). While these two cases may, at first, seem quite different, I hope to convey some of the remarkable similarities in constructing the other as enemy and making the journey toward violence. Less often, I will access the cases of 3) anti-abortion violence in the United States and 4) Israeli extremism, especially Yigal Amir's November 1995 assassination of Yitzhak Rabin.

Because time and history are collapsed into the present within such social movements, as Volkan (1997) has suggested, these cases will generate a number of references to events in both the present and an immediately salient decades- or centuries-old past. For example, while events in the seventh century might seem irrelevant, that Palestine was conquered for Islam by the Second Caliph (634–644), Umar ibn al-Khattab, is prominently featured in the preamble of the Hamas platform (1988) and is every bit as real to the believer today as it was nearly 1,400 years ago.

Primary sources of information will be accessed where possible and most frequently in the case of white separatism. Over the past four years, I have interviewed more than fifty individuals in the radical right in the United States,[11] and have attended a number of events, from cross lightings to religious services to picnics.[12] I have had briefer contact with perhaps three hundred and fifty others, accessed the knowledge of fourteen colleagues from diverse backgrounds (some formerly members of white separatist organizations) who have intimate familiarity with fifteen groups and more than seven hundred core members in those groups, and reviewed nearly one hundred thousand e-mail and Web pages. These data will represent, as Brannan, Esler, and Strindberg (2001) have admirably called for, a sincere effort to talk to "terrorists." Terrorism studies have far too long been overly reliant upon secondary sources. Mahmood (2001) has sharply captured this deficiency, referring to the study of "terrorism" as ". . . an Alice-in-Wonderland world, based on a concept no one can clearly define, *involving people no one can approach* [emphasis added], but centering on life-and-death issues whose importance no one dare ignore" (p. 526).

CONSTRUCTING THE ENEMY

Enemies do not just arise from the ether; they are socially and phenomenologically constructed from facts, be they actual or apparent, selectively or incompletely assembled, current or obsolete (Aho, 1994). Both accurate and inaccurate negative stereotypes are vital to understanding the construction of the enemy from "inside the narrative"; while the latter have been prominently addressed (Fiske, 1998), the former have been largely neglected in psychology (Jussim, McCauley, & Lee 1995). It is some collection of perceived facts, more or less wedded with an explanatory framework that assembles those facts in a particularly ominous and emotionally engaging arrangement, that gives rise to, and suggests important aspects in, the construction of the enemy other.

Although still vulnerable to the heuristics that may befall us all, those who would denigrate or attack a religio- or ethnopolitical enemy may be more cognitively complex than we'd anticipate (Durrheim & Dixon, 2001; Sidanius, 1985); we ignore this at our peril. One white separatist I interviewed, "Erik," purposely cultivated the "redneck," "simpleton" impression in public because it was clearly disarming; privately, Erik had a background of success in the military and in a technically demanding profession, had established contacts in Europe and the Arab world, and could eloquently discuss political philosophy and history. While Erik's accomplishments make him exceptional among those interviewed, it was not exceptional to find professionally and technically skilled white separatists. More impressively, Muhammad Abd al-Salam Faraj (1986), making the case for the primacy of *jihad* in *Al-Faridah al-Gha'ibah* (*The Neglected Duty*, justifying Sadat's assassination), raises and then deconstructs at least seventeen robust theological objections.[13] Faraj also ably argues the ways in which the individual duty of *jihad* (". . . fighting is prescribed for you," Koran 2.216) abrogates 114 other Koranic verses commanding Muslims to live in peace with the infidel. To understand how one comes to engage in violence against the enemy, one must first and foremost understand a collection of perceived facts and the explanatory religion, myth, or ideology by which those facts are often complexly put together.

Working largely off Aho's (1994) framework for our analysis, the enemy or evil other (however just or unjust the accusation may be) must first be labeled or named, derogatorily designated, and often branded with a dehumanizing moniker. President Bush's "terrorists" and "evil ones" are bin Laden's "faithful" and "vanguard Muslims." To bin Laden, Bush is the "head of international infidels."[14] For white separatists, people of color are "muds," Jews are "Satan's seed" or "parasites" in Aryan culture, and miscegenation produces "mongrels." For violent anti-abortionists, the "butchers" perpetrating the "genocide" against the unborn must be stopped and the "abortuaries" (clinics) put out of business.

Second, there must be legitimation of the name or label if it is to be meaningful or influential. This is often done with some sort of procedure or public degradation ceremony. Osama bin Laden has issued a number of *fatwas* and various commentaries over the past nine years, condemning and declaring war on America for its military presence in the Saudi peninsula, sanctions against Iraq, and support of Israeli brutality against Palestinians.[15] President Bush shored up his political capital in a speech to the nation on September 20, 2001, claiming al-Qaeda hates America essentially because Americans have "freedoms,"[16] declaring their path is that of "fascism, Nazism, and totalitarianism," and "exposing" al-Qaeda as a group that hides "in countries around the world to plot evil." White separatist Robert Mathews, before he was killed by federal law enforcement agents in December 1984, thought it necessary to issue a formal declaration of war against the U.S. government, some of which is included above; for many white separatists, Mathews is a hero and martyr, and the declaration of war remains in effect.[17]

Third, construction of the enemy must involve some sort of mythmaking (Aho, 1994) that often extends beyond the present or into the past; mythmaking in the present may express hindsight bias and appropriate historical fact to claim it is centuries old, the true tradition by which one's forebears lived and to which one has now been awakened. It is a way in which time can be collapsed and "chosen wounds and glories" made immediately relevant (Volkan, 1997). This mythmaking is of central importance for us because it is this process by which facts are framed and arranged, explanations produced, and predictions made; that is, by mythmaking, one comes to better satiate core social motives to understand one's world and control it (per S. Fiske, personal communications, September–December 2001). Importantly, one may be motivated by the merest illusion of control (see Pittman, 1998). Perhaps an example will illustrate how mythmaking can organize fact and history in ways that construct the enemy.

White separatists often see the white race as the evolutionary apex, without which European/Western civilization will not survive. Being the "fittest," however, is no guarantee of racial survival. Declining white birth rates and explosions in "Third World" populations have caused white Europeans or European-derived peoples to drop from 35 percent of the world's population in 1900 to approximately 10 to 15 percent of the world's population today (Buchanan, 2002; Goodrick-Clarke, 2002).[18] This decline is understandably distressing for those who perceive a common fate (see Brewer & Brown, 1998) and deem race to be important.[19] While prominent racialist religions such as Creativity and Wotanism largely make the case for racial survival from natural law-based perspectives (Klassen, 1973, 1981; Lane, 1999),[20] let me here very briefly discuss a theological Christian Identity explanation of what has happened.

In Christian Identity, which may have as many as fifty thousand adherents in the United States, there is an eternal battle between the Aryan "children of light," the blessed descendents of Adam through Seth (the true Israelites), and the "children of darkness," the modern Jews (tribal Khazars and impostors), the progeny of Cain (the original murderer).[21] In "two seedline" interpretations, Eve was literally seduced by Satan, giving rise to Adamic and Satanic seedlines: "And I will put enmity between thee and thy woman, and between *thy* seed and *her* seed" (italics added) (Genesis 3:15). Jesus is also believed by Identists to have identified Jewry's Satanic affiliation:

> If God were your Father, ye would love me . . . Ye are of *your* father the devil, and the lusts of your father ye will do. He was a murderer from the beginning, and abode not in the truth, because there is no truth in him. When he speaketh a lie, he speaketh of his own: for he is a liar, and the father of it. And because I tell *you* the truth, ye believe me not. (John 8:42–45)

Many an Identist has expressed to me a resignation to eventual violence against such a Satanic enemy; as one said, "The Jews are and always will be the Christ killers."[22]

In Identity, there is no Rapture, there will be no escape from the horrors of Revelations. As the world hurtles toward the "End Times," Jews are seen as continuing to engage, following their failed experiment with Communism, the destruction of the Adamic peoples. This is being done through leftist and leveling politics, secular humanism, media control and socialization, influences on education,[23] and secret societies that undermine (or outlaw) collective Aryan identity, discourage large families (thus, the declining birth rates), and encourage "race treason" and miscegenation (personal communications, R. Butler, July, 1998; The 11th Hour Remnant Messenger, no date).

A divine mandate to zealously guard racial purity and Adamic integrity is often derived from the example of Phinehas, who ran a javelin through an Israelite man and Midianite woman and so saved Israel from Yahweh's wrath (Numbers 25). Transmission of a divinely ordained "Phinehas priesthood" is traced through a number of historical and mythical figures, ranging from King Arthur to Robin Hood and William Wallace to John Wilkes Booth (Hoskins, 1997). More recently, members of the Order, the "Spokane Bank Bandits," and the Aryan Republican Army (see Hamm, 2002), for example, have all embraced Identity and/or the notion of a Phinehas priesthood. While other whites do not (yet) recognize the "truth" about who they are and the ongoing struggle, the violent Identist is confident he has done God's will, and has acted metaphorically as a white blood cell to cleanse the racial body of infection:

> Survival depends on the regenerated white blood cell, a cell rigidly judging everything and everyone by the ancient rules that ensure survival, a cell no longer misled, wooden, and ineffective. It is the day of the Phineas priest. (Hoskins, 1997, p. 64)

While such a belief may seem quite outlandish, perhaps we should attend to the warning of Peter Langan, a member of the Aryan Republican Army who has since renounced his Identity beliefs:

> I hear a lot of people talking about it . . . it's either a fake religion or a cult, but Christian Identity is a very viable religion. . . . they have a upbeat message to a certain segment of the population.[24]

Finally, in maintaining the existence of any enemy, Aho (1994) notes that ritual is necessary to reconfirm the truth of the myth. Psychologically, this approximates the self-fulfilling prophecy. For Hamas, Israel seeks only to oppress, divide, and further dispossess the Palestinians. Settlements and assassinations of community leaders provide proof of this and justify "martyrdom operations" in defense. To Israeli Prime Minister Ariel Sharon's administration, the Palestinians are violent and uncontrollable. Therefore, the IDF must maintain order in the occupied territories and protect vulnerable settlements. "Suicide missions" by Hamas confirm the need for IDF presence. In protracted conflicts, the violence cycles mimetically, maintaining the other as enemy and sustaining the immediate salience of explanatory myth with its ability to help one understand and, at least in small and sometimes only "spiritual" ways, control the world.

DEVIANT LEGITIMATION

Groebel (1989) insightfully advocates a scientific and multidimensional approach to the psychological comprehension of terrorism. Based upon his suggestions, it would seem a more complete understanding of religio- and ethnopolitical violence might be arrived at by using primary data, as possible, to explore 1) influential events in a society or culture, 2) explanatory ideologies and/or theologies, 3) personality and individual differences, and 4) group processes. We have thus far laid the groundwork upon which to integratively apply the domains of analyses Groebel suggests and propose a process of "deviant legitimation"[25] by which one moves toward and engages in violence.

At its most elemental level, deviant legitimation requires that two entities must exist for one to move toward political violence. To engage in the apparent slaughter of innocents requires the presence of a group that supports the actor's worldview; this will be discussed in greater detail later. Killing also requires a set of supportive beliefs that frame the killing as morally legitimate; similarly, Bandura (1990) has suggested the importance of "moral justification" in political killing. Furthermore, those would be "terrorists" seeking moral legitimation are rather "normally" socialized members of their societies or cultures, and they appear to have internalized the various norms and prohibitions against murder and other wrongful violence. That is, they are more "of us" than "not of us."

It is tempting to believe "terrorism" and acts of mass violence are necessarily the products of mental illness and aberration, deviance to be found lurking in the dark depths of the madman's mind, or, simply, evil. Such naming is comfortable, for it permits one to both identify with the "good" and keep the world intact, understandable, predictable, and otherwise rationally ordered. The evidence overwhelmingly suggests, however, that "terrorists" are not mentally ill or otherwise disordered (Crenshaw, 1990, 2001; Ruby, 2002b; Silke, 1998); Hoffman (2001), in his congressional testimony on September 26, 2001, characterized the September 11 attacks as being marked by their "professionalism and tradecraft," a far cry from political and theological characterizations of cowardice, madness, and evil. To further understand how it is that normally socialized, psychologically healthy individuals can come to see the killing of apparent innocents as legitimate and rational moral impulse, we must discuss killing.

When Killing Is Not Murder

In any given culture, all murder is killing, but not all killing is murder. For killing to not be murder, it seems that there must exist 1) special and rather severe circumstances, and 2) the killer must convincingly make the case that his killing was not murder per such circumstances. There are perhaps four ways to characterize killing that make it something less than murder. Further, these four characterizations appear to be universal, though their content may vary by culture. Killing is something less than murder when there is 1) mitigation (such as provocation), 2) an excuse (the killing was accidental and/or reasonably unforeseen), 3) justification (as is the case with self-defense), or 4) moral requirement or obligation. The latter might include defending vulnerable or threatened others, protecting sacred principles (whether "making the world safe for democracy" or ensuring application of the *shari'a*—Islamic law), or otherwise halting harmful or murderous acts of others before they can be successfully set in motion or completed. In arguing for the use of force to defend the unborn from abortion, Bray (1994) illustratively clarifies:

> Those who use lethal force to stop a murderer are not themselves committing murder. They kill, or terminate, or slay, or neutralize; they do not murder. (p. 175)

It is "justification" or "moral obligation" characterizations of killing that are most relevant to deviant legitimation. In an interview aired on al-Jazeera television in 1998, and again by the BBC on September 22, 2001, Osama bin Laden explained:

> We want our land to be freed of the enemies; we want our land to be freed of the Americans. God equipped living creatures with an instinctive zeal and they refuse to be intruded upon. . . . We are demanding a right given to all living creatures, not to mention the fact that it is a right for all human beings, including the Muslims. . . . We believe that the right to self-defence is to be enjoyed by all people.

To socially construct killing as justified or a moral obligation, the threat must further be seen as both imminent and not preventable by lesser means. Generally, permissible counterforce must be proportional to the attack, though culture and norms may provide grounds for disproportional counterforce or vengeance (French, 2001); in the United States, for example, there is broad support for use of retaliatory force that the Model Penal Code would deem excessive and criminal (Drummond, Vandello, & Darley, 2002).

The self to be defended may vary greatly. Triandis (1989) suggests that cultures vary in the importance placed on the private, public, or collective self. Markus and Kitayama (1991) describe culture-driven tendencies toward an independent or interdependent self, but it seems much more likely that we are often simultaneously degrees of both, seeking some optimal distinctiveness in a social self (Brewer, 1991). There appears to be significant variation of the self in response to culture and situation, such that certain self-aspects may become more or less salient and defining by context, mythmaking, or identity (Aho, 1994; Simon, 1998; Simon, Loewy, Sturmer, Weber, Freytag, Habig, et al., 1998; Volkan, 1997). It is the most salient, defining, and organizing self-aspect that may well determine whether an attack is interpreted as "personal" and invokes violent retaliation. Indeed, Drummond, Vandello, and Darley (2002) found that the level of retaliation justified was positively related to appraisal that an attack or affront is personal when directed against not only one's physical self, but also one's honor, family members, members of a secondary group, one's home, valued possessions, and culturally sustained beliefs and values.

In her volume on the social psychology of possessions, Dittmar (1992) declares that "*we are what we have*" (italics in original, p. 194). What is suggested by Dittmar and Drummond, Vandello, & Darley (2002) is that in addition to an independent and interdependent self, there may at times be an *interdimensional* self that is inextricable from inanimate entities, (sub)culturally located values and beliefs, ideas, or deity. The interdimensional self is not just a reflection of what we have, but also what has us! Some Muslims and Jews have a self-constructed interrelationship with the Haram al-Sharif or the Temple Mount. Intrusion by those not entitled, especially under arms or threat of arms, is religious insult and personal attack begging a forceful response (as with Ariel Sharon's September 2000 visit and the subsequent eruption of the al-Aqsa *intifada*). White separatists belong to their race, and therefore, "my skin is my [issued] uniform"; blood, soil, and honor, and their ability to invoke forceful defense, are no further than the racial self. The self is much more than just "I": "My Folk . . . is greater than I/My Race . . . is greater than I/Truth . . . is greater than I/Nevertheless, I am all of these" (McVan, 1997, p. 26). It is the interpersonal and interdimensional self, beyond the individual, that may well be found at the heart of justification and moral obligation characterizations of killing that make it not murder, and perhaps, even noble.

Delegitimating Discoveries

Being normally socialized, those who would kill know far more than the conditions under which killing may be just and, thus, socially acceptable; they also know how the society is to be appropriately structured and governed as well as the rules and norms by which the culture operates. Family, mosque, schools, and other institutions socialize youth to be functional in the culture. Sometimes, however, something goes wrong, and these culturally consistent beliefs, values, perceptions, and expectations are undermined, called into question, or even shattered. One's faith in the "system" or its ability to accommodate change may be shaken. These events, be they "tipping" events at the cultural/societal level (see Tellis, Szayna, & Winnefeld, 1997) or more private "triggering" events, are delegitimating discoveries (Darley & Drummond, 2002).[26] A broad body of research suggests perceptions of group (and not individual) deprivation are associated with collective social or political action (see Tyler & Smith, 1998); the reader should note that both cultural tipping and private triggering events presented herein target (or are perceived to target), in some way, a collective or interdimensional self beyond just the individual. A few illustrations will be helpful.

For many in the United States, including Oklahoma City bomber Timothy McVeigh (Hamm, 2002; Michel & Herbeck, 2001), events at Ruby Ridge (1992) and Waco (1993) destroyed faith in the federal government and guarantees of traditional American freedoms.[27] In August 1992, a federal siege of white separatist

Randy Weaver's residence over his failure to appear in court on minor weapons charges ended in the deaths of U.S. Marshal William Degan and Weaver's teenage son and wife. On August 22, 1992, FBI sniper Lon Horiuchi shot and killed Vicki Weaver as she held her ten-month-old daughter, Elisheba, in her arms. Despite findings by a Department of Justice task force and a Senate subcommittee that Horiuchi's shot was unconstitutional, Horiuchi has yet to face trial, and those dictating the rules of engagement have not faced substantial punishment or discipline (Dobratz & Shanks-Meile, 1997). Approaching the absurd, the government initially included Elisheba Weaver among those charged in Marshal Degan's death, making her probably the youngest person in U.S. history to be charged with the crime of murder. Also stunning are the lengths to which the government went in the Weaver case over such a minor violation of law, besieging a family with hundreds of agents, spending millions in the operation, and using U.S. Air Force F-4 reconnaissance flyovers (Aho, 1994). Ruby Ridge continues to motivate many in the American far right, demonstrating to them that the federal government will go to incredible lengths to murder its citizens (especially if they hold "politically incorrect" views) while remaining "above the law" and unaccountable to our judicial system.

At Waco, the Bureau of Alcohol, Tobacco, and Firearms and the FBI are seen by some as engaging in a government-led or -induced massacre of dozens of innocents, along with their children, who had been peacefully exercising their constitutional rights to worship freely and privately own firearms (see also Tabor & Gallagher, 1995; Wright, 1995, 1999). Relevantly, across fifteen groups on the far right, the belief that legislation in recent years has infringed Second Amendment constitutional guarantees of private firearms ownership was deemed the most important factor in the actual and potential use of violence. Sacred American values enshrined in the Bill of Rights are seen to be under attack by the very government responsible for maintaining and protecting them.

Bin Laden also experienced a delegitimating discovery that sent him careening on the path from loyal Saudi subject to global *jihad.* In the Wahabbist and Islamist worldviews, the House of al-Saud's primary duty is to protect the holy sites of Mecca and Medina. Stationing of non-Muslim U.S. military forces on Saudi soil during the Persian Gulf War generated concern; some Muslim clerics decreed that the Saudi royal family had betrayed its charge. The presence of the infidel was to many a far greater threat than the Iraqis.[28] In any event, bin Laden was a loyal subject during the Gulf War, and he apparently put faith in promises by Saudi and American leadership (including then Secretary of Defense Dick Cheney) that American forces would depart at war's end (Bodansky, 1999). They did not leave. Still, bin Laden sought to address the grievance nonviolently. Postwar, bin Laden was publicly supportive of the "Memorandum of Advice"; signed by more than one hundred Islamists and delivered to the Saudi government, it called for restoration of more strictly Muslim rule and questioned continued U.S. presence (Gause, 2001). These efforts were first met with official indifference, then a "crackdown" on Islamists. The House of al-Saud was now seen to be clearly apostate. Bin Laden and his family were threatened in various ways and many clerics were imprisoned and tortured; it was then that bin Laden fled to Sudan, became reintegrated into the network of *mujahideen* and "Afghan Arabs," and embraced *jihad* as the only remaining course of action (Bodansky, 1999; Gause, 2001; Nida'ul Islam, 1996). Bin Laden may not have been alone; fifteen of the September 11 terrorists hailed originally from Saudi Arabia.

Wright, Taylor, and Moghaddam (1990), Wright (2001), and Tellis et al. (1997) relevantly suggest that collective non-normative resistance may only arise when mechanisms of accommodation and change are perceived to be completely inaccessible. Exacerbating such frustration, groups may be prone to exaggerate perceptions of the victimizing collective injustice (Taylor, Wright, & Porter, 1994); other researchers have marked the importance of constructing a sufficiently severe injustice to continue along the path to violence (see White, 2001). One sees some of this in bin Laden's move to violence. This also appears to be the case for many in America's far right. Not only do those in the right believe the "common man" has no access to the moneyed landscape of American politics, but they further believe their concerns are unaddressed by any viable political party. The U.S. two-party system excludes a wide range of alternative views. This combination of a "broken" political process and undesirable outcomes by that process may be especially alienating (Tyler & Smith, 1998). Political access and accommodation are no longer plausible media of change. These are revelations that all is not well, a throwing off of a "false consciousness,"[29] a cognitive liberation revealing deprivation and injustice; only once recognized can injustice be countered through collective action (Dobratz & Shanks-Meile, 1997; Klandermans, 1997).

Individual triggering events may also erode faith in the "system" and its legitimacy, induce feelings of betrayal and victimization, and leave one open to extreme views in the search for an explanation. Several events may work counter, for example, to the ideal of the "American Dream" that if one works hard, one will prosper. Individuals have had small farms foreclosed upon no matter how hard they worked. A small Montana dairy farmer who had to close his operation because he was no longer "economically viable" in a world of large-scale multinational agribusiness eventually found a home in Christian Identity. Some females in white separatism have been sexually assaulted or raped by minorities, and men have had sisters or wives similarly victimized. One male became a white separatist after repeated bullying by a black gang of older teenagers was ended with a vicious, but effective, "skinhead" attack ("boot party"). Because of Affirmative Action policies, another man lost a state government job to a black man he felt was less qualified. "Lone Wolf" Benjamin Smith, affiliated with the World Church of the Creator, went on a suicidal shooting spree on the weekend of July 4, 1999; targeting ethnic minorities, he killed two and wounded nine. Smith was angry that church leader Matt Hale had been denied his license to practice law after passing the bar.[30] Whether by a cultural or societal tipping event or a more private triggering event, the world is rendered less understandable; explanations must be found to restore this understanding and permit one to act with efficacy to control one's life and surroundings.

Explaining Injustice

The individual encountering a delegitimating discovery experiences great dissonance between past positive beliefs about the society or culture and the one now being experienced. Maybe society's rules do not permit one to prosper after all. Maybe they do not ensure that justice prevails, or perhaps they have diverged from cultural truths. For the religious individual, the delegitimating discovery may be "evidence" the society suffers because it has deviated from divine will. Departure from the *shari'a*, collusion with the infidel in the death or deprivation of Muslims, and tolerance of apostate regimes have, for bin Laden, brought Allah's wrath upon Muslims; the people have gone astray and righteousness must be restored for the good of all (bin Laden is fond of referencing Koran 2.193, which bids one to fight until "there prevail justice and faith in God"). It is, in fact, not uncommon, even in rather mainstream religious systems, for believers to engineer cogent and psychologically functional explanations that simultaneously account for observations, imbue them with theological significance, and interpret God's intent (Ammerman, 1997). Ultimately, whatever the particular delegitimating discovery, explanations must be found, for as implied, they assuage fear, explain one's predicament, construct meaningful worlds, and inform solutions.

Explanatory views vary. They may be ideologies but are often much more. They may contain scapegoats, but these are a product of the mythmaking, not the explanation itself. The explanatory worldview must first explain why the individual is validly disenfranchised and discontented. That is, it must explain why following the cultural norms have not yielded success, why one's moral principles or values are not embraced by the polity, or why those in power are harming the governed or those they should beneficently serve. Second, the explanatory view must explain how it is that others are thriving, favorably represented, or able to advance their agenda and cause. Finally, any explanation must suggest some action(s) that might remedy the conditions that have produced the disadvantage. As one Wotanist suggested, "The Norse myths and sagas are a guide, a template for action."

Explanations identify key individuals or groups central to the injustice. Yigal Amir certainly held Yitzhak Rabin responsible for ceding part of Eretz Israel to the Arabs; at his arraignment, he explicitly stated he had killed Rabin for moving "to give our country to the Arabs." Anwar al-Sadat appeared to violate the *shari'a* by negotiating with the occupying Jewish infidel. Importantly, both Rabin and Sadat were in violation of the non-negotiable—"God's law." Former U.S. Attorney General Janet Reno, who authorized the FBI actions at Waco and implemented various gun control laws, seemed to some to exercise power in ways that infringed civil liberties while expanding police (and federal) powers. Clinton often spoke cheerfully that, in fifty years, there would be "no majority race left in America"; Buchanan (2002), echoing to a more mainstream audience a threat Mathews had invoked in his 1984 declaration of war (see opening quote), observed,

> It is a rarity in history that a people [college students hearing Clinton's remarks] would cheer news that they and their children would soon be

dispossessed of their inheritance as the majority in the nation their ancestors built. (p. 209)

These powerful figures, then, are identified as the perpetrators of one's discontent, harbingers of threat, and religious, cultural, or racial traitors, and their identification leads to a dawning realization of betrayal by an unjust, compromised, and dangerous system.

For the remainder of this section, I will focus on responses that explanations might suggest. Many actions might remedy the dire situation revealed by delegitimating discoveries. One may believe change is not possible by any means, and so seek to exit the intolerable situation and migrate elsewhere. The migration may provide a chance to regroup and reinvigorate the minority community, as was the case with Muslim emigration to Medina before the Prophet's triumphant return to Mecca. Doran (2001) makes a rather lucid case that the events of September 11 were intended to provoke U.S. and Western retaliation in ways that would advantageously (for Islamists) intensify the civil war between the "Believers" and corrupt apostate regimes. In a newly Islamist Saudi Arabia, bin Laden most certainly would return from exile as a triumphant hero.

The migration may also be an attempt to more permanently separate oneself from those that threaten. Fraternalistic deprivation has been associated with separatist attitudes in Quebec and Scotland (see Brewer & Brown, 1998). Mathews, leader of the Order, sought escape in remote Metaline Falls, Washington, and envisioned the establishment of a White American Bastion (Flynn & Gerhardt, 1990). More recently, many white separatists have advocated emigration to the Pacific Northwest under the "Northwest Imperative" or the "10% solution"; through an overwhelming white majority or by force of arms, the states of Washington, Oregon, Idaho, Montana, and Wyoming would be seized to form a white homeland. Lane (1999) suggests a separate racial community as well:

> People who allow others not of their race to live among them will perish, because the inevitable result of racial integration is racial interbreeding which destroys the characteristics and existence of a race. Forced integration is deliberate and malicious genocide, particularly for a People like the White race, who are now a small minority in the world. (p. 87)

While a white homeland has not come to fruition, pockets of receptive and disenfranchised citizens in the rural heartland and mountain west don't care for elites on the "edges" of the country. Some closed Christian Identity communities—such as Elohim City (Oklahoma), the Covenant, the Sword, and the Arm of the Lord (Arkansas, in the early to mid-1980s), and, until recently sued, the Church of Jesus Christ Christian–Aryan Nations (Idaho)—have successfully existed as private separatist enclaves. While the events of September 11 have brought the United States together, urban power centers like Los Angeles and New York still represent to many all that is wrong with the country—immorality, pornography, liberal politics, "socialist" tax policies, high-crime minority communities, overcrowding, pollution, and racial and ethnic mixing.

In a world with few remaining geographic frontiers, escape may not be possible. In the modern world, federal government is often everywhere within the state and enforces policy that counters separatism of any sort (this is not to say that there are no successful accommodations of minority rights movements). Faraj (1986) rejects *hijrah* (emigration) as a plausible strategy, deferring to the duty to fight (Koran 2.216). If one has rejected a government as illegitimate and sees no hope of change by any means, one may see separatism as the only option. However, if the government continues to intrude upon the separatist, the separatist may feel forced to violence, if only to secure the defensive separation and the integrity of the separatist's territorial claim.

Self-Defense as Criterion for Violence

Speech or actions that demean, insult, or attribute incompetence may necessitate a verbal response, a vote for change, or an attack on the other's character, but they do not justify killing. If, however, the other is taking actions that may destroy one's life or way of life, or that of ingroup others, the stakes are raised and one begins to access the justifications for violent self-defense. Recall here that the defended self may be inclusive of other people and entities, including those that are not aware of the threat or may not be able to defend themselves. When the other (be they foreign power, internal "alien," or traitor) threatens those of one's race, ethnicity, or religion, jeopardizing the future of "my people," God's plan, or what is best about us by various trends, actions, policies, or migration patterns, then a rather strong response may be in order.[31] Further facilitating a forceful defense, affective ingroup ties, when even minimal conflict is present, are associated with exaggerated negative evaluations of the outgroup (Jackson, 2002).

In any culture, in addition to justified violence, there may be instructive obligations to violence in defense of the sacred. U.S. military members take an oath to "support and defend" the Constitution against all enemies, "foreign and domestic." It is no surprise that many ex- and current military personnel in both racist and non-racist extremist politics see their paramilitary preparations and intentions as merely continued commitment to that oath. America, they believe, has deviated from its "patriots," not the other way around. One may also meaningfully argue that violating the *shari'a* or halakhic law destroys the pure and just life, disrupting an ordered creation, defying divine will, and denying the greater good. Here again, it may be understood that violent defense is mandated, whether to block a transgressor or restore righteousness; moral mandates, in turn, may lessen the import of adhering to a society's formal procedural justice requirements (Skitka & Houston, in press; Skitka & Mullen, 2002).

The individual perceiving threat seeks and is susceptible to those messages that might prove psychologically protective or esteem-saving. Terror management (TM) theory (Greenberg, Solomon, & Pyszczynski, 1997; Solomon, Greenberg, &

Pyszczynski, 2002) is instructive here. An existential crisis haunts us—we know we will die. We transcend our temporal selves, "cheat" our own death, by identifying with that which will outlive us, be it sacred writ or creed, deity, one's people, or other cultural institutions and world views. Consider the transcendence of heroic deeds implied in the following verse from the *Havamal* (see Griffin, 2001), popular in Wotanism: "Cattle die, and kinsmen die, /And so one dies oneself;/One thing I know that never dies:/The fame of a dead man's deeds" (p. 391). Relevant to our interests here, invoking the salience of one's mortality tightens one's bond to transcendent institutions and worldviews. Mortality salience has been robustly associated with ingroup identification, intergroup bias, and outgroup aggression (Greenberg, et al., 1997). Sometimes delegitimating discoveries or perceived threats undermine one's death-denying psychological apparatus and make one's own death salient, but more often it seems one must wrestle with symbolic (sometimes actual) death beyond oneself.

Let me, therefore, suggest that a collective mortality salience is also in effect when one is confronted with threat; psychologically functional explanations featuring esteem-saving ingroup identities and intergroup bias may be activated through collective mortality salience in perhaps three different ways. First, the imagined/ actual death of, or danger to, a valued or loved ingroup member may invoke or amplify a TM response, further binding the individual to group ideology and outcomes (S. Solomon, personal communications, November 2001). In seeing Vicki Weaver and her son killed at Ruby Ridge, many in America's right saw their own loved ones, their own "blood," at risk. Second, the imagined end of the ingroup (but not necessarily death of oneself or one's beliefs) may achieve the effect. Declining European dominance, populations, and birth rates seemed to cement racialist identities in a number of interviewees. Third, and perhaps less strongly, the threatened death of a (sub)culturally located ideal may indirectly imply collective death if the ideal is conflated with the collective. Consider McVan's (1997) seventh of the "14 Codes of the Aryan Ethic": "Treasure your history, heritage and racial identity, as your ancestors have entrusted; it falls with you, it will rise with you" (p. 50), or also, "A race dies when its ideals die" (p. 55).

It is important here to understand what may happen should one perceive sincere threat. If a person, organization, or other group is moving to enslave one, risking one's life or way of life, then violence is probably appropriate. If these ominous maneuvers are in their infancy, then there is likely time to warn others, to inform them of the growing threat, to awaken and cognitively liberate them with information. As social psychologists are well aware, however, rarely does message content alone persuade and bring about attitude change. The threat grows, and one also must constantly gauge the immediacy of the threat. As the sinister other comes closer to launching its assault or completing its encirclement, one's efforts must turn away from sounding the alarm and toward preparations to resist. One is not obliged to queue up for one's own slaughter or wait to respond until the enemy engages a massive strike or brings genocidal machinations to completion. Feelings of collective efficacy, that the situation can be changed by collective action (Bandura, 1997; Klandermans, 1997), combined with the threat presented by a delegitimated enemy (see Sprinzak, 1991), may produce unyielding resolve to embrace defensive violence. This is clearly reflected in comments by both Islamists and Jewish extremist Rabbi Meir Kahane, respectively:

> O (Ruler), servant of the two Holy Places (Mecca and Medina)
> If ye looked at us well
> Then you would realize that you only play with what is devotion
> Some people make their cheeks wet with tears
> in great quantities
> but our chests and throats become wet
> by torrents of our blood
>
> (Faraj, 1986, p. 184)

> I don't intend to sit quietly by while Arabs intend to liquidate my state—either by bullets or by having babies. It's important that you know what the name "Kahane" means to the Arabs. It means terror. (cited in Hoffman, 1998, p. 101–102)

Recall the white separatist concern about dwindling white populations and the reality that white people of European heritage are a shrinking global minority.[32] The decline is quickly reaching a "point of no return,"[33] and the U.S. and European governments and media label any mention of such concerns, or government and media complicity in these trends, as "hate speech." In a Pennsylvania community's "dialogue on race," a nineteen-year-old who claimed that "race-mixing is poison" was not invited to explain his position, respond to challenges, and continue participating—he was unfortunately instructed by a short-sighted professor to leave immediately. Nonviolent change has apparently been blocked outside of urging racially aware families to have more children. Perhaps the most commonly used phrase among those I've interviewed is "fourteen" or "for the fourteen words"; penned by Order member David Lane (who is serving a prison sentence of nearly two hundred years), they are: "We must secure the existence of our people and a future for White children." The reader would be correct in concluding that those embracing the imperative believe the existence of their people and their children's futures are in jeopardy. Presumably, if demographic trends continue, more racists will decide the time to warn others has passed, and the time for defensive violence is upon them.

Let's further consider how facts can be framed in ways consistent with myth, conspiracy theories, and narratives that construct imminent threat; to illustrate, I'll expound upon conspiracy theories about Jews, adding to earlier comments. Again, this is an attempt to phenomenologically understand, and I ask that you bear with me as I assemble the relevant worldview. In large portions of the white separatist movement, Adolf Hitler is admired. *Mein Kampf* is widely read by dedicated white separatists. While it is often recognized that his concerns were narrowly German, and World War II is seen as horrifically fratricidal (racially), Hitler is honored as a steadfast defender of Aryandom; he is referred to as the "Great One," for example, in *The Turner Diaries*, and some even carry his photo in their wallets alongside that of their family members. The reader will recall earlier mention of Jewish overrepresentation in the Bolshevik Revolution, European socialism, and Weimar politics (Ginsberg, 1993; MacDonald, 1998). Hitler's hatred of Jews is likely a product of his contempt for a Weimar Republic many Germans found shameful, and his fear that the Bolshevik "Red Terror" would be visited upon Germany. This contempt and fear, while extreme, does have some factual basis. Hitler (1925/1971) commented:

> In gaining political power, the Jew casts off the few cloaks that he still wears. The democratic people's Jew becomes the blood-Jew and tyrant. . . . The most frightful example . . . is offered by Russia, where he killed or starved about thirty million people with positively fanatical savagery, in part amid inhuman tortures, in order to give a gang of Jewish journalists and stock exchange bandits domination over a great people. (p. 326)

While Hitler's figures are grossly inflated, Rummel's (1994) analysis suggests that at the time *Mein Kampf* was published, as many as 5.4 million had already been slaughtered by a Soviet state that would eventually murder nearly 62 million.

As mentioned, Stalin and his successors eventually targeted Jews; among separatists, however, the belief is not that Jews (or Jewish elites) abandoned their "Communist" war on European gentiles, but rather that the strategy changed to one of "marching through the institutions." There is a body of fact, selectively attended to and assembled, that propagates the "Jewish threat," the concern that Jews seek to control and destroy white society through manipulations "behind the scenes." MacDonald (1998) relevantly suggests that through intellectual and political movements in the twentieth century, Jewish elites sought group strategies to end anti-Semitism while enhancing prospects for Jewish survival and prosperity both overtly and semi-cryptically.

White separatists are quick to point out that while liberal critics decry "white privilege," they overlook Jewish overrepresentation (per their 2.5 percent proportion of the U.S. populace) on wealth indices (1,000 percent), among the top 100 Wall Street executives (2,100 percent), in Ivy League admissions (1,700 percent), and in Republican and, especially, Democratic Party contributions (1,000 percent and 2,100 percent, respectively) (see MacDonald, 1998). The America-Israel Public Affairs Committee (AIPAC) and other Jewish/pro-Israeli organizations are notoriously powerful on Capitol Hill; racialists know well that speaking critically about Israel or U.S. policy on Israel, trotting out skeletons like the 1967 Israeli attack on the USS *Liberty* (which killed 34 and injured 171), or questioning the ethics of AIPAC's influence invite discrediting smears, accusations of prejudice, and various other sanctions, even if one is a congressman or a flag officer in the U.S. military (confidential personal communications; Bendersky, 2000; Hurley, 1999; MacDonald, 1998; Zacharia, 2000). Of greatest concern to most racialists is the fact that Jews compose an astounding 55 to 60 percent of the media elite (MacDonald, 2001), for it is media that shapes our "ways of seeing." More recent white separatist concerns revolve around a story Fox News broke in December 2001. In the ongoing "war on terrorism," at least sixty Israeli spies were apparently rounded up within the United States, and it was reported that Israeli intelligence may have had advance knowledge about the September 11 attacks, but did not share it (Cameron, 2001).[34] Another element of threat for racialists is to be found in interracial crime rates and inequities in "hate crimes" implementation.

In both conservative and white separatist subcultures, there is broad knowledge of "politically incorrect," and poorly publicized, information about race and crime in America. While blacks commit violent crimes at a rate approximately four times that of whites (per U.S. Federal Bureau of Investigation statistics), blacks commit crimes of interracial violence at a rate approximately fifty times that of whites, and blacks are better than one hundred times more likely than whites to commit interracial gang rapes and gang assaults (Buchanan, 2002; New Century Foundation, 1999).[35] A white assailant in an interracial crime of violence is almost twenty-eight times more likely to be charged with a "hate crime" than a black assailant (Perazzo, 2001). In the self-segregating world of prison life, one may become racially conscious, as did one man with whom I corresponded, when one is made aware of the black "intentions" behind the statistics and finds that when black prisoners say "Peace," they really mean "Planned Extermination of All Caucasoid Europeans."

While Americans are likely to be quite familiar with the grotesque dragging death of James Byrd in Texas and the vicious murder of Matthew Shepard in Wyoming, they are much less likely to know about the dragging death of white six-year-old Jake Robel by a black man, the rape and beating death of thirteen-year-old Jesse Dirkhising by two gay men, or the racist shooting spree by Ronald Taylor, a black man who killed three white men and wounded two others (Buchanan, 2002; Hutchinson, 2000). Jacobs and Potter (1998) have eloquently raised the issue that "hate crimes" legislation is, unfortunately, the continuation of identity politics and may be divisive in its consequences. Buchanan (2002) more assertively claims, "hate crimes are the cultural elite's way of racially profiling white males" (p. 67); this comment certainly implies media deception and seems almost to suggest a conspiracy.

As earlier indicated, my intention in the preceding paragraphs was to illustrate that a collage of facts assembled by many racial separatists is, as we shall see in a moment, consistent with (though not sufficient to prove) conspiracy theories that suggest profound and imminent threat. Indeed, the powerless (or those perceiving powerlessness) may be more motivated than the powerful to engage in accurate information-processing about the powerful (see Pittman, 1998); however, assembly of facts into theory about the behavior of others is often influenced by framing (Goffman, 1974) and influential mythmaking (Aho, 1994). A white separatist conspiracy theory, or explanatory worldview, goes something like this: Consistently across time, international Jewry, by placement in (and manipulation of) government, business, media, finance, and secret societies, seeks to destroy racial and ethnic awareness in all (especially Aryans) but Jews. By such position and influence, Jews seek to bring about a leveled, multicultural, miscegenating, immigrant-over-run, materialistic society in which feminism, abortion, and the decay of the traditional family contribute to declining Aryan birth rates and the eventual end of Aryans as they become hated minorities in their own lands. Further, because Jews control the media, it is virtually a "hate crime" for Aryans to point out an extortionist "Holocaust industry" (see Finkelstein, 2000) or raise the issue of racial enemies, while liberals (who ironically claim race does not exist) can openly declare that "the white race is the cancer of human history" (Sontag, cited in Buchanan, 2002, p. 55) and issue forth a call to "abolish the white race by any means necessary" (Ignatiev & Garvey, 1996). Jews in the media can also keep from public view information that might shock whites into racial consciousness, such as the magnitude of black assaults on whites or evidence that the Israelis knew in advance about the events of September 11 (while ensuring that Israel gains support for its attacks on Palestinians by likening its campaign to a timely U.S. "war on terror"). Lack of a mobilizing white racial consciousness will be especially catastrophic when the American ethnic civil war erupts (as envisioned by Chittum, 1996). This is a particularly bleak picture; what, white separatists ask, will be left of whites in a hundred years under such an unrelenting assault?

The point here is that what may at first seem to be incredible and outlandish explanations can be plausibly constructed from diverse bodies of factual information (they are not merely simple explanations of complex situations). The threat portrayed can be immense, imminent, and very real to the believer; private and collective mortality salience are invoked, ingroup affective ties tighten, perceptions of conflict exacerbate one's "positive hate" and intergroup bias, and violence results.[36] Those experiencing delegitimating discoveries and seeking explanations may be especially prone to acceptance of such explanatory theories. Abalakina-Papp, Stephan, Craig, and Gregory (1999) demonstrated that alienation and feelings of hostility, powerlessness, and disadvantage are related to acceptance of conspiracy theories. Blaming the (presumably illegitimate) "system" for disadvantage also has been associated with acceptance of conspiracy theories (Crocker, Luhtanen, Broadnax, & Blaine, 1999). Fortunately, it is also true that facts can be reframed in multiple other ways to construct and comprehend reality.

Defense-demanding threat is also readily identified in the Hamas (1988) platform:

> Our enemy . . . has resorted to breaking bones, opening fire on women and children and the old . . . it destroys houses, renders children orphans and issues oppressive judgments against thousands of young people who spend the best years of their youth in the darkness of prisons. The Nazism of the Jews does not skip women and children . . . They make war against people's livelihood, plunder their moneys, and threaten their honor. . . . Exiling people from their country is another way of killing them." (p. 20)

Also, and somewhat consistent with bin Laden's larger narrative that Islam is suffering an eighty-year decline under Western persecution and apostate leadership dating from the 1924 dismantling of the Caliphate,[37]

> World Zionism and Imperialist forces have been attempting, with smart moves and considered planning,[38] to push the Arab countries . . . out of the circle of conflict with Zionism, in order, ultimately, to isolate the Palestinian people. (p. 30)

Under such threat, nonviolent solutions and peace talks are seen to be hopeless:

> . . . the Islamic Resistance Movement . . . does not believe that those conferences are capable of responding to demands, or of restoring right or doing justice to the oppressed. Those conferences are no more than a means to appoint the nonbelievers as arbitrators in the lands of Islam.[39] Since when did the Unbelievers do justice to the Believers? (p. 12)

Accordingly, the only recourse left is that of defensive violence. Muslims cognizant of their duty "have raised the banner of Jihad in the face of the oppressors in order to extricate the country and the people from the [oppressor's] desecration, filth, and evil" (p. 5). When there is substantial pervasive threat constructed from the facts at hand, and nonviolent recourse does not appear to be an option, the necessity to defend oneself may be the criterion by which violence is permissible and killing is justified or even morally required.

The Importance of Groups

Groups are clearly an important psychological element in political violence (Pynchon & Borum, 1999). It is not often that individuals deal with grievance and on their own come to conclusions about hidden injustice.[40] Groups may enhance recognition of delegitimating discoveries, access to psychologically functional, if not always accurate, explanations and world views, and construction of the imminent threat that may justify defensive killing. As one white separatist described recruitment of angry youth, "We help them understand *why* they are angry and help them become racially aware." Other ethnographic work has suggested anomie as both something to which "skinhead" recruiters attend (and hope to capitalize upon) and a motivating factor for "joiners" (Blazak, 2001).

There is no doubt some are socialized, early in life, into extreme ideologies or theologies. Eric Rudolph, wanted for multiple bombings and murder in Georgia and Alabama, apparently spent some time during his youth at the Christian Identity Church of Israel (Missouri). I also witnessed socialization into racial theology in Christian Identity communities such as Elohim City (though it was well known that some youth frequently violated the "rules" and rebelled against the totality of Identity). Others socialized into racist ideologies attempted to hide this, seemingly in an impression management effort to appear independent. As one young man told me about his decisions to become a racialist, his friend, who had served multiple prison sentences for assault (and in the process had learned a great deal about knife fighting, which he, in turn, eagerly shared with other "race warriors"), cut him off in mid-sentence and corrected, "C'mon, your Dad's racist as fuck!" The first young man, momentarily embarrassed, admitted this was true. In an interesting twist on minority influence, a few young men had, through their struggles with various social institutions, apparently fostered racialist views in at least one parent.

As McCauley and Segal (1989) have noted, cult conversion models seem somewhat explanatory of terrorist/extremist recruitment. The combination of delegitimating discovery or other grievance, availability of a plausible explanatory worldview,[41] and presence of a social network that brings one to a group possessing the alternative view can be a powerful combination facilitating entry into the group (Galanter, 1999; Snow, Zurcher, & Eckland-Olson, 1980). Still, the vast majority of marginal group members never engage in violence; something else must be happening.

Many I interviewed in law enforcement likened the movement toward violence to entering a funnel. Many millions in the United States have a delegitimating discovery and publicly dislike various gun laws, federal actions at Waco, the Internal Revenue Service (tax collectors), and so on; they are all thrown into the top of the funnel, but very few "Tim McVeighs" pop out of the bottom. Many are spun out altogether; turnover in most marginal groups is quite high. Perhaps for most, the delegitimating discovery produces only a temporary "crisis of confidence" about the prevailing polity. For some few, though, there is eventually a "crisis of legitimacy" in which there is no hope of change without violence against the enemy and all its supporters (see Sprinzak, 1991). One does not become a "terrorist" overnight, however, and groups (or series of affiliations in McVeigh's case) seem to be important in the process of working deeper into the funnel.

Accordingly, let me extend the process of "double marginalization" (see McCauley & Segal, 1989) and Crenshaw's (1985) contention that individuals join a series of groups on the way to terrorism, and suggest that a process of "serial splintering" occurs to produce those who do engage in violence. This relatively lengthy process may occur in at least three ways. First, and what I have most commonly seen among white separatists, one moves out of the mainstream through various groups, repeatedly joining and then splintering away, sometimes with a few other like-minded individuals, and moving on to progressively more extreme alliances. The evolving separatist may, at times, display affiliations across multiple groups (Kaplan, 1997; White, 2001). Over time, the company one keeps is decidedly more committed to the cause. The extremist becomes increasingly isolated from "outsiders" with alternative views. Eventually, one is to be found in a small group in which violence previously unthinkable is now preferred. An example may help.

One interviewee began his political life as a leftist campus protester. He later joined the military, possibly to learn technical skills. Socialization in the military led him to conservative politics and organizations.[42] Disgust with Haitian refugees, what he saw as failure by leadership to equitably discipline blacks within the ranks, and observations that blacks were not learning technical skills quickly or proficiently began to make him racially aware. His politics and acquaintances became ultra-conservative. He later joined the Klan and rose through the ranks. Along the way, further isolating him from the mainstream, his wife divorced him, and he was fired from a civilian job for his racialist activities (events that may have further served as delegitimating discoveries). He began spending more time with racist acquaintances. In his Klan group, he tired of the ideological simplicity, noting that everything was "nigger, nigger, nigger, jew, jew, jew" with no political substance behind it. This man drifted through Identity and into Odinism (Wotanism). He later affiliated himself with White Aryan Resistance, built relationships with European racists, took funds from a foreign government hostile to the United States, and was associated with, though never charged in, a number of violent events. This pattern of serial splintering can also be seen in a number of "white power" individuals profiled in Kaplan (2000).

A second way serial splintering can occur is the case in which an entire organization changes, repeatedly splintering from previous versions of itself, and moving toward more extreme organizational culture and norms. This may occur because of 1) turnover in the group and/or entry of more extreme individuals or cliques (who, in turn, may be splintering as described in the preceding paragraphs), and 2) selective attendance to, and assimilation of, more extreme ideas, interpretations, or worldviews. Both of the above took place in the evolution of a quiet, rural Christian church, the Zarephath-Horeb Community Church, into a violent, isolated Christian Identity community, the Covenant, the Sword, and the Arm of the Lord (personal communications, K. Noble, June, 1998, May, 2000; Noble, 1998).

A third way serial splintering can occur is when one splinters from larger collectives to increasingly smaller subsets of the same movement or organization. This is perhaps the case in violence toward abortion doctors and clinics. There is some evidence to suggest one moves to increasingly intense Christian belief, perhaps embraces Christian Reconstructionism, becomes active in the pro-life movement, blockades abortion clinics, endures multiple arrests, and then eventually finds oneself among that small community that believes nothing remains to end the "genocide of the unborn" but the outright destruction of the clinics, the machinery, and the "butchers" performing the abortions. The embrace of violence is viewed as being in the greatest of traditions; time collapses as one becomes a Christian warrior for divine justice, following in the footsteps of Joan of Arc, John Brown, and Dietrich Bonhoeffer (Bray, 1994). Annually, this small community of people, endorsing what they see as heroic and divinely mandated use of violence to end abortion, comes together at the White Rose Banquet in Washington; there they celebrate the "sacrifice made by those incarcerated for defending the unborn" (Hill, 1997, p. 1).

For an individual searching for explanations in the wake of delegitimating discoveries or other grievances, groups are likely to wield informational influence (which helps one understand an ambiguous reality), while normative social influence may predominate once one has become part of the group, serving to build consensus and norms, promote conformity, suppress deviance from the cause, and keep one within a group that fulfills the social motive to belong (Asch, 1956; Deutsch & Gerard, 1955; S. Fiske, personal communications, September–December 2001; Schachter, 1951). The need to belong, paired with self-enhancement motives, can be quite powerful. Consider the case of "Dan," once convicted of possessing methamphetamine. Released from the criminal justice system and determined to stay "clean," he found in Christian Identity a supportive community that valued him for who he was—a white man. Further, norms against drug use in the congregation kept him away from drugs and old social networks, and he was clearly excited when talking about his new girlfriend, presents he bought for her, positive comments from family members, and how he kept his refrigerator full (in the past, a paycheck was immediately exhausted on drugs). His self-esteem soared. Baumeister (1997) and Crocker and Luhtanen (1990), however, would have us know that, when challenged, an unstable or unduly inflated (collective) self-esteem can produce violence. I spoke with Dan the day before an Aryan Nations parade; should anyone interfere with their expression of "white pride," he calmly assured me, he was ready to fight.

In small, like-minded, isolated groups, a number of dynamics can work to produce extreme or intense decisions and violent actions. It has long been known that small groups can produce norms and homogenize judgments about ambiguous phenomena; also, the norms formed in these groups may then stay with and influence individuals far into the future (Sherif, 1935), allowing one to even leave the group and yet execute behaviors consistent with the group's positions. Within the group, a phenomenon called "social implosion" may occur in which external social ties wither and members socially interact only with those in the group (Stark & Bainbridge, 1980). Given no access to other frames, arguments, or views, one's identity is conflated with the group's, and the group alone defines reality. Dissent or deviance, which threatens group survival and social support, are effectively suppressed. The socially imploded group wields incredible power in shaping behavior, be it pro-social or destructive.

When the need for consensus becomes dominant in a cohesive group (unity of thought and action may be seen as necessary for group success and survival), and if the motivating desire is to maintain extant social relationships (as may be the case with social implosion and isolation), groupthink can occur and produce poor decisions (see McCauley, 1998). Janis and Mann (1977) and Janis (1982) assert group insulation from competing views and high stress can produce a number of symptoms of groupthink, which I've qualitatively witnessed among white separatists; these include absolute belief in the morality of the cause and the group, inaccurate outgroup stereotypes, self-censorship, and illusions of unanimity. The group can also come to function as "ideologue," seeing its purpose as the articulation and embodiment of core values and norms (Hamm, 2002; t' Hart, Stern, & Sundelius, 1997). When groupthink occurs, the cause and its supporting ideology become unassailable; an assault on either is experienced as a personal attack on the interdimensional or collective self. Because an absolute morality is presumed and a moral mandate exists, the ends all too easily come to justify the means. It is no social accident that across fifteen extremist groups, beliefs that the cause is morally and ethically correct and that violence is sometimes necessary for the "greater good" increased significantly in importance for (and while) staying in the group.

Groups may easily become extreme or polarized in their decisions for a number of reasons (Brown, 2000). In a given group, it is likely there will be greater access to, and availability of, arguments supporting the dominant positions; this creates the illusion that the preponderance of the evidence on a given issue supports the *a priori* group perspective and groups move further in the direction of the initially preferred view (Burnstein & Vinokur, 1977). Even if outgroup views are available, ingroup arguments tend to be profoundly more persuasive (Mackie & Cooper, 1984). It also appears that ingroup members in cohesive groups strive to be the prototypical group member (Abrams, Wetherell, Cochrane, Hogg, & Turner, 1990; Hogg, Turner, & Davison, 1990); we can see here how important myth-making might be in defining the ideal to which group members aspire. Perhaps, then, it is also not surprising there is conflict within violent groups; as one white separatist observed, the problem with his movement is that "everyone wants to be the next Fuhrer."

Finally, it is worth noting that group isolation may occur in the midst of many, and may not be so easy to recognize as we'd believe. One need not geographically separate oneself, though that can surely be part of a serial splintering process. Virtual relations can monopolize one's attentions and give rise to cohesive, socially isolated groups populated by geographically dispersed individuals. Considerable reliance on alternative news sources, home schooling, Islamist *madrasahs*, closed religious/ritual systems, and alternative medicine may pull one away from competing social networks and constructions of reality. Even among many, countervailing influences may be nonexistent; the reader will readily recognize how rarely one encounters frank "belief talk" in work and various other social roles.

The Procedural Justice of Religio- and Ethnopolitical Violence

In most cultures, there are procedural safeguards that must be satisfied before one justly kills or harms. Whether satisfied by a single or multiple procedures, the components of these procedural safeguards are 1) proof standards (proof that some wrong has been done or someone has been threatened), 2) due process standards (subjecting proof standards and the information obtained to support them to critical scrutiny), and 3) measures to ensure consensus on the first two safeguards, and an appropriate response. Most readers will recognize that these safeguards are satisfied in U.S. criminal trials, with final consensus on a case and its disposition being provided by a body of unbiased jurors. Being normally socialized, those who would engage political violence are aware of the above and will seek to fulfill the requirements. Given the imminence of the threat and lack of access to formal institutions, the killer may truncate or informally seek fulfillment of the requirements, but in some way the requirements will be met. Deviant groups may, somewhat literally, "take the law into their own hands."

A number of examples of the above can be found. Common-law citizen's courts have tried and convicted public officials in absentia before calling on a militia to execute sentence. Others convened a "Continental Congress" prior to preparations for violence. McVeigh, when captured, wore a shirt displaying the words of

Thomas Jefferson: "The tree of liberty must be refreshed from time to time with the blood of patriots and tyrants" (Michel & Herbeck, 2001). In his car were copies of the Declaration of Independence, a clipping about the Battle of Lexington, a note that read "Obey the Constitution of the United States and we won't shoot you," a magazine article about the government "executions" (as he'd underlined) at Waco, and portions of *The Turner Diaries* (Griffin, 2001).[43] McVeigh (1998) also framed his act as a military operation, comparing the bombing of the Murrah building to U.S. bombing of Iraqi government buildings and employees. As Americans blamed Iraq for the death of "human shields" present at "legitimate" targets, so McVeigh blamed the U.S. government for the death of children at the Murrah building. In fact, McVeigh borrowed the U.S. government's very term and referred to the death of innocents as "collateral damage" (Michel & Herbeck, 2001). What, ultimately, was McVeigh's model? Consider his fondness for quoting late U.S. Supreme Court Justice Brandeis: "Our government is the potent, the omnipresent teacher. For good or ill, it teaches the whole people by its example'" (McVeigh, 1998, p. 23).

Did McVeigh achieve anything by the Oklahoma City bombing? He claimed federal agents abandoned the aggressive tactics used at Ruby Ridge and Waco as a result of the Murrah building bombing; at least one FBI agent agreed, in part (Michel & Herbeck, 2001). Of the several federal agents I have interviewed, almost all have said that no one now thinks about a federal standoff without considering the Oklahoma City bombing. Four months after the bombing, the federal government decided to settle out of court with Weaver for $3.1 million. One is left to wonder about aspects of both McVeigh's motivations and effect, but it is clear he saw his use of violence in the reasoned tradition of the country's "founding fathers."

Both Yigal Amir and the "team" that assassinated Sadat religiously delegitimized their respective governments in ways consistent with Sprinzak's (1991) framework (Alianak, 2000; Kelman, 2001). In Amir, grievance (the 1993 Oslo agreement blocked realization of Eretz Israel), an extremist state of mind, a radical ideology (arising from the *Gush Emunim*), and the desire to violently counter a threatening status quo all came together in the assassination of Rabin (Peleg, 1997; Sprinzak, 1999). In both assassinations, the leaders were considered apostate, nonviolent options were sincerely considered and rejected,[44] and religious authorities agreed there was proof of apostasy sufficient to condone a violent response (Alianak, 1998, 2000; Faraj, 1986). Sadat's assassins were supported not only by the rationale in *al-Faridah* and available *fatwas*, but attempted unsuccessfully to pursue even further religious consultation; tellingly, and suggesting yet another delegitimating discovery, their search was quickly abandoned because many of the clerics they sought were already in Sadat's prisons (Alianak, 1998). In Amir's case, a legitimate authority (rabbi) declared Rabin a *rodef* (pursuer or threat to the Jewish people); Amir commented during his trial, "I know Jewish law and *din rodef* means that you've tried everything else and nothing works then you *have to* [emphasis added] kill him" (Alianak, 1998, p. 7; Kelman, 2001). The assassins of both Rabin and Sadat, then, sought to adhere to culturally acceptable theological procedural justice requirements before engaging in violence.

In Islam, "defensive *jihad*" is an individual duty in the effort to repel aggression directed toward Muslim life and property, wherever those Muslims may be (Sivan, 1998). Consider the following comments by bin Laden (Nida'ul Islam, 1996):

> The evidence overwhelmingly shows America and Israel killing the weaker men, women, and children in the Muslim world and else-where. A few examples of this are seen in the recent Qana massacre in Lebanon, the death of more than six hundred thousand Iraqi children . . . which resulted from the boycotts and sanctions . . . their withhold-ing of arms from the Muslims of Bosnia Hercegovina leaving them prey to the Christian Serbians who massacred and raped . . . Our encouragement and call to Muslims to enter Jihad against the Ameri-can and Israeli occupiers are actions which we are engaging in as reli-gious obligations. (p. 5)

Bin Laden defines the threat and invokes obligation to fight (as expressed in the Koran and the *hadith*). In his 1998 *fatwa* for *jihad* against "Jews and Crusaders," bin Laden references the example of the Prophet, the sanctity of the now-occupied Arabian peninsula, and embraces what Faraj (1986) referred to as the "verse of the sword": "slay the pagans wherever ye find them" (Koran 9.5; later in the *fatwa*, the pagans to be attacked everywhere are identified as Americans). Time has collapsed, and bin Laden sees himself fighting against the pagans for a "true" Islam in a situa-tion no less urgent than that faced by the Prophet fourteen centuries ago. Further, on the 1998 World Islamic Front *fatwa*, five others are listed with titles such as "Shaykh" and "Amir"; a consensus among "informed" leaders about wrongs done, proof they have been done, and just response is communicated.

To summarize, it might be said that one is on the path to violence when there is a grievance or delegitimating discovery, an explanatory view that constructs or reveals threat, defensive rhetoric, culturally consistent time collapse that depicts the current struggle as epic or timeless, and increasing collective isolation (geographi-cally, socially, or virtually). At the same time, those on the path to religio- and eth-nopolitical violence remain much like the parent culture. They understand prevail-ing norms and appreciate the risk and magnitude of the events they are about to undertake. Interviewed separatists contemplating violence realized that it would end in 1) victory (which they realistically recognized as unlikely, at least in the near future), 2) forever fleeing law enforcement, 3) imprisonment, or 4) death. Before killing a doctor who performed abortions, Paul Hill (1997), a former clergyman, contemplated the act and its theological support for sixteen months. The killer and his group realize their views are in contradiction with most of the rest of the cul-ture; they are a deviant outgroup or counterculture. In one very important way, however, they are not deviant. In some way they will follow the rules for procedur-al justice established in the superordinate culture. The killer-to-be understands and will fulfill the procedural justice requirements producing the consensus necessary regarding the facts of harmful intent, imminence of the threat, and appropriate responses; this consensus will define a defensible response incorporating lethal violence in ways consistent with the parent culture.

When one sees, in another, grievance, perceptions of threat and need for defensive action, increasing isolation, and views of their struggle as epic or timeless, there is sound reason to be concerned. When there is also movement to fulfill procedural justice requirements for permissible killing in a way that mimics the broader society, perhaps those observing ought to both worry and proactively respond.

CONCLUSIONS

In this chapter, I have illustrated the ambiguity of "terrorism," suggesting, much like Zulaika and Douglass (1996), that "the word itself is an abuse . . . impoverishing language and thought by obliterating distinctions" (p. 98). Much more insight is to be gained from comparing culturally contextualized constructions of terrorism for those (sub)cultures engaged in conflict (Drummond & Darley, 2002). Such an approach promises to inform, in greater specificity, attempts at conflict resolution. Stepping beyond the politics of terrorism allowed me to then examine the general similarities, shared across cases, in the construction of the enemy and the path to violence. A process of deviant legitimation was proposed.

The journey from delegitimating discovery to religio- or ethnopolitical killing is one of considerable length, both psychologically and temporally. Deviant legitimation provides a means of understanding how it is that one may navigate that journey and arrive at that mental state in which only violent recourse remains. Deviant legitimation also suggests ways in which the movement toward violence may be countered. Timothy McVeigh, members of the Order, Osama bin Laden, Paul Hill, and Yigal Amir were often visible to family members, friends, and attentive authorities long before they completed their transition from mainstream citizen or respected soldier to "terrorist." Aspects of deviant legitimation such as rhetoric of self-defense as criterion for violence, serial splintering, and declarations or actions that fulfill, to some approximation, culturally endorsed procedural justice requirements for just violence can be recognized. Responses can, accordingly, be formulated.

In the days after September 11, President Pervez Musharraf of Pakistan laid down a challenge. Terrorists, he noted, are like the leaves on a tree; organizations like al-Qaeda are as branches. The United States and its coalition partners are well on the way to lopping off a large and menacing branch, but one must realize that other branches still grow and tender young leaves will emerge, mature, and weather any storm. The real challenge to ending terrorism, Musharraf reflected, is to somehow get to the roots and the soil from which the tree grows. "Terrorism," in other words, is not without cause. The case for anti-state violence is not without fact or cultural context—one cannot simplistically dismiss it as wrong, prejudiced, or evil, and, in the long run, either hope or bomb it away. McVeigh's attorney once commented, "Had the government conducted an investigation into the Waco tragedy in

1993, then the Murrah Federal Building would have never been bombed" (Hamm, 2002, p. xiii). Perhaps deviant legitimation provides a framing of violence that might reveal root causes and promote constructive pursuit of long-term solutions.

REFERENCES

Abalakina-Papp, M., Stephan, W. G., Craig, T., & Gregory, W. L. (1999). Beliefs in conspiracies [Abstract]. *Political Psychology, 20,* 637–647.

Abrams, D., Wetherell, M., Cochrane, S., Hogg, M. A., & Turner, J. C. (1990). Knowing what to think by knowing who you are: Self-categorization and the nature of norm formation, conformity and group polarization. *British Journal of Social Psychology, 29,* 97–119.

Abu-Rabi, I. M. (1996). *Intellectual origins of Islamic resurgence in the modern Arab world.* Albany, NY: State University of New York Press.

Ackerman, S. (2001). The illusion of balance: NPR's coverage of Mideast deaths doesn't match reality. Retrieved January 5, 2002, from http://www.fair.org/extra/0111/npr-mideast.html.

Ahmad, E. (1998, October 12). Terrorism: Theirs and ours. Presentation given at the University of Colorado, Boulder.

Aho, J. A. (1994). *This thing of darkness: A sociology of the enemy.* Seattle, WA: University of Washington Press.

Alianak, S. L. (1998, Winter). Religion, politics and assassination in the Middle East. *Orbis.* Retrieved October 18, 2001, from http://www.findarticles.com/cf_0/m2393/n3_vl60/20380795/print.jhtm.

Alianak, S. L. (2000, Spring). The mentality of messianic assassins. *Orbis.* Retrieved October 18, 2001, from http://www.findarticles.com/cf_0/m0365/2_44/61943114/print.jhtm.

Al-Qaeda (n.d.). *The Al-Qaeda manual* (U.S. Department of Justice, Trans.). Retrieved January 21, 2002, from http://www.fas.org/irp/world/para/manualpart1.html.

Ammerman, N. T. (1997). *Bible believers: Fundamentalists in the modern world.* New Brunswick, NJ: Rutgers University Press.

Asch, S. E. (1956). Studies of independence and conformity: I. A minority of one against a unanimous majority. *Psychological Monographs, 70.*

Associated Press (2001, December 30). Zimbabwe to name thousands of blacks to get farms of whites. *New York Times.* Retrieved December 31, 2001, from http://www.nytimes.com/2001/12/30/ International/africa/30ZIMB.html.

Baghdadi, G. (2001, December 16). Hamas is still defiant. *Time Europe.* Retrieved December 16, 2001, from http://www.time.com/time/europe/me/printout/0,9869,187759,00.html.

Bandura, A. (1990). Mechanisms of moral disengagement. In W. Reich (Ed.), *Origins of terrorism: Psychologies, ideologies, theologies, states of mind* (pp. 161–191). New York: Cambridge University Press.

Bandura, A. (1997). *Self-efficacy: The exercise of control.* New York: W. H. Freeman and Company.

Barghouti, M. (2002, January 16). Want security? End the occupation. *Washington Post.* Retrieved January 16, 2002, from http://www.washingtonpost.com/wp-dyn/articles/A51887-2002 Jan15.html.

Barkun, M. (1994). *Religion and the racist right: The origins of the Christian Identity movement.* Chapel Hill, NC: University of North Carolina Press.

Baumeister, R. F. (1997). *Evil: Inside human cruelty and violence.* New York: W. H. Freeman and Company.

Becker, H. S. (1963). *Outsiders: Studies in the sociology of deviance.* New York: Free Press.

Bendersky, J. W. (2000). *The "Jewish threat": Anti-Semitic politics of the U.S. Army.* New York: Basic Books.

Berger, S. R., & Sutphen, M. (2001). Commandeering the Palestinian cause: Bin Laden's belated concern. In J. F. Hoge, Jr., & G. Rose (Eds.), *How did this happen? Terrorism and the new war* (pp. 123–128). New York: PublicAffairs.

Blazak, R. (2001). White boys to terrorist men: Target recruitment of Nazi skinheads. *American Behavioral Scientist, 44,* 982–1000.

Bodansky, Y. (1999). *Bin Laden: The man who declared war on America.* Rocklin, CA: Forum.

Brannan, D. W., Esler, P. F., & Strindberg, N. T. A. (2001). Talking to "terrorists": Towards an independent analytical framework for the study of violent substate activism. *Studies in Conflict and Terrorism, 24,* 3–24.

Bray, M. (1994). *A time to kill: A study concerning the use of force and abortion.* Portland, OR: Advocates for Life Publications.

Brewer, M. B. (1991). The social self: On being the same and different at the same time. *Personality and Social Psychology Bulletin, 17,* 475–482.

Brewer, M. B., & Brown, R. J. (1998). Intergroup relations. In D. T. Gilbert, S. T. Fiske, & G. Lindzey (Eds.), *The handbook of social psychology, Vol. II* (4th ed., pp. 554–594). Boston: McGraw-Hill.

Brown, R. (2000). *Group processes: Dynamics within and between groups,* 2nd ed. Oxford, England: Blackwell Publishers.

Buchanan, P. J. (2002). *The death of the West: How dying populations and immigrant invasions imperil our country and civilization.* New York: St. Martin's Press.

Burns, J. F. (2002, January 8). Musharraf's bind: Pakistani wants to prevent war with India but without having to give in on Kashmir. *New York Times,* pp. A1, A10.

Burnstein, E., & Vinokur, A. (1977). Persuasive argumentation and social comparison as determinants of attitude polarization. *Journal of Experimental Social Psychology, 13,* 315–332.

Cameron, C. (2001, December 12). Suspected Israeli spies held by U.S. *Fox News.* Retrieved December 14, 2001, from http://www.foxnews.com/story/0,2933,40679,00.html.

Chittum, T. W. (1996). *Civil war two: The coming breakup of America.* Show Low, AZ: American Eagle Publications.

Cooper, H. H. A. (2001). Terrorism: The problem of definition revisited. *American Behavioral Scientist, 44,* 881–893.

Crenshaw, M. (1985). An organizational approach to the analysis of political terrorism. *Orbis, 29,* 465–489.

Crenshaw, M. (1988). The subjective reality of the terrorist: Ideological and psychological factors in terrorism. In R. O. Slater & M. Stohl (Eds.), *Current perspectives on international terrorism* (pp. 12–46). London: Macmillan Press, Ltd.

Crenshaw, M. (1990). The logic of terrorism: Terrorist behavior as a product of strategic choice. In W. Reich (Ed.), *Origins of terrorism: Psychologies, ideologies, theologies, states of mind* (pp. 7–24). Cambridge, England: Cambridge University Press.

Crenshaw, M. (2001, December 12). Suicide terror. Presentation given at a meeting of the Foreign Policy Research Institute, Philadelphia, PA.

Crocker, J., & Luhtanen, R. (1990). Collective self-esteem and ingroup bias. *Journal of Personality and Social Psychology, 58*, 60–67.

Crocker, J., Luhtanen, R., Broadnax, S., & Blaine, B. E. (1999). Belief in U.S. government conspiracies against blacks among black and white college students: Powerlessness or system blame? *Personality and Social Psychology Bulletin, 25*, 941–953.

Cuddy, A. J. C., Fiske, S. T., & Glick, P. (2002, February). Ambivalent stereotypes, predicted by power relations: Status and competition predict competence and warmth. Paper presented at the Third Annual Meeting of the Society for Personality and Social Psychology, Savannah, GA.

Darley, J. M., & Drummond, J. T. (2002). *Murder most foul or just violence? The case for deviant legitimation.* Unpublished manuscript. Princeton University, Princeton, NJ.

Derogy, J. (1990). *Resistance and revenge: The Armenian assassination of the Turkish leaders responsible for the 1915 massacres and deportations.* New Brunswick, NJ: Transaction Publishers.

Deutsch, M., & Gerard, H. B. (1955). A study of normative and informational social influences upon individual judgment. *Journal of Abnormal and Social Psychology, 51*, 629–636.

Dittmar, H. (1992). *The social psychology of material possessions: To have is to be.* New York: St. Martin's Press.

Dobratz, B. A., & Shanks-Meile, S. L. (1997). *"White power, white pride!" The white separatist movement in the United States.* New York: Twayne Publishers.

Doran, M. S. (2001). Somebody else's civil war: Ideology, rage, and the assault on America. In J. F. Hoge, Jr., & G. Rose (Eds.), *How did this happen? Terrorism and the new war* (pp. 31–52). New York: PublicAffairs.

Drummond, J. T. (2001). *Counterforce, other retaliatory violence, and firearms ownership: A preliminary report.* Unpublished manuscript, Princeton University, Princeton, NJ.

Drummond, J. T., & Darley, J. M. (2002). *Defining terrorism and the trouble with noncombatancy as criterion: Applying psychology to the "war on terror."* Unpublished manuscript, Princeton University, Princeton, N.J.

Drummond, J. T., Vandello, J. A., & Darley, J. M. (2002, February). *Virtuous defense or unwarranted violence? Behind the crosshairs of retaliatory force.* Poster session presented at the Third Annual Meeting of the Society for Personality and Social Psychology, Savannah, GA.

Durrheim, K., & Dixon, J. (2001). *Theories of culture in racist discourse.* Unpublished manuscript, University of Natal, Scottsville, South Africa.

The 11th Hour Remnant Messenger. (n.d.). *The Adamic race: Adam's pure blood seedline.* Author.

Ezekiel, R. S. (1995). *The racist mind: Portraits of American neo-Nazis and Klansmen.* New York: Viking.

Faraj, M. A. S. (1986). Al-Faridah al-Gha'ibah. In J. J. G. Jansen, *The neglected duty: The creed of Sadat's assassins and Islamic resurgence in the Middle East* (pp. 159–234). New York: Macmillan Publishing Company. (Original work distributed in 1980.)

Fazlollah, M., & Nicholas, P. (2001, December 16). U.S. overstates arrests in terrorism. *Philadelphia Inquirer*, pp. A1, A24.

Finkelstein, N. G. (2000). *The Holocaust industry: Reflections on the exploitation of Jewish suffering.* London: Verso.

Fiske, S. T. (1998). Stereotyping, prejudice, and discrimination. In D. T. Gilbert, S. T. Fiske, & G. Lindzey (Eds.), *The handbook of social psychology, Vol. II* (4th ed., pp. 357–411). Boston: McGraw-Hill.

Flynn, K., & Gerhardt, G. (1990). *The silent brotherhood.* New York: Signet.

French, P. A. (2001). *The virtues of vengeance.* Lawrence, KS: University Press of Kansas.

Galanter, M. (1999). *Cults: Faith, healing, and coercion.* New York: Oxford University Press.

Gamson, W. A. (1990). The success of the unruly. In W. A. Gamson (Ed.), *The strategy of social protests* (pp. 72–88). Belmont, CA: Wadsworth.

Gause, F. G., III (2001). The kingdom in the middle: Saudi Arabia's double game. In J. F. Hoge, Jr., & G. Rose (Eds.), *How did this happen: Terrorism and the new war* (pp. 109–122). New York: PublicAffairs.

Ginsberg, B. (1993). *The fatal embrace: Jews and the state.* Chicago: University of Chicago Press.

Goffman, E. (1974). *Frame analysis.* Cambridge: Harvard University Press.

Goodrick-Clarke, N. (2002). *Black sun: Aryan cults, esoteric nazism, and the politics of identity.* New York: New York University Press.

Greenberg, J., Solomon, S., & Pyszczynski, T. (1997). Terror management theory of self-esteem and cultural worldviews: Empirical assessments and conceptual refinements. In M. P. Zanna (Ed.), *Advances in experimental social psychology, Vol. 29* (pp. 61–139). San Diego, CA: Academic Press.

Griffin, R. S. (2001). *The fame of a dead man's deeds: An up-close portrait of white nationalist William Pierce.* Bloomington, IN: First Books.

Groebel, J. (1989). The problems and challenges of research on terrorism. In J. Groebel, & J. H. Goldstein (Eds.), *Terrorism: Psychological perspectives* (pp. 15–38). Seville, Spain: Publicaciones de la Universidad de Sevilla.

Gyatso, T. (1990). *Freedom in exile: The autobiography of the Dalai Lama.* New York: HarperPerennial.

Hamas. (1988). *The charter of Allah: The platform of the Islamic Resistance Movement (Hamas)* (R. Israeli, Trans.). Retrieved January 22, 2002, from http://www.fas.org/irp/world/para/ docs/880818.htm.

Hamm, M. S. (2002). *In bad company: America's terrorist underground.* Boston: Northeastern University Press.

Hill, P. J. (1997, December 22). *Why I shot an abortionist.* Retrieved November 2, 1998, from http://www.christiangallery.com/hill3.html.

Hitler, A. (1971). *Mein Kampf* (R. Manheim, Trans.). Boston: Houghton Mifflin. (Original work published 1925.)

Hoffman, B. (1998). *Inside terrorism.* New York: Columbia University Press.

Hoffman, B. (2001, September). *Testimony: Re-thinking terrorism in light of a war on terrorism.* Santa Monica, CA: Rand (Rand Publication No. CT-182).

Hogg, M. A., Turner, J. C., & Davison, B. (1990). Polarized norms and social frames of reference: A test of the self-categorization theory of group polarization. *Basic and Applied Social Psychology, 11*, 77–100.

Hoskins, R. K. (1997). *Vigilantes of Christendom: The history of the Phineas priesthood.* Lynchburg, VA: Virginia Publishing Company.

Hurley, A. (1999). *One nation under Israel.* Scottsdale, AZ: Truth Press.

Hutchinson, E. O. (2000, March 6). Why are black leaders silent on black hate crimes? *Salon.com.* Retrieved February 16, 2002, from http://www.salon.com/news/feature /2000/03/06/hate/index.html.

Ignatiev, N., & Garvey, J. (Eds.). (1996). *Race traitor.* New York: Routledge.

Jackson, J. W. (2002). Intergroup attitudes as a function of different dimensions of group identification and perceived intergroup conflict. *Self and Identity, 1*, 11–33.

Jacobs, J. B., & Potter, K. (1998). *Hate crimes: Criminal law & identity politics.* New York: Oxford University Press.

Janis, I. L. (1982). *Groupthink.* Boston: Houghton Mifflin.

Janis, I. L., & Mann, L. (1977). *Decision-making: A psychological analysis of conflict, choice and commitment.* New York: Free Press.

Jussim, L. J., McCauley, C. R., & Lee, Y. (1995). Why study stereotype accuracy and inaccuracy? In Y. Lee, L. J. Jussim, & C. R. McCauley (Eds.), *Stereotype accuracy: Toward appreciating group differences.* Washington, DC: American Psychological Association.

Kaplan, J. (1997). *Radical religion in America: Millenarian movements from the far right to the children of Noah.* Syracuse, NY: Syracuse University Press.

Kaplan, J. (Ed.). (2000). *Encyclopedia of white power: A sourcebook on the radical racist right.* Walnut Creek, CA: AltaMira Press.

Karon, T. (2001, December 11). Hamas explained. *Time.com.* Retrieved December 16, 2001, from http://www.time.com/time/world/printout/0,8816,188137,00.html.

Kelman, H. C. (2001). Reflections on social and psychological processes of legitimization and delegitimization. In J. T. Jost, & B. Major (Eds.), *The psychology of legitimacy: Emerging perspectives on ideology, justice, and intergroup relations* (pp. 54–73). Cambridge, England: Cambridge University Press.

Klandermans, B. (1997). *The social psychology of protest.* Oxford, England: Blackwell Publishers.

Klassen, B. (1973). *Nature's eternal religion.* Milwaukee, WI: Milwaukee Church of the Creator.

Klassen, B. (1981). *The white man's bible.* Lighthouse Point, FL: Church of the Creator.

Klein, A. (1990). Contemporary Tibet: Cultural genocide in progress. In C. Elchert (Ed.), *White lotus: An introduction to Tibetan culture* (pp. 45–55). Ithaca, NY: Snow Lion Publications.

Lane, D. (1999). *Deceived, damned & defiant: The revolutionary writings of David Lane.* St. Maries, ID: Fourteen Word Press.

Le Bon, G. (1982). *The psychology of socialism.* New Brunswick, NJ: Transaction Books. (Original work published 1899.)

Macdonald, A. (1978). *The Turner diaries.* Hillsboro, WV: National Vanguard Books.

Macdonald, A. (1989). *Hunter.* Hillsboro, WV: National Vanguard Books.

MacDonald, K. (1998). *The culture of critique: An evolutionary analysis of Jewish involvement in twentieth-century intellectual and political movements.* Westport, CT: Praeger.

MacDonald, K. (2001). *Preface to the first paperback edition of: The culture of critique: An evolutionary analysis of Jewish involvement in twentieth-century intellectual and political movements.* Retrieved November 11, 2001, from http://www.csulb.edu/~kmacd/Preface. htm.

MacDonald, K. (in press). Review of the book *The "Jewish threat": Anti-semitic politics of the U.S. Army. Occidental Quarterly.*

Mackie, D., & Cooper, J. (1984). Attitude polarization: Effects of group membership. *Journal of Personality and Social Psychology, 46,* 575–585.

Mahmood, C. K. (2001). Terrorism, myth, and the power of ethnographic praxis. *Journal of Contemporary Ethnography, 30,* 520–545.

Markus, H. R., & Kitayama, S. (1991). Culture and the self: Implications for cognition, emotion, and motivation. *Psychological Review, 98,* 224–253.

McCauley, C. (1998). Group dynamics in Janis's theory of groupthink: Backward and forward. *Organizational Behavior and Human Decision Processes, 73,* 142–162.

McCauley, C. R., & Segal, M. E. (1989). Terrorist individuals and terrorist groups: The normal psychology of extreme behavior. In J. Groebel, & J. H. Goldstein (Eds.), *Terrorism: Psychological perspectives* (pp. 39–64). Seville, Spain: Publicaciones de la Universidad de Sevilla.

McGreal, C. (2001, August 15). "Mugabe is behind this. In Europe you call it ethnic cleansing." *Guardian Unlimited.* Retrieved December 31, 2001, from http://www.guardian.co. uk/Archive/Article/0,4273,4239278,00.html.

McVan, R. (1997). *Creed of iron: Wotansvolk wisdom.* St. Maries, ID: Fourteen Word Press.

McVeigh, T. J. (1998, June). Hypocrisy: An essay. *Media Bypass,* 22–23.

Michel, L., & Herbeck, D. (2001). *American terrorist: Timothy McVeigh & the Oklahoma City bombing.* New York: ReganBooks.

Mutsaka, F. (2001, December 9). Mugabe's fascism revealed. *The Zimbabwe Standard Online.* Retrieved December 31, 2001, from http://www.mweb.co.zw/standard/index. php?id=3992&pubdate=2001-12-09.

National Vanguard Books (2000). *What is the National Alliance?* Hillsboro, WV: Author.

New Century Foundation (1999). *The color of crime: Race, crime, and violence in America.* Oakton, VA: Author.

Nida'ul Islam (1996, October–November). Mujahid Usamah bin Ladin talks exclusively to "Nida'ul Islam" about the new powder keg in the Middle East. Nida'ul Islam. Retrieved January 22, 2002, from http://www.islam.org.au/articles/15/LADIN.HTM.

Noble, K. (1998). *Tabernacle of hate: Why they bombed Oklahoma City.* Prescott, Ontario, Canada: Voyageur Publishing.

Palestinian Central Bureau of Statistics (2002). *Killed Palestinians (martyrs) in Al-Aqsa uprising (intifada), by week and age group.* Retrieved January 3, 2002, from http://www.pcbs. org/english/martyrs1/table2_e.htm.

Peleg, S. (1997). They shoot prime ministers too, don't they? Religious violence in Israel: Premises, dynamics, and prospects. *Studies in Conflict & Terrorism, 20,* 227–247.

Perazzo, J. (2001, August 30). The truth about hate crime statistics. *FrontPageMagazine. com.* Retrieved February 16, 2002, from http://www.frontpagemag.com/columnists/ perazzo/jp08-30-01p.htm.

Pierce, W. (2002, January 12). *What is moral?* National Vanguard Books ADV-list.

Pipes, D. (1997). *Conspiracy: How the paranoid style flourishes and where it comes from.* New York: Free Press.

Pipes, R. (1990). *The Russian revolution.* New York: Alfred A. Knopf.

Pipes, R. (1993). *Russia under the Bolshevik regime.* New York: Alfred A. Knopf.

Pittman, T. S. (1998). Motivation. In D. T. Gilbert, S. T. Fiske, & G. Lindzey (Eds.), *The handbook of social psychology, Vol. I* (4th ed., pp. 549–590). Boston: McGraw-Hill.

Pynchon, M. R., & Borum, R. (1999). Assessing threats of targeted group violence: Contributions from social psychology. *Behavioral Sciences and the Law, 17,* 339–355.

Redbeard, R. (1996). *Might is right.* Bensinville, IL: M.H.P. & Co. (Original work published 1896.)

Ruby, C. L. (2002a). The definition of terrorism. *Analyses of Social Issues and Public Policy, 2,* 9–14.

Ruby, C. L. (2002b). Are terrorists mentally deranged? *Analyses of Social Issues and Public Policy, 2,* 15–26.

Rummel, R. J. (1994). *Death by government.* New Brunswick, NJ: Transaction Publishers.

Said, E. (2001, December 20–26). Israel's dead end: Edward Said wonders: Is Israel more secure now? *Al-Ahram Weekly On-line.* Retrieved December 30, 2001, from http://www.ahram.org.eg/weekly/ 2001/565/op1.htm.

Satel, S. (2001, December). Medicine's race problem. *Policy Review.* Retrieved January 6, 2002, from http://www.policyreview.org/DEC01/satel_print.html.

Schachter, S. (1951). Deviation, rejection, and communication. *Journal of Abnormal and Social Psychology, 46,* 190–207.

Shahak, I. (1994). *Jewish history, Jewish religion: The weight of three thousand years.* London: Pluto Press.

Sherif, M. (1935). A study of some social factors in perception. *Archives of Psychology, 187.*

Sidanius, J. (1985). Cognitive functioning and sociopolitical ideology revisited. *Political Psychology, 6,* 637–662.

Sidanius, J., & Pratto, F. (1999). *Social dominance.* Cambridge, England: Cambridge University Press.

Silke, A. (1998). Cheshire-Cat logic: The recurring theme of terrorist abnormality in psychological research. *Psychology Crime & Law, 4,* 51–69.

Simon, B. (1998). Individuals, groups, and social change: On the relationship between individual and collective self-interpretations and collective action. In C. Sedikides, J. Schopler, & C. A. Insko (Eds.), *Intergroup cognition and intergroup behavior* (pp. 257–281). Mahwah, NJ: Lawrence Erlbaum Associates.

Simon, B., Loewy, M., Sturmer, S., Weber, U., Freytag, P., Habig, C., Kampmeier, C., & Spahlinger, P. (1998). Collective identification and social movement participation. *Journal of Personality and Social Psychology, 74,* 646–658.

Sivan, E. (1998, Spring). The holy war tradition in Islam. *Orbis.* Retrieved October 18, 2001, from http://www.findarticles.com/cf_0/m0365/n2_v42/20575545/print.jhtm.

Skitka, L. J., & Houston, D. (in press). When due process is of no consequence: Moral mandates and presumed defendant guilt or innocence. *Social Justice Research.*

Skitka, L. J., & Mullen, E. (2002). The dark side of moral conviction. *Analyses of Social Issues and Public Policy, 2,* 35–41.

Slater, J. (2001). What went wrong? The collapse of the Israeli-Palestinian peace process. *Political Science Quarterly, 116,* 171–199.

Snow, D. A., Rochford, E. B., Jr., Worden, S. K., & Benford, R. D. (1986). Frame alignment processes, micromobilization, and movement participation. *American Sociological Review, 51,* 464–481.

Snow, D. A., Zurcher, L. A., Jr., & Eckland-Olson, S. (1980). Social networks and social movements: A microstructural approach to differential recruitment. *American Sociological Review, 45,* 787–801.

Solomon, S., Greenberg, J., & Pyszczynski, T. (2002). *Fear of death and social behavior: The anatomy of human destructiveness.* Unpublished manuscript. Brooklyn College, New York.

Sontag, D. (2001, July 26). Quest for Mideast peace: How and why it failed. *New York Times.* Retrieved December 24, 2001, from http://www.nytimes.com/2001/07/26/International/26MIDE.html.

Sprinzak, E. (1991). The process of delegitimation: Towards a linkage theory of political terrorism. In C. McCauley (Ed.), *Terrorism research and public policy* (pp. 50–68). London: Frank Cass.

Sprinzak, E. (1999). *Brother against brother: Violence and extremism in Israeli politics from Altalena to the Rabin assassination.* New York: Free Press.

Stark, R., & Bainbridge, W. S. (1980). Networks of faith: Interpersonal bonds and recruitment of cults and sects. *American Journal of Sociology, 85,* 1376–1395.

Staub, E. (1999). The origins and prevention of genocide, mass killing, and other collective violence. *Peace and Conflict: Journal of Peace Psychology, 5,* 303–341.

Stern, J. (2001). *The prospect of domestic bioterrorism.* Retrieved from http://www.cdc.gov/ncidod/EID/vol5no4/stern.htm.

Stoddard, L. (1981). *The rising tide of colour against white world-supremacy.* Brighton, England: Historical Review Press. (Original work published 1920.)

Swarns, R. (2001, December 25). Zimbabwe opposition party members killed. *New York Times.* Retrieved December 31, 2001, from http://www.nytimes.com/2001/12/25/international/africa/25ZIMB.html?pagewanted=prin.

Taylor, D. M., Wright, S. C., & Porter, L. (1994). Dimensions of perceived discrimination: The personal/group discrimination discrepancy. In M. P. Zanna, & J. M. Olson (Eds.), *The psychology of prejudice.* Hillsdale, NJ: Erlbaum.

Tabor, J. D., & Gallagher, E. V. (1995). *Why Waco? Cults and the battle for religious freedom in America.* Berkeley: University of California Press.

Tellis, A. J., Szayna, T. S., & Winnefeld, J. A. (1997). *Anticipating ethnic conflict.* Santa Monica, CA: Rand.

't Hart, P., Stern, E. K., & Sundelius, B. (1997). *Beyond groupthink.* Ann Arbor: University of Michigan Press.

Thompson, C. E., & Carter, R. T. (1997). *Racial identity theory: Applications to individual, group, and organizational interventions.* Mahwah, NJ: Lawrence Erlbaum Associates.

Triandis, H. C. (1989). The self and social behavior in differing cultural contexts. *Psychological Review, 96,* 506–520.

Tripathi, R. C., & Srivastava, R. (1981). Relative deprivation and intergroup attitudes. *European Journal of Social Psychology, 11,* 313–318.

Tyler, T. R., & Smith, H. J. (1998). Social justice and social movements. In D. T. Gilbert, S. T. Fiske, & G. Lindzey (Eds.), *The handbook of social psychology, Vol. I* (4th ed., pp. 549–590). Boston: McGraw-Hill.

Volkan, V. (1997). *Bloodlines: From ethnic pride to ethnic terrorism.* New York: Farrar, Straus, & Giroux.

White, J. R. (2001). Political eschatology: A theology of antigovernment extremism. *American Behavioral Scientist, 44,* 937–956.

Wright, S. A. (Ed.). (1995). *Armageddon in Waco: Critical perspectives on the Branch Davidian conflict.* Chicago: University of Chicago Press.

Wright, S. A. (1999). Anatomy of a government massacre: Abuses of hostage-barricade protocols during the Waco standoff. *Terrorism and Political Violence, 11,* 39–68.

Wright, S. C. (2001). Restricted intergroup boundaries: Tokenism, ambiguity, and the tolerance of injustice. In J. T. Jost, & B. Major (Eds.), *The psychology of legitimacy: Emerging perspectives on ideology, justice, and intergroup relations* (pp. 223–254). Cambridge, England: Cambridge University Press.

Wright, S. C., Taylor, D. M., & Moghaddam, F. M. (1990). Responding to membership in a disadvantaged group: From acceptance to collective protest. *Journal of Personality and Social Psychology, 58,* 994–1003.

Yassin, A. (2001). *Message from Sheikh Ahmed Yassin to Arab and Islamic peoples in general and to the Palestinian people in particular on the advent of the holy month of Ramadan.* Retrieved January 22, 2002, from http://www.palestine-info.com/daily_news/Yassin2.htm.

Zacharia, J. (2000, September 27). Bush campaign steps back from supporter's criticism of Israel. *Jerusalem Post.* Retrieved December 7, 2001, from http://www.mideastfacts.com/Moorer_GeorgeW.html.

Zulaika, J., & Douglass, W. A. (1996). *Terror and taboo: The follies, fables, and faces of terrorism.* New York: Routledge.

NOTES

1.   The Order, inspired by the organization of the same name in *The Turner Diaries,* was responsible for, among other things, the June 1984 murder of Jewish radio personality Alan Berg in Denver, Colorado, and the July 1984, $3.8 million robbery of an armored car near Ukiah, California. The majority of the $3.8 million was never recovered, likely being used to fund various white separatist organizations.

2.   Pierce, under pseudonym, is the author of *The Turner Diaries* (MacDonald, 1978) and *Hunter* (MacDonald, 1989). In Stern's defense, there is little doubt by either "watchdogs" or those in the white separatist movement that Pierce was interested in building a viable racial political movement (see also National Vanguard Books, 2000), and this may well have included "building bombers" rather than bombs. Pierce also was known to have associated in some capacity with individuals such as Robert Mathews, Timothy McVeigh, and serial racist murderer Joseph Paul Franklin, to whom *Hunter* is dedicated (Flynn & Gerhardt, 1990; Griffin, 2001). Nonetheless, labeling Pierce (a man living freely in West Virginia until his death on July 23, 2002) a "terrorist" amounts to little more than informed speculation presented as fact.

3.   Sheikh Muhammad Hussein Fadlallah, associated with Hezbollah for some twenty-five years, has been accused in the past of ordering such attacks as the truck bomb that killed 241 U.S. Marines in Beirut in 1983. In seeming contrast, he has openly condemned the attacks of September 11, 2001, largely on the basis of who was killed where in "aggressive combat" versus a more defensive interpretation of the duty of *jihad* per the *shari'a* or Islamic law.

4.   Due to PRC policies promoting massive Han Chinese immigration to various locations on the Tibetan plateau, ethnic Tibetans have become, in many places, a pronounced

and disadvantaged minority; for example, as long as a decade ago, Hans already outnumbered Tibetans in the Lhasa Valley by a ratio of 7 to 1. There is nothing autonomous and increasingly little that is Tibetan about the PRC's "Tibet Autonomous Region."

5.　I am also raising this controversial issue here due to its relevance to later phenomenological discussions of white separatism. White separatist claims that "Communism is Jewish" are inaccurate today, but the claim has some basis in fact. Lenin and half his first Politburo were of Jewish origin (Pipes, 1997). Lenin was known to generally hold ethnic Russians in low esteem and once remarked to Gorky, "An intelligent Russian is almost always a Jew or someone with Jewish blood in his veins" (Pipes, 1990, p. 352). Two thirds of the triumvirate (Kamenev and Zinoviev) succeeding Lenin were Jewish (Ginsberg, 1993). Influencing Hitler's racial views, in addition to widespread anti-Semitism and open publication of the spurious *Protocols of the Elders of Zion*, were 1) the mass violence perpetrated by the noticeably Jewish Bolshevik regime in Russia, 2) Jewish overrepresentation in Weimar politics (including Jewish authorship of the Weimar constitution by socialist Hugo Preuss), and 3) Jewish economic opportunism during the Weimar era (Jewish firms accounted for about 80 percent of department/chain store sales) (Ginsberg, 1993). Pipes (1993) also documents disproportionate Jewish representation in European communist revolutions and unrest post-World War I. For example, Jews made up 95 percent of the leading figures in Kun's 1919 dictatorship in Hungary. Comments about the prevalence and goals of Jews in the early Soviet regime, whether by Winston Churchill, U.S./British intelligence, or the U.S. State Department (Bendersky, 2000; Pipes, 1997), are not just possible expressions of anti-Semitism, but actually reflect the ethnic makeup of the regime and allied polity in Europe and the United States. Pipes (1993) dismisses such heavy Jewish representation as similar to that in other elite and professional occupations. He makes the claim that many in revolutionary politics did not ethnically identify as Jews. MacDonald (1998), however, deconstructs Pipes' assertions, plausibly illustrating a conflation of political orientation and ethnicity during the era in question.

6.　The four are Sean McBride, Menachem Begin, Yasir Arafat, and Nelson Mandela. Accordingly, Zulaika and Douglass (1996) question the notion that talking to a terrorist is contaminating or compromising, and, it follows, underscore the inadequacy and poorly informed nature of policies that categorically dismiss discourse or negotiations with terrorists.

7.　The global "war on terror" is revealing a number of brutally opportunistic governments. Human Rights Watch (HRW) reported in January, 2002, that a number of governments have used the anti-terror campaign to defend abusive military actions and crackdowns on political opposition. Among HRW's most notable violators are Russia, Uzbekistan, Egypt, Israel, and Zimbabwe. In the United States and western Europe, HRW notes some anti-terror measures "are threatening long-held human rights principles" while policies long in place demonstrate an "apparent disregard for grave civilian suffering caused by sanctions against Iraq."

8.　There is yet another case, which, because of its rarity, may be minimally informative. While the events of September 11, 2001, are appropriately condemned globally, there may be cases of terrorism that are applauded almost as widely. The case which most comes to mind is the campaign conducted by the Armenian Dashnaktsutiune to assassinate and destroy Turkish leadership responsible for the World War I Armenian genocide (Derogy, 1990).

9.　While some in Hamas are sincerely fighting a defensive struggle for the liberation of Palestine and the occupied territories, it is worth noting that others likely fight to defend Islam and its perceived lands, and they seek nothing less than the destruction of Israel. In the preamble of the platform of Hamas (1988), the words of Hassan al-Banna (who founded the Muslim Brotherhood in Egypt in 1928) are used to clearly convey such intentions: "Israel will rise and will remain erect until Islam eliminates it . . ." (p. 2).

10.   There is little doubt many of these Palestinians were militants, but some likely were not. In any event, there has been nothing even approximating due process or presentation of evidence to support the killing of these individuals.

11.   The "radical right" is far more diverse than is often noted, and many factions stand in opposition to each other. There is a great deal of infighting, something that may not be all that uncommon in extremist politics (R. Abelson, personal communications, April, 2001; Dobratz & Shanks-Meile, 1997; McCauley & Segal, 1989). Also, it should be understood that not all in the radical right are racist; the author is aware of a number of "constitutional militias" for whom perceived government divergence from a strict and literalist interpretation of the U.S. Constitution, and not race, is the basis for grievance.

12.   Some may be struck by my choice of words here. Following the lead of Dobratz & Shanks-Meile (1997), and for reasons they state, the term "white separatist," while imperfect, is the most accurate description. Of course, some separatists are also supremacists. Within the white separatist movement, "cross lighting" is the preferred term and can, in fact, be a powerful part of a private religious service. Even some white separatists, however, endorse the more (sociologically) profane "cross burning" when it is done as a political act or to intimidate political and racial enemies.

13.   The discourse referenced likely reflects the fruit of lengthy debate within the clerical community, and more specifically, among Islamist clerics. The importance of the group cannot be dismissed; group polarization and groupthink will be later addressed.

14.   I must emphasize here that I am not equating President Bush to bin Laden, but rather illustrating similarities in the social construction of the enemy other.

15.   Remarkably, Berger and Sutphen (2001) write that "until it served his larger purposes after the September 11 attacks, bin Laden had been no champion of the Palestinian cause" (p. 124). While the Palestinian cause usually ranks about third on bin Laden's lists of grievances, it is clear he cares deeply about the issue. The Berger and Sutphen comment reflects either ignorance or deception, and given that Berger was Clinton's national security adviser from 1997 to 2001, the former is unlikely. Separating bin Laden from the Israeli-Palestinian question (and, in the process, divorcing any rationale for the September 11 attacks from perceptions of U.S. foreign policy on Israel and the Palestinian Authority) is, however, a clever way of mobilizing public support legitimating bin Laden as an irrational, deceptive, and terrifying enemy.

16.   Interestingly, an article appeared in the Kuwaiti paper *Al-Watan* eleven days before the events of September 11, presenting an Islamic justification for killing "noncombatants." The justification is grounded in the fact that citizens in democracies surrender noncombatancy because they vote, pay taxes, are all potential soldiers, and otherwise voluntarily support their governments' actions in myriad ways. The reader should not be surprised; in an experimental effort, "normal" American undergraduates withdrew non-combatancy status from individuals, including taxpayers, minimally placed in a "causal chain" of violence (Drummond & Darley, 2002).

17.   It was not unusual to see a photo of Mathews prominently displayed in white separatist homes in a way much like photos of the IRA's Bobby Sands are displayed in some Irish-American homes.

18.   The alarm of racial decline and general predictions about what has demographically occurred were sounded by a number of writers widely read early in the twentieth century. In *The Rising Tide of Colour Against White World-Supremacy*, Stoddard (1920/1981) warns ". . .

colored triumphs of arms are less to be dreaded than more enduring conquests like migrations which would swamp whole populations and turn countries now white into colored man's lands irretrievably lost to the white world" (p. vi). It takes little imagination to see how prophetic Stoddard must seem to the white separatist who is presently barraged by commentary suggesting whites may be a minority in the United States and many European countries by the middle of the twenty-first century.

19. While race may largely be a social construction, it is important to understand that what is socially constructed is no less real to the believer. Though infrequently discussed, however, there is some question about the extent to which race is only socially constructed. Definitions of race that account for both biological factors and associated social constructions, such as racial identity theory's concept of *sociorace*, may prove helpful conceptualizations (Thompson & Carter, 1997). While completion of the human genome project has encouraged many to declare that genetically there is no difference between the races, small genetic differences can be profoundly meaningful; this is not lost on those familiar with genetics research, including some who are white separatists. Understanding the importance of small differences flies in the face of naïve political bantering along the line of "there is no such thing as race because people are 99.9 percent the same." Satel (2001) notes, ". . . facts, however, paint a more complex picture . . . race does have biological dimensions, and if we regard it solely as a social construct, we may forfeit opportunities . . ." (p. 2)—medically, in the cases she addresses. It is not that such information should be used to harm, Satel argues, but precisely the opposite. Finally, claiming there is no such thing as race underestimates the cognitive abilities of some who are racial or ethnopolitical separatists. In doing so, it is mainstream science and media which, revealing their ignorance, or worse, deceptive intentions, bolster the separatist's perception that they have come upon a "forbidden truth." Such findings in science may be best left to informed, honest, and open discussion that is kept free of all political agendas and maneuvering.

20. Wotanism (also known as Asatru) is a return the Norse pantheon of gods, atavistic archetypes that have now been awakened. In Creativity, the "guiding principle of all [one's] actions shall be: What is best for the White Race?" (Klassen, 1973, p. 256). Both appeal to the laws of nature and social Darwinism. Aryandom is seen as having become deracinated, soft (feminized), duped by a pacific, universalist Judeo-Christian ethic: ". . . Jewish books are for the Jews/And Jew Messiahs too/ . . . A dying God upon a cross/Is reason gone insane" (Redbeard, 1896/1996, p. 47). Aryans have failed to respect maxims that might is right (the white race is foolishly surrendering advantage), survival of one's own kind is the first law of nature, and demographics are destiny (the white race is failing to reproduce itself). Governments of the world's "white" nations are also seen as failing to heed nature's laws, and, along with "Jewish" media, are complicit in racial demise by promoting egalitarian social, economic, and family structures and values that lead to declining birth rates and promotion of miscegenating, multicultural societies now drowning in a dusky tide of immigrating "mud people." Since the masses have no racial awareness, they do not perceive the mounting threat to racial survival and continuation of Western civilization. As many racists reported, "the people are sheeple, the masses are asses."

21. It is interesting to note that Jewish extremists may mirror such accusations, considering Gentiles, for example, to be among the Satanic animals (Shahak, 1994). For an impressive treatment of Christian Identity, see Barkun (1994).

22. Shahak (1994) reveals that Hebrew publications of the Maimonidean *Book of Knowledge* do identify Jesus of Nazareth as among the "prime examples of 'infidels' who must be exterminated . . . " (p. 24). The more widely read among the white separatist movement are intimately familiar with Shahak's (1994) work. Here again, we see that "extreme"

beliefs are often not groundless.

23.   The Frankfurt School is particularly cited as having a destructive influence on education in the United States. While not racist authors, Buchanan (2002) and MacDonald (1998) both address, similarly to white separatist discourse, the undesirable influence of the Frankfurt School. Also threatening is the less than empty claim both make that Adorno's work on *The Authoritarian Personality* managed to effectively pathologize "traditional" family structures.

24.   In the same interview, Langan also refers to Christian Identity as Anglo-Zionism. Because Identists see themselves as the true Israelites, and may faithfully adhere to Mosaic law (R. Millar, personal communication, June, 1998; K. Noble, personal communications, June, 1998, May, 2000; Noble, 1998), the reader will not be surprised to know that in many ways Identity appears like the belief one finds in extreme Jewish groups such as Kach and Gush Emunim. Observations about Dr. Baruch Goldstein, and Goldstein's own comments preceding his massacre of twenty-nine Muslim worshippers in the Cave of the Patriarchs on February 25, 1994, are similar to some of Kerry Noble's thoughts when he, as a leader of The Covenant, The Sword, and the Arm of the Lord, went to Kansas City in the summer of 1984 with a bomb intended to kill fifty to sixty people (Noble, 1998; Sprinzak, 1999). Both intended to do God's will, arrest what they saw as a process of decay, directly strike against enemy others, and awaken their co-ethnics. Goldstein acted, while Noble essentially found he could not dehumanize the intended victims enough to bring himself to detonate the device.

25.   The author wishes to acknowledge the assistance, insight, and original ideas provided by John Darley. Deviant legitimation as explanatory process for violence is the product of nearly two years of conversations between the author and Darley, most of which is reflected in Darley and Drummond (2002). Any errors in making the case for deviant legitimation are solely the fault of the author. The term "deviant" is here used sociologically. An act or process is not inherently deviant, but rather, the attribution of deviance comes about as an application of values, rules, norms, and sanctions by the empowered in a given culture. Deviant behavior is that which others so label. Determining deviance, as most anyone crusading for the survival of their co-ethnics or religious community would attest to, is a rather relativistic and politically charged activity (Becker, 1963).

26.   See Staub (1999) for the role "difficult life conditions" may play as instigators of violence. Also, Tripathi and Srivastava (1981) have found that deprivation is associated with less positive intergroup attitudes.

27.   Other delegitimating discoveries on a cultural or societal level I've witnessed along the path to extremist U.S. politics include: immigration policy change in 1965, desegregation, the declining birth rates and populations for European-derived peoples, overrepresentation of Jews in the Clinton administration, the Clinton administration's security-compromising relations with the PRC, cases of what seem to be unevenly applied "hate (thought) crimes" legislation (because people are differentially judged and sentenced not by their acts but by thoughts associated with acts), changes in the Bureau of Land Management's "wise use" policies for ranchers, feelings of government betrayal/abandonment of Vietnam "Agent Orange" veterans and Vietnam Missing in Action/Prisoners of War, and seeming government abandonment and lack of urgency in dealing with "Gulf War Syndrome" veterans.

28.   Consider the following related by an intelligence officer. As the first Scud missiles struck Israel during the Persian Gulf War, the Saudi officers in a command post began to cheer. American personnel were stunned and asked about the strange behavior of cheering for their enemy. The Saudi officers responded that the Americans "did not understand," that the fight with Iraq was merely a squabble among Arab neighbors. The real enemy, they clari-

fied, was Israel. Bin Laden has suggested on many occasions the enemy is the broader infidel, the "Jews and Crusaders."

29. As used here, false consciousness may be grounded in class, race, gender, and so on. Overcoming one's false consciousness requires some awakening, some realization liberating in its qualities. Accordingly, Marx and Engels challenge the working class ("Working men of all countries, unite"), racists plead "wake up, white people . . . wake up or die," and feminists are well aware that women must first recognize gender inequity before they can act to end it.

30. In June 2000, the U.S. Supreme Court refused to hear Hale's appeal to the state of Illinois's denial of his law license. For some Creators, justice is not now to be found through our legal system—not even the highest court in the nation would permit the "politically incorrect" to have their day in court. Lack of capacity or will to accommodate such grievance may well encourage some to resort to other than peaceful means of redress. Conversations and e-mail exchanges with Creators following the Smith shootings revealed their thoughts that the government or ZOG (Zionist Occupational Government) had, by their actions, invited the violent response. While Hale and the Church of the Creator claim they do not endorse violence (though they simultaneously embrace the slogan of RAHOWA—Racial Holy War), Smith is now considered to be a martyr in white separatism. Reflecting upon the racial make-up of the nation's founders and Smith's rejection of a multicultural society, White Aryan Resistance now claims the Fourth of July as "Aryan Independence Day."

31. Consistent with this thread, White (2001) suggests that theological "terrorists" respond to a "perceived terminal threat to religious values and attitudes." Violence that annihilates the perceived threat is not necessarily needed, however; sometimes violence sufficient to demonstrate that one has the will and capacity to resort to violence may function defensively and influence the enemy (Ezekiel, 1995; see Hill, 1997). The use of violence has been associated with success in social movements (Gamson, 1990); it is reasonable bin Laden might endorse violence as a viable means to pressure the United States to leave the Arabian peninsula—the United States left Somalia and Beirut after suffering casualties.

32. Most racialists or racial loyalists, as they often refer to themselves, are disgusted with government suggestions that whites are a majority. Government is biased, they point out. In most all matters, the focus is increasingly global. On issues of race, European culture, and Western civilization, however, the government continues to ignore global context. This "political correctness," they argue, keeps the white masses ignorant of the reality of pending extinction.

33. Racists note that only two to three percent of the world's population consists of white women of childbearing age and younger. Given projections of declining birthrates and rapidly rising median age in the U.S. and European nations, this is expected to only decrease in the coming decades. If the future of a people is "in the wombs of its women," they query, at what point does the number of childbearing or younger women fall below some critical threshold, some critical mass necessary to sustain the race in sufficient numbers to propagate its culture and sustain its defense?

34. This incident is particularly troublesome. The report by Carl Cameron that I referenced in the text, and apparently others, were quickly pulled from Fox's archives. All articles on the issue are now unavailable. Further suggesting deception, the Web site notice that Cameron's article was no longer available recently displayed an altered date for the article's original issue. That is, I have, in hard copy, an article published on December 12, retrieved on December 14, and as of February 13, 2002, now unavailable, but supposedly dated December 21, 2001. Repeated requests for Fox to explain or place me in contact with Cameron have been met with silence.

35.   Based on proportions of the population, one would expect black on white crime to occur at roughly six times the rate of white on black crime. That considered, black on white violence still occurs at a rate eight times that of white on black violence. Additionally, Buchanan (2002) reports similarly disparate rates of interracial violence in the United Kingdom.

36.   "Positive hate" was a term I heard used in a speech by Charles Lee of the White Camelia Knights of the Ku Klux Klan. Positive hate is hate for that which threatens one's kind. It is hate that arises out of pride and love of one's "own." Its elements of ingroup bias and outgroup hostility under threat or conflict are remarkably consistent with experimental findings in mortality salience research and that of Jackson (2002). Tom Metzger, of White Aryan Resistance, has also talked often about the need for a racist to hate out of one's love for one's race, for hate without love, he opines, will consume one in directionless rage.

37.   The following is to be found in the introduction of *The Al-Qaeda Manual*: Martyrs were killed, women were widowed, children were orphaned, men were handcuffed, chaste women's heads were shaved, harlots' heads were crowned, atrocities were inflicted on the innocent, gifts were given to the wicked, virgins were raped. . . . After the fall of our orthodox caliphates on March 3, 1924, and after expelling the colonialists, our Islamic nation was afflicted with apostate rulers who took over . . . (Al-Qaeda, no date).

38.   Note here that, as with white separatists, Jews are seen to be a cunning and capable enemy. This is consistent with the findings of Cuddy, Fiske, and Glick (2002) that negative stereotype content, and even envy (some white separatists have commented that Aryans should have the ethnic/racial solidarity they perceive Jews to display), are associated with competitors/outgroups seen as competent but emotionally cold (ruthless).

39.   Historic Palestine is considered by Hamas to be Islamic land. Recall that al-Khattab conquered Palestine for Islam in the seventh century. It is also from the Haram-al-Sharif (site of the al-Aqsa mosque) that the Prophet ascended to the Heavens.

40.   Society generally refers to these as "paranoids," or, in the event they are correct, "visionaries."

41.   The proffered view must be plausible to the potential recruit. The theory that "Jews control the world" would have been of little use to Yigal Amir.

42.   This movement across the ideological spectrum might seem quite strange, but in fact is consistent with the concept of "ideological asymmetry" proposed by Sidanius and Pratto (1999). That is, there is a correlation between being privileged or empowered in a social system and embracing hierarchy enhancing and maintaining ideologies. For those who perceive themselves to be relatively powerless, the correlation does not exist, and they likely search for that ideology, whatever its orientation, which will address grievance or the perceived source of one's powerlessness. In the years preceding Hitler's consolidation of power, privileged Germans moved to embrace national socialism as it became clear Hitler would leave private industrial empires relatively intact (compared with the Strasser brothers, Hitler de-emphasized the "socialism" in "national socialism"); for the disenfranchised in the street, however, large numbers embraced both fascist ideologies and communism as they sought to radically better their condition.

43.   A source close to McVeigh notes he was drawn to *The Turner Diaries* because the tipping event in the book is a U.S. government ban on private possession of firearms. Others have suggested McVeigh associated with the Aryan Republican Army and other white separatists (Hamm, 2002); McVeigh was reprimanded for a racial slur while in the U.S. Army, but the extent to which primarily racist beliefs motivated McVeigh is uncertain.

44.   For Amir, the theological rulings and traditions trumped an acceptable secular response. As Amir told the commission investigating the assassination, "What's all this crap

about democracy? There is democracy, but there is also Judaism" (Alianak, 1998, p. 5).

The author would like to sincerely thank John Darley, Kevin MacDonald, Clark McCauley, Kerry Noble, and Jean Rosenfeld for their encouragement, insightful comments, challenging questions, and helpful suggestions. The author would also like to express gratitude to those many white separatists who have shared their views and perspectives. Of course, responsibility for chapter content and any error rests solely with the author. Finally, the views expressed in this chapter are those of the author and do not reflect the official policy or position of the United States Air Force, Department of Defense, or the U.S. government.

5

Terrorist Beliefs and Terrorist Lives

Ted G. Goertzel

Are terrorists rational actors who find themselves forced to use desperate measures in response to extreme provocations? Or are they driven by demons of the mind? Are the evils they so righteously denounce carefully selected to externalize feelings buried within their own psyches? Experts disagree. Psychologist Martha Crenshaw (1998) defends the rationality of the terrorist. She argues that terrorism "displays a collective rationality" and that "efficacy is the primary standard by which terrorism is compared with other methods of achieving political goals" (p. 9). In reply, psychiatrist Jerrold Post (1998) insists that "political terrorists are driven to commit acts of violence as a consequence of psychological forces, and that their special psycho-logic is constructed to rationalize acts they are psychologically compelled to commit" (p. 25).

Of course, Crenshaw and Post offer opposite positions as a means of sharpening the argument. Everyone's behavior is a combination of rational and emotional responses to a set of social, economic, and political circumstances. There is no question that terrorists engage in a good deal of rational thinking. They vary their strategies and tactics to fit changing political circumstances and historical conjunctures. They respond to social trends, becoming more active at some times and less active at others. But terrorists also choose to run risks of death, torture, or imprisonment. Sometimes they deliberately sacrifice their own lives.

These sacrifices are not rational if we think of individuals as purely selfish beings. For the person who is motivated entirely by self-interest, it is more rational to be a "free rider" who benefits when someone else makes sacrifices for the common good. But people are not always selfish. We praise soldiers, fire fighters, and police officers when they risk their lives for the good of society, and give them the benefit of the doubt with regard to any hidden psychological motives they may have. Terrorists and revolutionaries, also, are praised as heroes by the people whose causes they champion.

Terrorists and revolutionaries must make sociological and political judgments, as well as personal ones. It is one thing to risk or sacrifice one's life for a worthy cause, another to sacrifice it for a cause that history will view as misguided or counterproductive. The causes terrorists and revolutionaries espouse often fail, and cause unnecessary human suffering in the process. The eagerness with which terrorists risk injury, death, or imprisonment in the pursuit of doubtful causes suggests such unconscious motives as self-hatred or a need to be punished. But it is much easier to make these judgments with hindsight than it is in the heat of a conflict.

Terrorists think rationally, but they think within the limits of belief systems that may be irrational. Unlike the delusions of psychotics, these belief systems are social constructs shared by large numbers of people. Terrorist belief systems are rigid and simplistic, and they are defended with great emotional intensity. Anyone who wishes to remain within a terrorist group must limit his[1] thinking to the parameters of the group's belief system. As Post (2001) observes:

> Considering the diversity of causes to which terrorists are committed, the uniformity of their rhetoric is striking. Polarizing and absolutist, it is a rhetoric of "us versus them." It is rhetoric without nuance, without shades of gray. "They," the establishment, are the source of all evil in vivid contrast to "us," the freedom fighters, consumed by righteous rage. And, if "they" are the source of our problems, it follows ineluctably in the special psycho-logic of the terrorist, that "they" must be destroyed. It is the only just and moral thing to do. Once one accepts the basic premises, the logical reasoning is flawless.

There have been a great many psychological studies of people who adhere to extremist belief systems. Unfortunately, most of these studies have relied on superficial questionnaire instruments, such as scales of the "authoritarian personality," that have been shown to have serious methodological flaws (Martin, 2001). More insight has come from studies that use projective psychological tests and qualitative interviews. Rothman and Lichter (1982) used projective tests to probe the unconscious minds of New Left activists in the United States. They found them to be characterized by weakened self-esteem, injured narcissism, and paranoid tendencies. The tests showed that many activists were motivated by a preoccupation with power, which attracted them to ideologies that answered their doubts and offered clear and unambiguous answers to their problems. Similar traits were found in studies of West German terrorists (Kellen, 1998), Italian radical youth (Ferracuti, 1998), and members of the Shining Path movement in Peru (Cáceres, 1989). The findings of these and similar studies are summarized well by Post (2001):

Terrorists as individuals for the most part do not demonstrate serious psychopathology. While there is no one personality type, it is the impression that there is a disproportionate representation among terrorists of individuals who are aggressive and action-oriented and place greater than normal reliance on the psychological mechanisms of externalization and splitting. There is suggestive data indicating that many terrorists come from the margins of society and have not been particularly successful in their personal, educational and vocational lives. The combination of the personal feelings of inadequacy with the reliance on the psychological mechanisms of externalization and splitting make especially attractive a group of like-minded individuals whose credo is "It's not us; it's them. They are the cause of our problems."

People who join terrorist movements make a strong commitment to a rigid belief system, but they may adopt their rigid beliefs for a variety of reasons. Some are filled with so much anger and frustration that they jump on the first bandwagon that comes along. Others spend years in study and analysis before selecting a certain set of beliefs to make sense of a complex world. Still others adopt terrorist beliefs as powerful ideological tools for organizing and manipulating other people. Perhaps most have some mixture of these three motives.

THREE TYPES OF TERRORISTS

Since no one personality type characterizes all terrorists, it may be useful to construct a typology of terrorist personalities. Three types of terrorists come readily to mind: the political strategist, the radical theorist, and the militant activist.

The political strategist's goal is to win power so as to impose his will on society. His behavior fits rational choice theory well, since he has a clearly defined goal and the discipline to subordinate his personal needs to whatever is necessary to achieve power. He has no special interest in terrorism as an end in itself, but is quite willing to use it if he thinks it is the best way to achieve his goals. In democratic societies, political organizers are less likely to resort to terrorism because they have opportunities to seek power nonviolently. Terrorism is a high-risk strategy used when safer alternatives are not available. Well-known political strategists include Vladimir Lenin, Carlos Marighela, and Osama bin Laden.

The radical theorist is more interested in ideas than in power. He would rather be true to his beliefs than win power by compromising them. The nobility of a lost cause appeals to him, especially when it receives attention in the media. The worst fate he can imagine is to be ignored. There is often no need for the radical theorist to become personally involved in terrorist conspiracies or violent acts. This is especially true in democratic societies that permit free expression of revolutionary sympathies and sometimes even reward radical theorists with prestigious publications, speaking tours, and academic sinecures. We may think of these intellectuals as "terrorist sympathizers" or "armchair terrorists" rather than as terrorists per se. But even if they remain distant from the action, radical theorists play an important role in terrorist social movements. They refine and develop the belief systems and defend them from critical assault. They fill the pages of publications that sympathize with or promote terrorism. It is to them that more militant activists turn when they need help in defending their beliefs or assuaging any doubts that they may have.

Radical theorists are quite skilled in constructing rational justifications for their ideas. This means that rational choice theory is little help in explaining their behavior, except in the sense that they may be rationally pursuing intellectual careers. For them, the ideas are ends in themselves rather than the means of achieving any other goal. Psychodynamic theories may offer some insights into their motivations, but they can often be better understood with such approaches as script theory (Goertzel, 1992; Tomkins, 1963, 1987), which give causal priority to the ideas themselves. Well-known radical theorists include Leon Trotsky, Theodore Kaczynski, and Abimael Guzmán.

Militant activists fit the popular image of "terrorist" most closely, and they also fit the psychodynamic model much better than the other two types. They are drawn to violence as an end in itself, either as a means of venting anger or as a source of excitement and adventure. For them, the theories are useful as rationalizations for doing what they want to do anyway. Well-known militant activists include Joseph Stalin, Timothy McVeigh, Velupillai Prabhakaran, and Bommi Baumann.

In Marxist parlance, these types are often referred to as Leninist, Trotskyist, and Stalinist (Wolfe, 1964). But historical individuals are more complex than any typology, and no successful terrorist fits any theoretical type perfectly. Lenin wrote serious theoretical works in addition to leading a movement, Trotsky put his writing aside to lead the Red Army, and even Stalin wrote theoretical monographs, or perhaps had them ghostwritten. When push came to shove, however, Lenin adapted his theories to political necessity, while Trotsky remained loyal to his failed theory of world revolution (Goertzel, 1992). Stalin's brutality won in the end, although we can only speculate about what would have happened if Lenin had not died prematurely. There is something to the idea that every revolutionary movement needs its Lenin, its Trotsky, and its Stalin. Each of these types has a different mix of rational and emotional motivations.

BIOGRAPHICAL SKETCHES

The following biographical sketches explore the combination of psychological, social, economic, and political forces that led several historically important individuals into terrorist careers. The sketches are drawn from published biographies and autobiographies, and the depth of psychological insight varies depending on the quality of the available information.

Timothy McVeigh

The Oklahoma City bomber, Timothy McVeigh, was driven to terrorism by emotional needs, with only a thin veneer of rational thinking. In a revealing biography based on extensive interviews, Michel and Herbeck (2001) portray a man filled with rage and frustration caused by a troubled relationship with his mother, problems with bullies in school, and difficulties in establishing relationships with women. He collected guns and spent many hours in target practice. He joined the Army and had a successful military career, including combat in Iraq. However, he became disenchanted with Army life because of the lack of idealism, discipline, and respect for authority among the soldiers and officers. He was disgusted by the fact that many of them treated the Army as a job, not as a sacred cause.

The major crisis of McVeigh's life came when he failed to pass the physical examination for the Green Beret special forces, a unit that might have lived up to his high standards. He left the Army but failed to make a successful adaptation to civilian life. He became involved with gun-rights activists who viewed the United States government as the enemy. His biographers observe that "united by the common thread of personal failure," McVeigh and his friend James Nichols "took their anger at the system to new heights of defiance. They renounced their citizenship and the law of the land" (Michel & Herbeck, 2001, p. 129).

Although McVeigh was not an intellectual in any sense, he did feel the need of an ideology to justify his anger. He found inspiration in the novel *The Turner Diaries,* which was widely read by radical gun-rights activists. The novel is about a gun enthusiast who used a truck bomb to destroy FBI headquarters in Washington. Its author, Andrew MacDonald, an official of the American Nazi Party, advocates killing blacks and Jews. McVeigh's destruction of the Oklahoma City federal building was modeled on this story.

McVeigh's tactical goal in the Oklahoma City bombing was to have a large "body count" so as make a powerful statement and prove his potency as a soldier. He saw his action as analogous to the Hiroshima bombing, which killed hundreds of thousands of innocent civilians but was generally regarded as justified because it served the worthy cause of ending World War II. He was not overtly suicidal, but he did not care if he lived or died. He left many clues, such as using a traceable telephone card and driving without a license plate, to make it easy for the authorities to catch him. The court-appointed psychiatrist who examined McVeigh did not find that he was delusional. He was, Michel and Herbeck (2001) conclude, "an essentially decent person who had allowed rage to build up inside him to the point that he had lashed out in one terrible, violent act" (p. 290).

Theodore Kaczynski

After his arrest, Timothy McVeigh happened to be held in the same federal penitentiary as Theodore Kaczynski, better known as the Unabomber. The court-appointed psychiatrist decided that Kaczynski merited a psychiatric diagnosis of paranoid schizophrenia because his delusions of persecution were so persistent

(Johnson, 1998). If this diagnosis is valid, he was an exception to the generalization that people with serious mental illnesses do not make effective terrorists. He is the exception that proves the rule, since he acted as an isolated individual and had great difficulty functioning as a member of any kind of organization. He was quite capable of sustained intellectual work.

In their prison conversations, Kaczynski and McVeigh found that their views of the world were quite consistent. Although Kaczynski was nominally on the "left" and McVeigh on the "right," Kaczynski observed that "certain rebellious elements on the American right and left respectively had more in common with one another than is commonly realized" (Michel & Herbeck, 2001, p. 399). They both hated the American establishment and believed that killing was justified to defeat it. The Oklahoma City bombing was, in Kaczynski's view, "unnecessarily inhumane" because the large number of killings of innocent civilians, including children, distracted attention from the message. McVeigh saw the point. His bombing had been inspired by *The Turner Diaries.* Later he read *Unintended Consequences,* a novel by John Ross, a gun-rights advocate from St. Louis. If he had read *Unintended Consequences* first, he might have modeled himself on that novel's protagonist who assassinated carefully selected government officials.

Kaczynski and McVeigh also had much in common on a personal level. Both were shy young men who had great difficulty establishing relationships with women. Both were picked on by bullies in school, Kaczynski after he had skipped a grade because of his high academic ability. Kaczynski felt abused by his family, McVeigh felt abused by his mother although not by his father. Both were filled with anger and felt the need for an ideology to justify that anger. Neither cared much whether he lived or died, but both cared a great deal about what people thought of them. Both adamantly opposed using an insanity defense at their trials.

There are also important differences between the two men. Kaczynski was more intelligent and intellectual and much more of a loner. He took much greater precautions against getting caught. He spent his life writing a lengthy monograph denouncing industrial society and its cultural perversions. But his writings were not very original, nor was he connected to the scholarly or journalistic worlds in ways that would have enabled him to win an audience for his ideas. So he used terrorism as a means of drawing attention to his ideas. His terrorism consisted of sending bombs through the mail to scientists or business people he hated for their involvement in technological society.

Was Kaczynski irrational? His writing (Kaczynski, 2002) is certainly rational enough, and not unlike that of many other social critics. But it was irrational for him to believe that technological society could be stopped by sending a few bombs in the mail, just as it was irrational for McVeigh to believe that blowing up the federal building in Oklahoma City would build sympathy for his grievances. Kaczynski certainly pursued his tactical objectives rationally, and succeeded in getting his manifesto published in the *New York Times* and the *Washington Post,* giving it far wider circulation than the scholarly monographs from which it was derived. A rational choice theorist might argue that Kaczynski calculated that even a small chance of saving the earth from total devastation justified the harm he caused to a handful of individuals. But by this loose standard almost any behavior could be called rational, and the theory loses any explanatory power.

Bommi Baumann

Not all terrorists are shy, reclusive young men who have trouble meeting women. West German terrorist Michael "Bommi" Baumann was a fun-loving, long-haired young man who "preferred running after a girl over running after work, naturally, you get more out of it and she does too!" (Baumann, 1979, p. 23) He found working as an apprentice construction worker tedious, and gravitated to Berlin's counterculture, where he enjoyed rock music, drugs, and plenty of liberated sex. He and his friends looked down on the conventional working-class neighborhoods where "cars are more important than places for children to play" (p. 31). In his autobiography, he recalls that one day he was visiting just such a neighborhood, where a lot of policemen lived, and "my whole disgust toward these object relationships just went through me, and I started slashing tires. I did them to the tune of about a hundred. In other words, I slashed the tires of about a hundred cars with a knife, a kind of stiletto" (p. 31). He kept doing this until he was caught and served jail time.

Baumann says that he came from a working-class environment where fighting was common and that for him "violence was a perfectly adequate means, I've never had any hang-ups about it" (p. 27). Indeed, he was fascinated by it. He and his friends took pleasure in the actions of Charles Manson and his "family" in California, who tortured and murdered the actress Sharon Tate and her friends. He remembers "at that time we didn't think Charles Manson was so bad. Somehow we found him quite funny" (p. 65). Baumann's fascination with Manson was shared by Bernardine Dohrn, one of the leaders of the Weathermen in the United States, who remarked: "Dig it, first they killed those pigs, then they ate dinner in the same room with them, then they even shoved a fork in the victim's stomach! Wild!" (Sprinzak, 1998, p. 70).

Baumann rose above petty hooliganism by reading radical literature—Robert Williams, Regis Debray, Eldridge Cleaver—and dedicated himself to the struggle against the Vietnam war. Was this a rational decision? Certainly more so than McVeigh's or Kaczynski's. Baumann had no illusions that the left would win the struggle against capitalism in Germany. Focusing on Vietnam allied him with a cause that had a chance of succeeding, and in fact did succeed. The only problem is that, when the war ended, the rationale for his terrorist career ended. So he and his friends looked around for another cause they could identify with and settled on Palestine. This cause provided a sufficient rationalization for continuing his terrorist actions.

Eventually Baumann tired of terrorism as a lifestyle, although he did not completely abandon the belief system. He simply became bored with living in safe houses and being isolated from the fun-loving counterculture community. Life underground made it difficult to sustain meaningful relationships with women, and he came to feel that a stable relationship was more important to him than the cause. He concluded that "making a decision for terrorism is something already psychologically programmed. Today, I can see that—for myself—it was only the fear of love, from which one flees into absolute violence. If I had checked out the dimension of love for myself before hand, I wouldn't have done it" (Baumann, 1979, p. 115).

Baumann is an example of the militant activist for whom the excitement of violent struggle was the chief motivator. He saw the parallel between his life and that of Stalin, observing that "Stalin was actually a type like us: he made it, one of the few who made it. But then it got heavy" (p. 116).

Velupillai Prabhakaran

Baumann's love of violence pales in comparison to that of Velupillai Prabhakaran, the founder of the Liberation Tigers of Tamil Eelam. Prabhakaran's mother was "deeply religious and very fond of him," but "his thin-lipped father was a strict and upright man who demanded absolute discipline" (Swamy, 1994, p. 49). His father is also described as "doting" and as a man who took very close interest in his children's education. But the young Velupillai found his father's attentions stifling. He was bored with school, and was inspired by exciting tales of Indian struggles against the British.

He also had a taste for killing animals. Swamy (1994) reports that "his love for the catapult, while the other boys were more interested in sports, was legendary and took him to the world of marksmanship. His earliest victims were chameleons, squirrels and birds which he felled or killed with pebbles" (p. 51). His early associates remember him as "a shy and quiet young man with big piercing eyes who always appeared to be itching for action" (p. 51).

He quickly became famous by murdering Alfred Duriappah, the Tamil mayor of Jaffna and the leader of a moderate Tamil political party. After this killing, Prabhakaran lived underground with a group of young men who were inspired by his daring. One of these young men recalled that "Prabhakaran would take slow steps with a revolver tucked into his shirt, take a sudden u-turn, whip out the revolver in a flash and fire at the imaginary enemy. He never got tired of it. He thought it was fascinating" (Swamy, 1994, p. 59). He was particularly proud of a pistol he took from a police official he murdered.

Prabhakaran had a "near total disinterest in Marxist politics and ideology" (Swamy, 1994, p. 69). When an interviewer suggested that it was important to politicize people before beginning armed struggle, he responded "What people, people, you talk about? We have to do some actions first. People will follow us. You armchair intellectuals are afraid of blood. No struggle will take place without killings" (Swamy, 1994, p. 69). He conceded, however, that every movement needs ideological manifestos, so he recruited a journalist, Anton Balasingham (1983), to write them.

Abimael Guzmán

If theory meant little to Prabhakaran, it meant everything to Abimael Guzmán, the founder and leader of the Sendero Luminoso (Shining Path) movement in Peru. Guzmán was the illegitimate son of a prosperous businessman. His mother died when he was five, and he lived with uncles until he was of high school age, when he went to live with his father. He was a top student at an exclusive Catholic high school. Although he had plenty of money and enjoyed spending it, he "was aloof and obscure. He was a loner. He never asked questions in class, never attended parties, and never had girlfriends" (Strong, 1992, p. 5). He consistently received top grades, and went on to study law and philosophy at the National University of San Agustin in Arequipa.

At the university, he was captivated by a charismatic philosophy professor, a specialist on Kant who had abandoned Marxism out of revulsion for Stalinism. Guzmán adopted his professor's love for learning, but not his anti-Stalinism. Strong (1992) reports:

> Books are the cornerstone of his universe. A voracious reader in his youth, Guzmán has such respect for the written word that he all but eschews personal experience. With the delight of a philosopher and mathematician, he encounters in Marxism-Leninism, and especially in Maoism, a set of laws that satisfies his quest for scientific truth and his hunger for social justice. (p. 23)

After earning two doctorates, one in philosophy and one in law, Guzmán was offered the chance to run the philosophy faculty at the University of San Cristobal de Huamanga in Ayacucho, an impoverished, largely Indian town in the Andes. He was a great success as a professor, and rose to an administrative position, which allowed him to fill the university with his political associates. His students became the core of his political movement.

Although he was moved by the poverty of the Indians in Ayacucho, his first political activism had nothing to do with the peasantry. It was an attack on a female Peace Corps volunteer who was attending the University and who had, for some reason, slapped another student in class. The students threatened a nation-wide strike and forced the Peace Corps to leave Peru. Even after his capture in 1992, after leading a movement that terrorized the country and led to the death of 27,000 people, Guzmán (1993) bragged about this incident because "this was the first victorious battle against a powerful enemy, which makes one feel strong and capable of great achievements." The benefits were clearly psychological and symbolic, the Peace Corps volunteer had "humiliated her classmates and offended Peruvians." She had to be punished.

Guzmán became intensely involved in doctrinal disputes within the Communist movement, where he was frequently denounced as a "Trotskyist" because of his championing of ideological and theoretical purity over tactical opportunism. He did not join any Trotskyist faction, however, but became a Maoist and had the opportunity to visit Albania and China. He met Chairman Mao, and aspired to be the Mao of Peru.

Guzmán's greatest strengths were his intellectual persistence and his skill as an organizer. He was not an original thinker or an especially charismatic personality. A man who knew him when he was a young professor said, "I remember him as a rather cold, inexpressive person. Always very correctly dressed. Not given to gesticulation. Not a talker. But the students who were taught by him spoke very highly of him. They said he was the most intelligent of all their teachers" (New Internationalist, 2000). Guzmán did not abandon his didactic role when he became a guerrilla leader. Trainees in his guerrilla warfare mountain school spent as much time reading literature and philosophy as learning military techniques. The reading list was quite sophisticated, including excerpts from Shakespeare's *Julius Caesar* and *Macbeth,* Washington Irving's *Mahomet and His Successors,* and *Prometheus Bound* by Aeschylus (Gorriti Ellenborgen, 1999, pp. 21–36).

Guzmán adopted terror as a deliberate political and military tactic. He argued that "only by agreeing to accept for themselves, and especially for others, higher casualties and a much more intense level of suffering than the enemy, could the party erase the tactical and material disadvantage it had with the enemy" (Gorriti Ellenborgen, 1999, p. 56). Shining Path activists went out of their way to be brutal, torturing victims to death in public squares in the middle of villages, sometimes cutting their heads off and sewing them back on backwards before hanging them from trees, frequently hanging dead dogs from trees as warnings. These acts were intended to impress everyone with their ferocity. Much of their terrorism was directed at social workers, priests, and leftist activists from other political parties who were considered dangerous because they disagreed on Marxist doctrine (Ron, 2001).

For the followers of Sendero Luminoso, terrorism was also a way of communicating angry feelings and guaranteeing that they would not be ignored. Peruvian psychiatrist Saul Peña thought that:

> Sendero says it very clearly, the only way to resist and to regain power is with violence . . . if a person becomes violent, one way to understand this is that he is trying to communicate a level of violence so that we will understand the daily violence that was committed against him. The violence which is expressed in the present is a way of expressing that which they have lived and felt in the past. (Salazar, 1989, p. 48)

This description may apply better to Sendero's followers (Cáceres, 1989) than to Guzmán himself, since he had a middle-class lifestyle and there is no evidence that he suffered from violence of any kind as a child. Some observers speculate that anger at his father for the stigma of illegitimacy, and at his mother for dying when he was five, were at the root of his anger at the capitalist world (Caretas, 1992).

But millions of people in Peru and elsewhere go through similar life experiences without becoming terrorists.

We cannot say that Guzmán, like McVeigh and Kaczynski, adopted political strategies that were so far out of touch with reality that they were bound to fail. He clearly calculated that the use of brutal terrorist methods would intimidate his competitors and make his movement a focal point of Peruvian and world attention. Social contradictions in Peru were acute enough, and the government was corrupt and ineffective enough, that it certainly seemed possible for him to win power, as Mao and Pol Pot did. Even though his movement collapsed after his arrest in 1992, it succeeded in transforming him from an obscure professor at a provincial university to an important actor on the stage of history.

Osama bin Laden

In his exultation about the World Trade Center bombing, Osama bin Laden (2001) identified himself and his agents with "God Almighty," and proclaimed:

> What the United States tastes today is a very small thing compared to what we have tasted for tens of years. Our nation has been tasting this humiliation and contempt for more than 80 years. Its sons are being killed, its blood is being shed, its holy places are being attacked, and it is not being ruled according to what God has decreed. Despite this, nobody cares.

Bin Laden's rhetoric follows the terrorist ideological script, as described above by Post (2001) perfectly. It is polarizing and absolutist, a rhetoric of us versus them, with no shades of gray. Most revealing, however, is his lament that "nobody cares." The terrorist attacks forced the whole world to pay attention to his complaints. Bin Laden and his organization are quite sophisticated in their use of mass media, so it is impossible to know how sincere he is in his rhetoric. But many of his followers are sincere enough to sacrifice their lives to make sure their agonies are heard.

Biographical information about bin Laden (Frontline, 2001; Robinson, 2002) is limited and open to different interpretations. His father was dedicated to his family, but as one of fifty-four children, Osama's time with his father was unavoidably limited. His father, a wealthy construction entrepreneur, had three "permanent" wives and filled the fourth slot permitted under Muslim law with temporary incumbents; "discarded" wives were kept in the family compound and continued to be supported financially. Osama's mother was one of these, an attractive young Syrian woman who had quickly lost favor with his father. Osama was not close to his mother, but was raised mostly by servants.

This kind of family life is not abnormal in Saudi Arabia, however, and most of bin Laden's brothers have led conventional lives. He seems always to have been an outsider within the family. He swung from one lifestyle to another, at times being a bookworm, then experimenting with hedonistic pleasures abroad, then getting heavily involved in religion and radical politics. Robinson (2002) reports:

> He was shy—a characteristic some interpreted as weakness. He isolated himself and was reluctant to participate in family life. Because of this he was both unpopular and shunned as a playmate by his brothers. Confused and hurt, he sought attention through silly childish antics and mischief. But, when his father was nearby, Osama was clever enough to transform himself into a dutiful, well-behaved son. (p. 78)

His father, however, died when he was ten years old, leaving him adrift in the world.

At first, bin Laden was focused primarily on Saudi politics. He strongly opposed the Saudi government's alliance with the United States against Saddam Hussein, believing that it should rely instead on radical Muslim *mujahideen*. The Saudi government correctly saw this as a losing strategy, and sent bin Laden into exile. He sought to become a leader of Muslim civilization against the West, and found that focusing on Palestine, rather than on internal Saudi politics, was much more effective in motivating followers.

From his point of view, bin Laden's attacks on the World Trade Center and Pentagon cannot be viewed as irrational. They brought him the fame and recognition he craved, and there was certainly a chance that they might have succeeded in uniting much of the Muslim world under his leadership. Indeed, he and his advisors might well have been guided by the work of Harvard professor Samuel Huntington, who posited the clash of civilizations as the emerging trend in world history. Bin Laden clearly sought to be the leader of the Muslim civilization against the predominantly Christian civilization of the West. If the Western leaders had not read the same books and carefully avoided casting the conflict as one between Muslims and the West, he might have succeeded. Many of the young men who have sacrificed their lives to his holy war are unquestionably driven by personal frustrations, a lust for adventure, and sincere religious beliefs. Bin Laden shares some of these motivations, but he is most important for his skill in organizing and manipulating the emotions of others.

CONCLUSIONS

Among the cases we have examined, Bommi Baumann and Velupillai Prabhakaran were drawn to terrorism by a love of violence. They were militant activists first. Prabhakaran developed skills as a political strategist, but he never had much taste for theory. Baumann developed literary and theoretical skills as he drifted away from activism and politics. Theodore Kaczynski and Timothy McVeigh certainly had political ideologies, but these were secondary to their psychological pathology. Abimael Guzmán was first and foremost a theorist, but he developed considerable organizational and political skills. Osama bin Laden is primarily a political strategist, drawn to terrorism as a way of winning power and changing the world.

Effective terrorists have a combination of emotional, intellectual, and political drives. Those emotionally inclined to violence, but without ideology or politics, may lash out at neighbors or coworkers, but they are unlikely to be disciplined enough to carry out effective terrorist activities. Radical theorists and political strategists without violent psychological inclinations are likely to find other, less dangerous outlets for their skills. It is the combination of all three drives that is the most potent.

Although an isolated individual may occasionally carry out a highly destructive act, terrorism is much more dangerous when it is carried out by an organized group. Terrorist movements grow out of movements for social change. Organizing such a movement is a complex matter, and requires the contributions of individuals with a variety of traits and skills. The first stage in the development of a social movement is a period of mobilization of discontent. Intellectuals are very important at this stage because they formulate the movement's doctrine, helping people to understand how their unhappiness is rooted in a common social problem.

As the movement grows, its participants want to do more than understand and express their discontent. They want to take action to change things. The movement enters a stage of sharpening objectives and strategies, where political and organizational skills are more essential. There is typically a good deal of conflict among the supporters of a movement about how to accomplish its goals (Goertzel, 1992). Terrorist factions typically emerge at this stage in the development of a movement. Extremists use terror to distinguish themselves and to assert leadership. Typically, this stage lasts for a few years, after which terrorist activity is likely to decline, either because the movement is suppressed, or because it develops a strong, centralized leadership that finds other strategies more effective.

The large majority of people who sympathize with, support, or are active in a social movement do not commit terrorist acts. The actual terrorists are likely to be recruited from the ranks of troubled young men, men like Bommi Baumann and Velupillai Prabhakaran, whose anger is so great that they are willing to take great risks to express it. The larger social movement encourages these men to believe that their anger is caused by an external enemy and that they are justified in engaging in terrorism against that enemy.

Fighting terrorism involves psychological counseling to help troubled youth, reformist measures to ameliorate social problems, and repressive measures that make rebellion too costly (Lemann, 2001). The hard-core terrorists are highly resistant to both reformist and repressive measures, but they are nevertheless likely to become discouraged when support for the broader social movement withers away. With time, they also often mature and get past the psychological storms that led them to terrorism.

A visitor to Ayacucho in 2000 found former Sendero activists to be a discouraged lot, understandably, since most of them are serving long terms in prison. One woman, who had taken part in Sendero "actions" in 1989 and 1990 when she was fifteen and sixteen years old, said "I think the path I took was incorrect. But I never had bad intentions, I didn't join Sendero in order to kill people" (New Internationalist, 2000). When asked about her hopes for the future, she said "I hope that others do not make the mistakes I made."

Remarks of this sort are often made by terrorists who look back on their periods of activism. William Harris, one of the leaders of the Symbionese Liberation Army that became famous by kidnapping Patricia Hearst in 1974, now observes that "I'm older, no longer self-destructive and unwilling to go to jail. We were a bunch of amateurs. I wish everyone would forget us" (Sterngold, 2002, p. 26). Bernardine Dohrn, who once rejoiced in Charles Manson's exploits, grew up to become director of the Children and Family Justice Center at Northwestern University. Her husband, fellow Weatherman activist Bill Ayers, became a professor of education at the University of Chicago. Attempting to explain his past, Ayers (2001) wrote, "the psychological answer, I think, was that we were young with an edge of certainty and arrogance that I would be hard-pressed to re-create or even fully understand again. The moral justification requires remembering the context of the times" (p. 258).

These terrorists have had the good fortune of being able to grow out of their terrorist stage and go on with normal lives. Others, like Weatherman Kathy Boudin and many of Guzmán's comrades, have had to do their personal growth in prison. Many others lost their lives, as did many of their victims.

REFERENCES

Ayers, B. (2001). *Fugitive days: A memoir*. Boston: Beacon.

Balasingham, A. S. (1983). *Liberation Tigers and Tamil Eelam freedom struggle*. Madras, India: Liberation Tigers of Tamil Eelam.

Baumann, M. (1979). *Terror or love? Bommi Baumann's own story of his life as a West German urban guerrilla*. New York: Grove Press.

Bin Laden, O. (2001). Bin Laden's warning: Full text. Retrieved October 8, 2001 from: http://news.bbc.co.uk/hi/english/world/south_asia/newsid_1585000/1585636.stm.

Cáceres Velásquez, A. (1989). *Buscando el sendero*. Lima, Peru: Caribe.

Caretas. (1992, October 8). Guzman por dentro. *Caretas, 1231*, 16–18, 20–21.

Crenshaw, M. (1998). The logic of terrorism: Terrorist behavior as a product of strategic choice. In W. Reich (Ed.), *Origins of terrorism: Psychologies, ideologies, theologies, states of mind* (pp. 7–24). Washington, DC: Woodrow Wilson Center Press.

Ferracuti, F. (1998). Ideology and repentance: Terrorism in Italy. In W. Reich (Ed.), *Origins of terrorism: psychologies, ideologies, theologies, states of mind* (pp. 59–64). Washington, DC: Woodrow Wilson Center Press.

Frontline. (2001). A biography of Osama bin Laden. Retrieved January 18, 2002, from http://www.pbs.org/wgbh/pages/frontline/shows/binladen/who/bio.html.

Goertzel, T. (1992). *Turncoats and true believers*. Buffalo, NY: Prometheus Books.

Gorriti Ellenborgen, G. (1999). *The shining path: A history of the millenarian war in Peru*. Chapel Hill, NC: University of North Carolina Press.

Guzmán, A. (1993). Exclusive comments. *World Affairs, 156*. Retrieved January 10, 2002, from Academic Search Premier database.

Johnson, S. C. Psychological evaluation of Theodore Kaczynski. Retrieved January 9, 2002, from http://www.courttv.com/trials/unabomber/documents/psychological.html.

Kaczynski, T. (2002). Industrial society and its future. Retrieved January 9, 2002, from http://www.panix.com/~clays/Una.

Kellen, K. (1998). Ideology and rebellion: Terrorism in West Germany. In W. Reich (Ed.), *Origins of terrorism: psychologies, ideologies, theologies, states of mind* (pp. 43–58). Washington, DC: Woodrow Wilson Center Press.

Lemann, M. (2001, October 29). What terrorists want. *New Yorker, 77,* 36–41.

Martin, J. L. (2001). The authoritarian personality, 50 years later: What lessons are there for political psychology? *Political Psychology, 22,* 1–26.

Michel, L., & Herbeck, D. (2001). *American terrorist: Timothy McVeigh and the Oklahoma City bombing.* New York: ReganBooks.

New Internationalist. (2000). Shining bloodstained path. *New Internationalist, 321,* 18–22. Retrieved January 10, 2002, from Academic Search Premier database.

Post, J. (1998). Terrorist psycho-logic: Terrorist behavior as a product of psychological forces. In W. Reich (Ed.), *Origins of Terrorism: Psychologies, ideologies, theologies, states of mind* (pp. 25–42). Washington, DC: Woodrow Wilson Center Press.

Post, J. (2001, November). Terrorist organization and motivation. Testimony prepared for Subcommittee on Emerging Threats and Capabilities, Senate Armed Services Committee. Retrieved October 15, 2001, from Academic Search Premier database.

Robinson, A. (2002). *Bin Laden: Behind the mask of the terrorist.* New York: Arcade.

Ron, J. (2001). Ideology in context: Explaining Sendero Luminoso's tactical escalation. *Journal of Peace, 38,* 569–592.

Rothman, S. & Lichter, R. (1982). *Roots of radicalism: Jews, Christians and the new left.* New York: Oxford University Press.

Salazar del Alcázar, H. (1989). La otredad de Sendero: una entrevista. *Quehacer, 62,* 44–50.

Sprinzak, E. (1998). Extreme left terrorism in a democracy. In W. Reich (Ed.), *Origins of terrorism: Psychologies, ideologies, theologies, states of mind* (pp. 65–85). Washington, DC: Woodrow Wilson Center Press.

Starn, O. (1995). Maoism in the Andes: The Communist party of Peru—Shining Path and the refusal of history. *Journal of Latin American Studies, 27,* 399–422.

Sterngold, J. (2002, January 17). Four former radicals are charged in 1975 killing in bank robbery. *New York Times,* pp. 1, 26.

Strong, S. (1992). *Shining Path: Terror and revolution in Peru.* New York: Times Books.

Swamy, N. (1994). *Tigers of Lanka, from boys to guerrillas.* Delhi, India: Konark Publishers.

Tomkins, S. (1963). Left and right: A basic dimension of personality and ideology. In R. White (Ed.), *The Study of Lives* (pp. 399–411). New York: Atherton.

Tomkins, S. (1987). Script theory. In J. Aronoff, A. I. Rabin, & R. Zucker (Eds.), *The emergence of personality.* New York: Springer.

Wolfe, B. D. (1964). *Three who made a revolution.* New York: Dial Press.

NOTE

1. In this chapter, when "he" or "his" are presented in an unspecified way, one should also read "she" and "her."

6

Psychological Concepts of the "Other": Embracing the Compass of the Self

Steve S. Olweean

At a time when the threat of terrorism and seemingly irreconcilable clashes of cultures dominate our attention, one can overlook the fact that similar discord based on conflicting views of each other and even the essence of human nature has plagued humankind since its beginnings (May, 1982). For the most part, any temporary outcomes of such past clashes have not been determined by the strength of a "right" reality, but instead by the military and economic might of one of the parties. While this fact may speak to the value of one physical or economic strength over another, it contributes little if anything to the comparison of the value of ideas or perspectives of particular groups. No major collision of worldviews was decided by one side suddenly seeing the "truth" of the "other." In fact, most conflicts have done little to settle such arguments, even long after the encounter has ended. The temporary nature of physical dominance in human history unfortunately provides many new opportunities for "revisiting" disagreements.

To understand this chronic dilemma and find answers that all can endorse, it is helpful to use more than shortsighted vision and to address the larger, underlying dynamics of how we form ideas and perceptions of each other.

The concept of the "other" is probably one of the most elemental and enduring aspects of human interactions. As a means of distinguishing who is "not us" and, conversely, who we are, it provides an invaluable model of our separate identity. Like the related process of stereotyping, it brings order to our lives by routinely sorting and categorizing into simpler, more manageable clusters the overwhelming multitude of situations that flood our daily life. As is the case with habitual processes, the concept is allocated to a less than fully conscious state.

As a mechanism, this process is neither good nor bad. It just is. Judgments in terms of being good or bad, healthy or harmful, come only as a result of examining how the process is put to use through our interactions with the rest of the "selves" we coexist with in the world—i.e., our behavior. Since this psychological process is highly subjective, judgment of behavior requires objective, universal standards to be valid.

A problem comes when we confuse comparisons of opposite and conflicting absolutes—good and evil, right and wrong, superior and inferior, civilized and uncivilized—with the group identities of "us" and "them." Such misguided comparison can lead to the failure of reason and logic and set the stage for grievous mistakes and injustices.

This article attempts to point to this dilemma of human relationships and raise difficult questions. It invites others to explore these issues with the hope of finding viable solutions. Particularly given the current state of global affairs, it is no stretch to say that addressing such all-too-human psychological and historical questions is not simply desirable but vital to our survival.

THE "OTHER" AS A PROCESS

Rather than being an actual and specific entity, the "other" can better be understood as an expression of a fundamental psychological process that helps us get our bearings and make sense of ourselves within the context of the world in which we live. It is a reference point. If we know where north is, we also know where south, east, and west are.

The earliest example of this process occurs when we are children. We discover that our parents, and through them the world, are not simply extensions of ourselves, but instead are separate and distinct beings, with separate needs, preferences, and characteristics. At its beginnings, then, the "other" is made up of those closest and most available to us—our parents, siblings, and family. From there we continue in our quest to define what is us and what is not us—generalizing and becoming increasingly more sophisticated in how we conceive of and relate to the "other," all the while asserting our own authentic identity. If there is an "other," by definition, there must be a "we," and visa versa.

Life then expands in quantum leaps, and we struggle to make sense of this new, shifting reality as other strangers enter into what is now becoming a shared existence. We begin to attach meaning to this phenomenon, and from those meanings come beliefs and belief systems connected to ourselves, others, and the world. As we form core group identities with those closest and most familiar to us, our parents, family, community, and society profoundly influence these belief systems. The qualitative nature of those beliefs defines the context for what we can expect of new others in general (Harman, 1984).

When our beliefs are based on a premise of security and confidence, these beliefs provide a receptive context for new experiences of others and an appreciation for diversity in these strangers. This posture serves us well in creating and maintaining healthy, cooperative, and mutually valuing relationships with new people we encounter who are different from us.

When there is a pervasive insecurity at the core of our belief, this insecurity is reflected onto new and potential "others," particularly those less predictable and less familiar to our life experience. From this perspective, being "not like us," "different," or "an outsider" is seen as less than desirable or comfortable, and there is a tendency to distance and to avoid forming relationships.

When the beliefs are strongly fear-based, this heightened sense of vulnerability leads to an excessive discriminating vigilance for potential danger. Anything deviating from the norm carries a substantial degree of potential risk or threat that can promote resistance, opposition, and even aggression. In extreme cases, fear-based beliefs can be expressed in striking out through violence and war.

Much can be said about the formation and modification of both positive and negative belief systems. For this discussion, reference is simply made to a powerful energetic link between interpreted meanings of profound life experiences and primary needs associated with them. The strength of the link is based on a perceived maximum benefit to or protection of those vital needs that is provided by the attached meaning.

Once this bond occurs, an internal drive is activated to maintain and perpetuate the belief against threats to its validity. New outside information is filtered by a highly subjective screen that tends to match the presumptions of the belief. In extreme cases, this can create a nearly closed system. Any forced challenge to the belief from the outside is met with similar resistance. An example might be the need for acceptance coupled with early painful rejection by primary figures, forming a belief that one is not acceptable and resulting in self-defeating behaviors intended to avoid being exposed to the pain of future rejections. In this case, forcing an individual into situations where there is even high probability for acceptance is resisted by the person as too threatening to a defensive belief now heavily relied on for the more vital purpose of avoiding expected rejection at all costs.

A belief system is vulnerable, however, to internal dissonance when conflicting information is allowed into the internal database of facts. When contradictory facts are present at this level, especially when absolute beliefs are involved, the person must—in order to reduce internal dissonance and maintain harmony—revisit the original meaning and go through the process of making sense of it again, incorporating new information.

It is through this opportunity to reevaluate old, entrenched, negative beliefs that such beliefs can be modified and reframed in a more positive, healthy context. The assumption, of course, is that there is a powerful, natural drive toward internal harmony, and that the character of this harmony is one of health and "goodness" (Rogers, 1982). This assumption will be addressed later in this chapter.

A strong negative belief, particularly an absolute one, must be continually nurtured. It demands repeated confirmation and vigilance in seeking out proof around us, as well as agreement with others with whom we identify. If there is either a dwindling of proof or a difficult-to-dismiss contradiction, we experience some degree of uncertainty. Even if we feel 90 percent certain of an absolute, we cannot avoid feeling the 10 percent of doubt. It is this crack in the door of our negative beliefs that offers the most hope for change.

The focus in healing negative belief systems, then, is on the resistance to allowing new and accurate information into an individual's deep experience. It is important to keep in mind that compelling negative beliefs are usually attached to powerful defensive emotions and energy, sometimes literally even to survival. Full-frontal assaults on these beliefs invariably fall into the trap of feeding them (as in using force against a force field; the field draws from the very energy expended to confront and eliminate it). Paradoxically, in the process of resisting attack, the subjective screen may tighten further to distort and ward off threatening contradictory facts from the outside. In some cases, fear and anger attached to negative absolutes may even trigger aggression.

What is more effective and lasting in the long run is to introduce a less threatening, subtle exposure to new facts that can be digested and absorbed with less internal chaos. This discreet flow of new information has the effect of challenging and eroding the belief as the new information accumulates. The person is more in control of the process and therefore the process does not activate a defensive stance. The key, then, is to let truth seep in methodically to shift the balance of proof, with a minimum of threat or force, to let a healthy dissonance set in.

CONTAINER VERSUS CONTENT

For the purpose of this discussion, I would like to offer a metaphor of the "other" as both a vessel and the content of that vessel.

As a vessel, the "other" is remarkably stable, durable, and active. Since its purpose is not time- or situation-limited, but rather part of an ongoing psychological process, it is fixed. At the same time, as the particular content or occupant of this vessel, it is just as remarkably changeable, tenuous, and situational—even interchangeable to the point of being contradictory.

As a container, if the current content alters significantly or even ceases to exist, the container persists in functioning by simply finding another more workable occupant and replacing it. The character of the vessel (identification) goes unchanged, while the character of the content (what is identified) is always in various stages of flux. When a person is placed in the vessel, differences are emphasized and inflated, while likenesses are minimized or denied. When the person is removed, the reverse process occurs to return the person to a neutral to positive standing with us. The criteria are highly fluid and relative, adjusting up or down depending on the circumstances.

There are examples throughout our history of an "other" transforming to become not only a "non-other," but a "we." On a global level, one example is the relationships of Germany, Japan, and Italy with the United States, Britain, France, and the Soviet Union during and after World War II. A more recent example is the relationship between the former Soviet Union and the West. Each has been included in its counterpart's vessel of the "other," epitomizing the most extreme characterizations of evil, immorality, and certainly the treacherous "enemy." In current times, these groups see each other as allies, as friends, and even as part of the core of "us" in a new global community. On an everyday basis, the average American is comfortable with the Japanese language appearing regularly in electronic and automotive literature and even on various components of our most commonly used technology. At the time of Pearl Harbor in the 1940s, this exposure would have conjured up images of an evil and barbaric alien. Then there is the image of John F. Kennedy standing before cheering crowds at the Berlin Wall, supporting Germans occupied by the Soviet Union by declaring "I am a Berliner."

Old movies depicting nefarious stereotypes of these societies are now considered politically incorrect and even embarrassing. Of course, it should be noted there is now a plethora of new "other"-depicting movies that repeat the same extremist dynamics of demonizing and dehumanizing entire groups of people based on such common characteristics as ethnicity and religion.

Although the nations mentioned above no longer consider each other enemies (i.e., are not the current "occupants"), each continues to maintain and operate a vigorous vessel of the "other." Ironically, a good deal of the current content of these vessels is the same (that is, they share current adversaries).

A more dramatic example of the "other's" situational pliability as an entity, and its lack of universal or stable criteria, is from my childhood—one to which many might relate. I recall numerous visits to movie theaters to see "alien invasion" movies. They were scary and exciting, and seemed to tap into all the right fears that my friends and I shared. A common scenario, which struck me as an astonishing shift even then, was the immediate uniting of all the world against a larger, even "more" alien "other." The image was of an "other" so different and unknown to us that it literally went off the charts, relegating all human differences on all levels to the less than trivial. Any semblance of adversity, competition, or suspicion between the people of Earth was mutually dropped with such obvious and logical ease that it was almost unnecessary to explain it in the plot. It just made simple, uncomplicated sense to both the characters in the movie and the audience watching. In some stories, other species were even included. "Us" was defined as simply all living beings of this planet. I remember sharing a momentary exuberance with all those in the theater as there was only one "us" on Earth, and I must admit to a bit of disorientation when the trance state quickly receded as we all walked out into the newly reestablished "reality." This brief shift in paradigm that allows us to experience a deep and, for the moment, highly logical sense of belonging to each other is not an uncommon phenomenon. In therapy we call such moments breakthroughs; in spiritual traditions, enlightenment. Yet we can tend to relegate such as experience to fantasy and to the "unreal"; not unlike the way in which our negative belief systems screen out contradicting data. The question is: Which is trance and which is real?

If what appear to be enormous and irreconcilable differences in one moment shrink to less than insignificant in the face of a much larger difference, how can we make absolute life decisions based on them? If a perception of "other" is fear-based (and therefore to a great degree distorted), and if the content identity of that vessel at any given time can so easily and radically switch, what are the implications of categorical, far-reaching, and irreversible actions toward those who simply happen to be the most current occupants of the vessel?

COMPLICATING FACTORS CONTRIBUTING TO DESTRUCTIVE USE

How does a neutral process so frequently result in such destructive consequences in our relationships? Part of the answer may have to do with several compounding factors.

Subconscious Quality of the Process

This process operates for the most part outside our clear awareness at a subconscious level. As such it is highly vulnerable to influences of which we may not be aware. Because we cannot monitor these influences serious distortions in how we identify and characterize others are possible. If these distorted and incorrect perceptions are accepted as reality and unwittingly acted upon, our actions will likely be equally distorted and incorrect. In extreme cases, these actions may be experienced as unjust, cruel, and inhumane. As long as this process remains outside our awareness, mistakes based on distortions can be repeated to the detriment of others and ourselves. When we collectively share distortions, there is the potential for even more harm. Among ten key propositions listed in research findings reported by Willis Harman (1984) is the statement that "Unconscious beliefs held collectively are the most fundamental cause of the global dilemmas that beset the world, and thus a major contributor to non-peace" (p. 81).

Self-Defensiveness

Inner Conflict: Denial to Avoid Psychic Pain

After the fact, individuals who "know" themselves to be basically good and just can find it intolerable to wrestle with the self-blame and guilt of having done something wrong and unjust. To reduce inner conflict and threat to self-esteem, it is often easier to deny the reality of these actions or, if this is not possible, to justify or minimize their effect on others and thus avoid responsibility. Unfortunately, the price of short-term relief from psychic distress is continuous repetition of our mistakes.

Conflict With the Outside: Denial to Avoid Blame, Shame, and Judgment

If we define our world in absolutes, such as good and evil, there is little room for admitting and correcting our own wrongs. This difficulty is further compounded when competition for affixing blame and evil intent exists between groups who identify each other as the "other." Within these "one-of-us-must-be-wrong" adversarial relationships, because we carry a "known true sense" of our basic goodness, we can feel compelled to protect ourselves against all odds from losing ground and having our mistakes used to prove unfairly our ultimate "wrongness."

To maintain validity as the "good guys" in a conflict, there is pressure to defend against any accusations to the contrary, even those accusations we may know to be true to some extent, and to instead prove the "other" worse by comparison. As the accuser focuses on and even exaggerates wrongs, we deny, minimize, or dismiss the same as insignificant, excusable, or even righteous.

Again, the price of successfully avoiding responsibility and losing out in the short term allows us to turn a blind eye to the repetition of mistakes that are contrary to our own self-image as well as to how we are viewed by others. A resulting irony is that this route eventually ensures that all sides increasingly experience some degree of wrong.

Self-Fulfilling Prophesy and Victim Identity

A tragic result of acting on distorted negative stereotypes is that the practice continually creates a factual history of proof on all sides of the wrongness of the perpetrating "other" and the rightness of the victimized "us," and that it actively supports the mutually exclusive negative belief systems.

After a while all sides have a body of concrete grievances that support their correct stance and view of the "other," as well as their justification in responding to unjust wrongs. Retaliation and retribution are superimposed onto offensives until there is no discernable beginning, no end—only competing blames and accusations that feed the destructive cycle.

Taking on the identity of victim places us in the role of someone wronged who deserves justice, and allows for a self-righteous perspective that can eventually rationalize inhumane treatment of others identified as the perpetrators of our victimization. There are examples in psychotherapy of individuals who are past victims themselves becoming perpetrators. On a societal level this paradoxical dynamic is less studied.

If we select any society or culture in recent history that has been identified as a perpetrator against another (and I exclude some absolute dictators whose individual motives may not represent the overall population), invariably that group carries a deeply held myth of itself as victim, martyr, or even champion of a higher good— sometimes the good of all.

Bosnians and Kosovars point to crimes against humanity perpetrated on them in the Balkan wars at the end of the last century. Serbs point to their massacre as defenders of Europe by Eastern invaders generations earlier. Arabs point to the loss of their homeland and a devalued daily life of brutal oppression and trauma. Jews point to the pogroms of Russia and Nazi concentration camps. Americans point to Pearl Harbor and most recently the tragedy of September 11, 2001. Iranians point to a reign of terror by a Shah twice placed in power by a Western government intent on maintaining its oil supply. The list goes on, and there appears to be no lack of tragic cultural myths in the world community.

A society tends to sees itself as inherently good and just, with little tolerance for a conflicting viewpoint. If it engages in hostile or oppressive behavior toward others, this behavior is usually linked, correctly or incorrectly, to past wrongs (often including physical, psychological, and emotional injuries) at the hands of those it is attacking, or at the hands of another community that this group somehow represents. It is fair to say that such unresolved communal wounds are one of the most—if not the most—powerful fuels of war and violence between groups. Such wounds also contribute the most to creating and validating negative stereotypes.

Entire cultures can take on the identity of tragic victim and unwittingly use this energy of fear to become the perpetrators. When two groups in conflict each bear a deeply embedded ethos of victim, there is the greatest danger of blind, brutal treatment toward a dehumanized and demonized "other." Absolute wrongness allows for absolute righteousness, and inhumane treatment allows for inhumane treatment in the guise of just retribution toward evildoers.

Exploitation and Manipulation

This dilemma is further complicated when individuals or groups intentionally decide to exploit it for their own particular purposes. Manipulation may be by an individual, by small groups, or by larger groups with access to important institutions, such as the media. A look at the long history of institutional propaganda offers many examples of the latter.

Polarization is created or fueled for self gain by those exploiting parties, often to the detriment of the very "us" group they are attempting to incite. The motivations can vary, including seeking power, political or financial gain, justification and support for antisocial behaviors, or personal revenge.

Those who engage in terror—whether they be a lone individual such as Timothy McVeigh, small renegade groups, large networks, or even governments—rely on fanning the flames of "enemy" to build support for their actions. If they are successful in getting an opposing group, such as the U.S. government, to engage in the same practices of demonizing and dehumanizing innocent groups that are somehow associated with these terrorists, and particularly to use unilateral violence and oppressive measures against them, the terrorists succeed in producing new and intense "truths" that validate belief in the presence of an evil, oppressing "other." For example, retaliatory violence that assumes that "collateral damage" in the "other" community (i.e., innocent victims) is necessary and acceptable in protection of a more valued "us" can galvanize portions of the world on a scale that terrorists are unable to achieve in any other way.

The sad result is an escalation of the malevolent "other" on both sides. A further result is the creation of a powerful inducement within another generation of alienated and newly victimized individuals to join the ranks of what terrorists conveniently portray as "freedom fighters." The lines blur for the average person in societies on the receiving end of violence and oppression in their desperate daily lives. The formula of fear, despair, and a deep victim identity can easily lead to endorsing and even embracing violence both as an expression of their pain and the only viable means of achieving security and justice (May, 1984).

As one illustration, in recent times some cunning terrorists have relied on the West's xenophobia and ignorance of Islam—as well as the ignorance of some minorities in Muslim communities who know little of the faith and rely instead on biased interpretations—and have shrouded themselves in the label of Islam while operating in complete opposition to its beliefs. The fact that their actions are clearly un-Islamic is missed, as is the Orwellian double-speak. The unfortunate corresponding use of negative stereotypes, as well as such divisive and destructive labels as "crusade," and "evil Islamic terrorists," by U.S. government leaders and a sensationalizing media only serves to play into this polarizing game of the terrorists. At some point, to an outside observer the rhetoric on both sides sounds remarkably similar, whether it be from a U.S. president or an al-Qaeda leader.

In the wake of the September 11 attacks on the United States, there is currently a greater focus on this particular situation, but these kinds of manipulation dynamics are not new and have a long history that spans many centuries, many places, and many "others."

THE BEGINNINGS OF SOLUTIONS

A more intense multidisciplinary and cross-cultural exploration of these dynamics is needed. I stress the multicultural perspective in particular since what we are addressing is highly subjective and any one cultural view necessarily carries with it a certain amount of biased baggage. By helping each other see our respective tinted lenses and blind spots, we can better gain insight into the multifaceted nature of this process, and into practical solutions for transforming its misuse in our relationships.

Acknowledging and Accepting Our Human Process

The most consistent trait of the "other" as a vessel is that it exists for a purpose beyond and even independent of any identified "characteristics" of a particular group contained in it at any given time. It is a function in itself that operates as a point of reference for our self-definition. It exists because the holder of the vessel exists.

The key component of any solution for problems resulting from its misuse, then, must be our unconditional, even compassionate acknowledgment and acceptance of this fundamental aspect of our human psyche. Only then can we expect to be in conscious control of how it affects our behavior toward others in the world.

There needs to be, in fact, an appreciation for the essential task the "other" accomplishes in helping make sense of who we are in relation to the rest of reality. Without it we would certainly flounder in our journey to define ourselves in a vast universe, and to deny it unnecessarily places us at odds not only with others but with ourselves. Denying it, in fact, is the crux of the problem.

In our humanness, as long as we experience an unconscious fear of the unknown and some degree of stress, insecurity, and vulnerability in our psyche, there is the likelihood of some degree of discrimination and intolerance in our thoughts of others. It is not just impractical to expect that we can totally eliminate such thoughts, it is detrimental. To demand this dooms us to failure, self-condemnation, and denial, and undermines our contact with and control over our human process.

Just as we may periodically experience other uncomfortable impulses or bad thoughts within our inner subjective world that are in direct opposition to what we actually intend to do in the outer world, there are times when we can and do internally judge others in less than fair or less than unbiased ways. These instances are sometimes clustered into what can be called prejudices. Prejudice here is defined as a negative opinion of a person's qualities and intentions, based on a lack of direct, specific knowledge and relying instead on fear-based group stereotypes and illogical, overly generalized assumptions.

When this process goes unacknowledged it can operate outside the peripheral vision of our awareness and can influence our actions without our knowledge. To admit and even forgive ourselves for these simply human failings allows us to take conscious responsibility for monitoring and controlling how this is reflected in our actual treatment of others in the real world. It also allows for empathy. Awareness forces us to see the uncompromised connection between our purposeful actions and our "known" sense of goodness and compassion to transcend any prejudice and bias.

For, in the final analysis, the true reflection of our integrity and goodness as an individual rests on the "knowing intent" of expressing fundamentally human characteristics, particularly when they impact on the lives of others.

Sensitizing and Familiarizing

If an underlying assumption is that the unknown "other" is suspect and to be feared, it can seem wise to keep a safe distance. At the same time, to know accurately where safety is we need to know where this unknown is and where it is not. Stereotypical tools help to locate this danger quickly. Unfortunately, putting distance between us and the unknown prevents us from learning anything directly about the members of this group. As a result, the very distorted tools we use to identify danger become the only known characteristics of the "other."

Perceptions of irreconcilable differences and adversity come from an inability to validate the other person's experience personally. Sensitivity training is not so much for the purpose of simply discovering and squelching bad or politically incorrect habits in relating with others. Instead it is intended to allow us a firsthand glimpse of our behavior on the receiving end—a personal experience of what it is like to be the objectified and estranged "other," and particularly the one we create ourselves. There is obvious truth to clichés like "walk a mile in my shoes."

It is even more important to experience ourselves as valuable, good, and right at the same time that someone quite different from us can be equally valuable, good, and right. The opportunity for both to be true and mutually inclusive—without the need to define our positive identity through contrast with a negative "other"— can free us from a lie that says "one of us must be wrong for the other to be right."

Once this discovery is accomplished, "common sense" kicks in and there is a natural moderation in behavior based on understanding the context and impact of our actions toward others. At that point, how we treat others becomes more of a known indication and even support of our own self-worth, respect, and sense of goodness.

Direct personal familiarity is an obvious and natural way to remove barriers and increase understanding. When understanding increases, stereotypical assumptions and generalities decrease. Moving from the unknown, strange, and mysterious to the known, recognized, and predictable reduces anxiety and opens us to someone else's experience. Establishing a common base of understanding also yields a sense of security and thus allows us to appreciate and even savor diversity. As the unknown shrinks we feel increasingly safer, more optimistic, and at ease (Olwean & Friedman, 1997).

This understanding does not require, however, that what becomes known be the same as us; just that it be familiar. A mistake that is often assumed is that we must "us-ize" the world community to make it more and more like "us" than like "them." The question that invariably comes up with this kind of thinking is whose "us" does this refer to? Any solution that involves eliminating the "other" by absorbing it is unrealistic and, for those identified as the "other," can be viewed on a psychic level as a kind of genocide. We don't have to look far to see powerful reactions to attempts to us-ize the world culture through Western commercial influence. The term "McDonaldizing" is a bitter one in most regions of the world, symbolizing an economic hijacking of the local social/cultural identity.

In the case of the United States and Western Europe, the "other" happens to comprise the vast majority of the world, and the percentage is only rising. Not only is it irrational that the West attempt to offer itself as the most appropriate model of the global community when it is such a minority, it is irrational that any particular culture do this.

A group maintains its sense of well being and a healthy balance with other groups when the primary decisions regarding its development and evolution are determined from within, not when it is pressured from outside, and particularly not when the perceived motivation is to supplant its identity with another's. Again, on a psychic level, such imposed transformation can be experienced as invasion and a marginalizing of members within their own group, as well as within the world at large.

A more natural and acceptable alternative is actively cultivating a positive concept of "otherness." A positive "otherness" allows for a higher tolerance of and appreciation for diversity, for more inclusiveness rather than exclusiveness, for celebrating great variety in human expression without diminishing or threatening our deep sense of belonging at the most basic level of our humanity (Friedman, 1984).

Of course there is a serious conflict if this basic, binding "core" is held to be sinful or evil (i.e., as in original sin) rather than good, benevolent, and trustworthy. If the former, then we have little basis for our belonging except in opposition to and exclusion of others we *don't* belong to. The combination of the psychological process of the "other" and an assumption of basic sin/evil in humans sets the stage for an unfortunately antagonistic, no-win relationship in humankind; just as the combination of a compass and an assumption of north as basically evil sets the stage for continually validating the presence of evil at every turn. It is hard to imagine peace on earth and goodwill toward all within such a view of reality.

Universal Standards of Behavior

A Universal Declaration of Human Rights already exists. Global commitment to this declaration is a necessity; it must be built on, expanded, and followed by all. The leaders of the world need to lead this effort. In addition to this declaration, however, something more radical is called for. There needs to be a commitment to new universal standards, to a Universal Declaration of Basic Human Worth and Basic Human Goodness.

This idea may be radical for many reasons, not the least being some religious interpretations of basic human nature. However, I propose that without such standards we will continually see the wrong actions of individuals used as indictments of entire groups of innocent people. This is not only unjust, it is inefficient and contrary to the overall good because it takes the focus and responsibility for specific actions away from the individual who knowingly perpetrates them, where it belongs, and puts this focus and responsibility on the group. Doing this prevents that group from itself holding the individual accountable for acts against society according to the group's own standards. The group's natural methods of regulating itself and maintaining its moral character are effectively disabled.

Guilt by association, proximity, appearance, or simply birth, becomes an impossible quagmire. An absurd Catch-22 results that traps everyone involved.

In the short term, innocents of this group must accept guilt and punishment, and place themselves at risk. The natural, healthy forces within a group that monitor and control unhealthy, destructive, and antisocial behavior toward others are more than just seriously compromised—they are eliminated. The group is forced to unite in self-defense against an outside threat. The siege mentality becomes predominant. Under these circumstances the mindset that "a house under attack cannot be divided" is a straightforward and certainly reasonable rule to say the least. A house under attack doesn't have time or opportunity to disagree or censure its members. It would take extraordinary courage, inner strength, and fortitude—let alone a willingness for tremendous risk taking—to stand up and side with the opponent group on principle. Yet when this siege mentality is created we can often miss the obvious logic and see this behavior as complicit evidence of group guilt. If the group is then condemned, threatened, and humiliated on the world stage, this attention only galvanizes and complicates things further.

In the long term, innocents of this group must deny reality and create an ongoing delusion of guilt in order to satisfy the opposing group of "others," that is, the group must agree to collectively go insane. To do this they must also agree to be less valuable, less good, and self-hating. To succeed at this would result in their becoming culturally, morally, psychologically, and spiritually bankrupt.

Regardless of one's spiritual or philosophical leanings, a core premise contributing to the need to identify evil in others is the belief that humans are fundamentally sinful or even evil. From some religious perspectives, the saving grace is in divine intervention to correct this. It is no wonder, then, that those seen outside this grace (i.e., nonbelievers) are experienced as suspect and carrying the highest potential for evil in the world. Furthermore, if they are perceived as less good, less chosen, and thus less valued in God's eyes, we can feel absolved in judging them as such ourselves.

What is missed here is that endorsing such a simplistic view of the world—as essentially divided between Satan's people and God's people—cuts both ways, and under such a premise we cannot avoid also finding ourselves labeled as the most available approximation of evil by another religious dogma. From this same worldview, if untempered evil exists in those not in community with believers (i.e., us), then it becomes important to be vigilant of this danger. If it is not easily identified or found, then it becomes important to be more vigilant; to look harder, until it is indeed, found. Then, of course, there is the question of what to do about the evil when we find it.

It may be a radical idea that if we agree evil exists in and of itself in the hearts of all humans (rather than resulting from acts of "ungood" or "emptiness of good"), we are then compelled to look for it, rarely within ourselves and most often in others. If fear of this evil unknown and the alien are at the source of justified acts of violence and oppression against others, then perhaps a case is made for creating our own evil in the world, among ourselves, by demonizing the "other." As Pogo said, "We have met the enemy, and he is us."

I propose we consider what the world would look like if there were no evil groups, societies, cultures, religions, races, nations, and so forth, but rather simply a potential for evil (i.e., cruel) actions by individuals. I propose that we judge the actions of individuals as good or bad, and that we hold the individuals who perpetrate them accountable.

The basic universal rules that could be proposed as part of a universal declaration would logically include:

- All life is equally valuable and sacred. No innocent life can be part of a plan for "collateral damage."

- People are essentially good and worthy.
- Actions are judged good/bad, right/wrong, constructive/destructive.
- People are individually responsible for their actions and behavior, and blame can only be laid on those individuals knowingly and purposely involved in perpetrating an evil act.
- No one can be "born" into guilt, or guilty by association of race, culture, society, spiritual belief, gender, etc.

Eliminating Justified Violence

Universal standards of humane and inhumane treatment allow the best opportunity for common, worldwide endorsement and support. For example, the world should agree that an act of violence, oppression, and humiliation is an act of violence, oppression, and humiliation no matter *who* does it. This standard removes the slippery slope of "just wars," "justified retribution," and the objectified, self-absolving, and inhumane concept of "collateral damage." If this is not addressed, then:

- One group's violence and terror is another's righteous defense.
- One group's terrorist is another's hero, freedom fighter, and martyr.
- One group's collateral damage is another's odious, horrific, and inhumane massacre of innocents.

By removing justifying labels we better stem the flow of violence in our lives and stop contributing new proofs that strengthen the very negative belief systems we are trying to heal in the world.

As violence clearly invites violence, it seems obvious that any universal code must remove violence as an acceptable tool in dealing with each other. A global commitment to nonviolent means of resolving conflicts is required and, just as important, a global commitment to nonviolent means of punishing crimes against society. Violence justified on any level leaves the field open for violence on any level. A society that validates and employs killing, torture, and physical abuse as appropriate punishment simply proves that, with established power and authority, violence is a viable means to an end. A mistake is made in assuming a monopoly on defining that power and authority. History offers countless examples of contenders for such a right—contenders who are invariably associated with creating the very victim identities that feed the image of a feared "other" in the world. Hitler, as just one prime example, defined his power and authority in assuming the "right" of life and death over others.

It is not only reasonable to expect that premeditated violence be officially outlawed, it is unreasonable not to. I would point out that this does not refer to issues of imminent self-defense. Although there certainly may be different views, for the purposes here what is at issue is the model of acceptable universal behavior toward others when we have conscious choices. I propose that to choose violence by design is to lose the integrity of our moral authority.

Transforming the Group Ethos From Martyrdom to Confident Compassion

Just as we would counsel individuals against chronically dwelling on past wrongs and losses and instead to move forward in defining their lives in positive terms that enhance the ability to relate in healthier ways with others, it is important that communities and groups find ways to do the same. Grieving is also an essential human process that needs to be guided in a way that leads to resolution and reconciliation with the world.

The final result must be a reestablished confidence in the goodness of life and a compassion for ourselves and others. This would seem to be the most worthy testament of our honoring of the dead and acts of supreme contribution to our communities and the world. It is not served by institutionalizing hatred and the demonizing of others that provide negative energy for future human tragedy.

Many emotional "hot points" serve as profound and deeply held symbols of a group's ethos. Too often these hot points are memorials to wars and acts of violence where there has been a tragic loss of life, and these memorials serve to galvanize the identity of the victim and just retribution. What is needed are more memorials to struggling toward peace and understanding together; memorials in the tradition of visionaries like Gandhi, Mother Teresa, and Martin Luther King Jr. The task here is to find healthier, more confident ways of celebrating our group esteem and paying tribute to our history without doing so at the cost of demonizing another group.

HOPE

The "other" has been part of us since our beginning. Whether the differences identified have been family, tribal, cultural, religious, gender, or a multitude of other differences, we have sought to distinguish between us and them, we and they, you and me.

Even as we have created the "other" it has confounded and plagued us with a sense of fear for the unknown that shares our world. It is a vague, shadowy fear that always seems to be rumbling in the background. When we define the struggle as between forces of light and dark, our metaphors betray the true story behind our fears—a struggle between the light of knowledge and familiarity and the dark of the unknown and alien.

If there is any culprit, then I would propose it is ignorance defined as evil. While the task of overcoming evil at every turn can be daunting for mere humans, there is great hope for finding practical solutions for overcoming ignorance.

What is needed is a profound shift in our collective consciousness. A shift that is quite possible if we can but be aware of the trance state out of which we operate, and if we can purposely begin to make the shift together. The reward is a future that honors our common human bond and celebrates a constantly evolving treasure house of amazingly varied expressions of this humanity; where diversity becomes desirable, liberating, and, paradoxically, reassuring.

REFERENCES

Friedman, M. (1984). The nuclear threat and the hidden human image. *Journal of Humanistic Psychology, 24,* 65–76.

Harman, W. (1984). Peace on earth: The impossible dream become possible. *Journal of Humanistic Psychology, 24,* 77–92.

May, R. (1982). The problem of evil: An open letter to Carl Rogers. *Journal of Humanistic Psychology, 22,* 10–21.

May, R. (1984). The destiny of America. In T. Greening (Ed.), *American politics and humanistic psychology* (pp. 7–11). San Francisco: Saybrook.

Olweean, S., & Friedman, S. (1997). Sharing tools for personal/global harmony. *Journal of Humanistic Psychology, 37,* 64–70.

Rogers, C. (1982). Notes on Rollo May. *Journal of Humanistic Psychology, 22,* 85–90.

7

The Soul of a Terrorist:
Reflections on Our War With the "Other"

Sharif Abdullah

INTRODUCTION

What motivates people to strap plastic explosives to their bodies, go to a public place, and detonate? Are they soulless criminals? Are they insane fanatics? Or is something else going on?

My goal is to help us see what is right in front of our faces. I make no claim to be able to see the future; my ability is to see and articulate the *now*. I make no claim of special knowledge; my talent lies in being able to articulate the obvious.

My authority to write on the subject of terrorism is threefold:

- I have had an up-close view of a society locked in a vain attempt to solve its terrorism problem with increasing levels of violence. For half of the year, I live in steamy, tropical Sri Lanka, the teardrop hanging off the tip of India, so far from my home in Portland, Oregon, that, no matter which way I leave the island, I'm returning home. I have had a series of near misses with bombings, ambushes, and mortar attacks. I have seen the effects of terrorism firsthand.

- I have talked to many of the young men and women who are so willing to give their own lives—and take the lives of others—for a cause. I have visited slums, refugee camps, and other places of despair around the world. I have seen firsthand the violence that violence has produced.

- I have had the soul of a terrorist. In my youth, I personally experienced the anger, the alienation, and the emptiness that led me to a series of violent encounters with the "white power structure" in Camden, New Jersey. For years, I mistakenly believed that whites were the problem and that violence was the solution.

The reflections in this chapter are designed to help us reframe our thinking about the issue of terrorism, to help us see the issue with new eyes and a new heart.

THE WAR THAT CAN NEVER BE WON

A car blows up on a busy street. An innocuous shopping bag in a department store contains deadly explosives. Biological agents are delivered in the daily mail. Sniper bullets pierce the windshields of passing vehicles. Men with machetes hack to death the people of a different race. Men in uniform carry young boys away, as mass graves fill up in hidden locations. And death rains down from shattered skyscrapers in Lower Manhattan.

Terrorist incidents such as these have escalated over the past fifty years, and various governments have been fighting this unique form of violence with violence of their own.

Despite America's well-publicized entry into the battle, the "war on terrorism" has been going on for quite some time. The British government's violent confrontation with the Irish Republican Army (IRA) terrorists lasted more than three decades. The Israeli government has met violence with violence for generations. The Sri Lankan government has been fighting terrorists for almost two decades.

The American "war on terrorism" is only a few months old. Is there anything the United States can learn from the bloody conflicts in other lands? Can America head off decades of pain and suffering by looking for lessons in Sri Lanka, Northern Ireland, and Israel?

THE OPPOSITE OF SERENDIB

The Arab traders who visited the island of Sri Lanka in ancient times called it *Serendib*, the land of happy surprises. (*Serendib* is the root of the word "serendipity.") Presently, however, Sri Lanka is anything but happy.

My reason for being in Sri Lanka is simple: to help stop the two decades of debilitating war that is sapping the vitality and civility of an otherwise beautiful island. I do this through the application of the philosophy of inclusivity, a search for a "third-way" solution that does not support either party to the current struggle. Our goal is to permanently break the cycles of victim–villain–violence. I work with Sarvodaya, a forty-year-old self-help development organization based on Gandhian and Buddhist principles. Sarvodaya's goal is to end terrorism and other forms of violence, through nonviolence and spiritual awakening.

Sarvodaya is succeeding where twenty years of military confrontation have not. Sarvodaya's success in helping to move this island nation beyond war and terror lies in one simple fact: Sarvodaya does not use and has utterly renounced the use of violence.

In the Sarvodaya model, the way to end terrorism is to change the consciousness of the terrorist. (In the violence model, the way to change consciousness is to put a bullet through the brain of one's opponent. In a world where there are multiple opponents who are increasingly likely to shoot back, the violence model has diminishing returns.) Sarvodaya's approach is to change consciousness by meeting violence with compassion and loving-kindness. Through a massive meditation campaign, Sarvodaya's goal is to change the "psycho-sphere," the field of human thought. Through this approach, Sarvodaya intends to make violence unthinkable and peace inevitable.

WHO IS A "TERRORIST"?

In order to tackle terrorism, we must first define it. For the purpose of this writing, terrorism means:

- Intentionally inflicting pain, suffering, and death on civilians and/or other noncombatants, for the purpose of achieving an aim
- Inflicting pain, suffering, and death on civilians and/or other non-combatants, in callous disregard of their human and civil rights
- Creating an atmosphere of fear and horror, through the use and/or threat of violence

Terrorism is not an ideology; it is a specific type or brand of violence. If you accept the definition of terrorist as a person or group who intentionally inflicts pain, suffering, and death on a group of defenseless civilians in order to achieve a purpose, then terrorism is largely a twentieth-century phenomenon.

Prior to the twentieth century, most wars were fought in somebody's cow pasture—civilians just got in the way of a good fight. Of course, if the military objective was to seize a certain castle, and if that castle happened to be filled with civilians, the civilians caught hell. Furthermore, civilians caught hell *after* the war, when they were incorporated into the society of the victor (sometimes as citizens, often as slaves.)

As far back as the Mahabharata, there were rules of war—and targeting civilians as combatants was considered wrong. (It was also considered wrong to defend oneself by hiding behind unarmed civilians.)

Something happened, however, around the turn of the last century. Unarmed civilians became not collateral targets, or subsequent targets, but primary targets. This shift took full force in World War II, when both Allied and Axis powers targeted entire cities for destruction. The Japanese were guilty of the infamous "Rape of Nanking," the Germans for Auschwitz and the other extermination camps, and the United States for the one terrorist event that has been unequalled in all human history: the destruction of the civilian cities of Hiroshima and Nagasaki by atomic bombs.

NON-STATE TERRORISM

The examples above represent "state terrorism": the terrorizing of civilians by a nation or state. Another form of terrorism involves para-state, or proto-state, organizations.

This form of terrorism also has an unfortunately long and rich history. Activities of para-state organizations are considered criminal until the members take over, change the laws, and become "heroes." For example, a group of colonists dressed up like Native Americans and trashed an English vessel loaded with valuable cargo. They went on to become founders of America's democracy, and their violent act was called a party. In an act not unlike the World Trade Center atrocity, Golda Meir, Menachem Begin, and others blew up the King David Hotel in Palestine, killing scores of innocent civilians. They went on to become the political leaders of the state of Israel.

In America, the most notorious of the non-state terrorists is the Ku Klux Klan. For more than one hundred years, they heaped death, destruction, and terror upon African American populations, primarily in the South. The image of the white-robed night riders still strikes terror in the hearts of many African Americans.

STARING INTO THE SOUL OF THE TERRORIST

These definitions and historical facts do nothing to help us understand the motivation of the terrorist.

This is not the first time the United States has faced suicide attackers. In World War II, one of the most potent weapons in the Pacific theater was the Japanese kamikaze pilot—the original "smart bomb." But the kamikaze pilot was not the same as the modern terrorist, for one fundamental reason: The Japanese pilot was not motivated by anger, hatred, powerlessness, and emptiness. These pilots were soldiers, not terrorists.

What is the difference? What motivates a terrorist? How do terrorists differ from soldiers? In general, terrorists feel:

- Very angry—an anger based on hurt, pain, and suffering
- Unheard—they feel that their beliefs, perspectives, or reality have not been considered or respected
- Powerless without resorting to violence
- Under attack and forced to fight back—terrorists generally see themselves as victims
- Defeated—that they have already lost, have nothing left to lose, and are therefore committed to a "lose-lose" scenario

THE LAND OF THE BLIND

Let me describe an act of terrorism, an act that I classify as "evil." Although fictitious, it is based on real-life events.

It's 1983. A woman has just put her children to bed, combed her daughters' hair and tucked in her son. She is about to turn out the light and go to sleep when she hears a faint whistling sound. The next thing she knows, her house explodes in a fireball. She is crushed under the wreckage, losing the use of her legs. Up and down her narrow street are the sounds of other explosions: ten, twenty, thirty, or more.

One of her daughters is killed; the other loses an arm and a leg. Muhammad, her son, though battered and cut, escapes serious injury. The surviving daughter, being maimed, has no chance of getting married. Mother and daughter become street beggars in a city filled with street beggars.

Does any of this sound "evil"? It does to me.

Twenty miles away, on the battleship *New Jersey*, a young man (we'll call him Jimmy) loads the firing coordinates into the battleship's huge twenty-inch guns. For the third night in a row, Jimmy directs the firing of the *New Jersey*'s artillery into residential neighborhoods *suspected* of harboring anti-government fighters. He knows he is firing cannon shells on unarmed and unprotected civilians, people who have nowhere to run, no way to escape.

Is this an "evil act"? I think so. And, more importantly, the woman's surviving son thinks so.

> As soon as he is old enough, Muhammad joins Hamas, or al-Qaeda, or Black September, or any of the other groups that proliferate in the Middle East. He doesn't join because of religion, or political ideology, or because he believes his cause will succeed. He joins to avenge his mother, avenge his sisters, and to punish the evildoers. Us.

Gandhi said, "An eye for an eye leaves the whole world blind." Welcome to the Land of the Blind.

> Almost twenty years later, Jimmy (now married with children of his own) looks at his television in horror as planes slam into the World Trade Center. He wonders how those people could be so evil as to kill innocent civilians and destroy buildings like that. He has forgotten, justified, or dismissed his own actions in killing innocent civilians and destroying their homes. Jimmy doesn't know that one of the pilots is Muhammad.

Jimmy, Muhammad, and all the rest of us are caught in a web of mutuality. The fact that we don't see it doesn't mean the web isn't there. The glue on this web is violence.

Muhammad took his action because he was angry and felt powerless. In general, Americans have no idea that such anger exists. Most Americans have a viewpoint, a perspective that does not allow them to see or hear the angry and powerless masses. Or, they hear the anger yet ignore it, feeling that these angry people can't possibly hurt them in their middle-class, gated communities, their gated lives.

Like Muhammad, most of us, in the face of pain, want to hurt back. We want to find the perpetrators and make them hurt the way we are hurting. We believe it's the only way to relieve our pain.

I was one of those pain-filled, angry people. I have felt as angry and powerless as Muhammad. I have had the experience of feeling victimized by an entire society. As an African American, growing up in the inner-city ghetto, I struggled to get the larger white society to take notice of the problems of our communities, atrocities that were happening in plain view but that were invisible to middle-class white Americans. My attempts became increasingly militant, increasingly violent. I became convinced that violence was the only language that would jolt white America out of its complacency. On the third floor of my organization's headquarters in Camden, New Jersey, that "jolt" took the form of a small bomb factory. I still remember the recipe for homemade napalm.

Anger and fear favors the extremists. It is extremism that fuels the world's violence. The extremists on all sides gain from conflict. As long as this is true, the conflict will continue. Extremists benefit from the atrocities committed by the "other"—they gain a false sense of righteousness and justification.

We must isolate the extremists. We must not allow extremists on any side to dictate the dialogue on war and peace. We must understand that the purpose of violence is polarization and separation—we must refuse to be separated from the "other."

WHO IS THE "OTHER"?

However, while isolating the extremists, we must not separate from the "other."

Who is the "other"? Simply, the "other" is the person or group with whom you find it hardest to practice inclusivity, the group from whom you feel the most separation. This may be a person of a different ethnicity, class, religion, and/or ideology. This may be a parent or a spouse.

All of us have some one who is, for us, the "other." All of us experience degrees of separation from other people. The challenge of the twenty-first century is to not act on our feelings of separation. Our challenge is to act as if we are all brothers and sisters, not strangers and enemies.

To defuse the terrorist, we must understand the mind of the terrorist. To understand the mind of the "other," we must understand our own mind. The seeds of terrorism lie within each of us.

There are some very, very angry people in the world. Part of their anger is in not being heard. People who feel unheard will do anything to get attention. In their minds, *any* attention, even negative attention, is better than no attention at all.

Some of those angry people are Middle Eastern, like the September 11th attackers. Some of those angry people are white Americans, like Timothy McVeigh (the Oklahoma City bomber) and Theodore Kaczynski (the so-called Unabomber). Some terrorists look and act just like me—or you. To stare terrorism in the face is to look in the mirror.

The perpetrators of violence around the world all believe that their brand of violence is good, just, and necessary. The perpetrators of violence all believe that they oppose evil people, and that the only way they can stop that evil is to perpetrate violence. Each violent person, for the "other," is a terrorist.

So, George Bush believes that Osama bin Laden is evil. Bush is willing to kill to stop bin Laden's actions. He is willing to risk the lives of innocent civilians in his efforts to stop bin Laden. It can't be helped.

And, Osama bin Laden believes that George Bush is evil. Bin Laden is willing to kill to stop the actions of Bush. He is willing to risk and expend the lives of innocent civilians to stop Bush. It can't be helped.

And, Timothy McVeigh believed that the U.S. government was evil. McVeigh was willing to kill to stop the actions of the government. He was willing to risk and expend the lives of innocent civilians to stop the government. McVeigh believed it couldn't be helped.

While the American public so myopically focuses on bin Laden and al-Qaeda, we have pushed from our consciousness our own homegrown version of the Taliban. They are called the Christian Identity movement. There are hundreds of thousands of them, right in this country.

We don't have to go halfway around the world looking for terrorists. We don't have to single out people with foreign-sounding names or wearing turbans on their heads. The terrorists are with us. The terrorists live within.

ENDING TERRORISM MEANS TRANSFORMING OUR BELIEFS

How we deal with terrorists depends on our beliefs about the usefulness of violence.

For example, at the height of the Vietnam War, the U.S. strategy was widely articulated as "bombing the North Vietnamese to the bargaining table." That was one way of looking at it. Another way to perceive it was that the bargaining table was inevitable, and the bombing campaigns just delayed the negotiations.

This difference in point of view is a fundamental issue. It is an issue of belief and perception. It doesn't really matter what we *see*; what matters is what we *believe* about what we see.

In Vietnam, it was clear that first there was bombing and then there was negotiating. How you put the two together (violence-as-necessary or violence-as-obstacle) describes your fundamental belief about the nature of violence. In the Vietnam example, if you believe in violence-as-necessary to resolve conflict, you will see the bombings as a prelude to peace. If you believe in violence-as-obstacle to peace, you will see the bombing of North Vietnam as an unnecessary waste of lives and time.

Using places like Northern Ireland, Israel, and Sri Lanka as examples, the world has more than one hundred years of experience in attempting to combat terrorism with violence. Has it worked? Does the world become a safer place when we fight violence with violence? Have we learned anything from this experience? Your answer will be determined solely by your beliefs about the usefulness of violence.

From the violence-as-necessary viewpoint, America's "war on terrorism" is right on course. We have significantly hurt al-Qaeda and will continue to do so.

From the violence-as-obstacle viewpoint, since September 11, America has done nothing that will reduce the threat of terrorism in the future, and everything to guarantee that terrorist attacks will expand and increase in the future. Yes, we have significantly hurt al-Qaeda—and that hurt will be the launchpad for the next waves of violence.

Do you think the current U.S. get-tough policy with terrorists will yield the results we want? Viewed from the perspective of one hundred years of experience, there is no evidence that a get-tough policy yields anything other than increased levels of violence. Getting tough yields toughness, not security.

Consider the following examples:

- Israel: Every time Israel gets tough with the Palestine Liberation Organization (PLO) and/or Hamas, Palestinian violence has increased. Every time.

- Sri Lanka: Every time the Sri Lankan government got tough with the Tamil Tigers, the rate of suicide bombings went up. Every time.

- Northern Ireland: Every time the British government got tough with the IRA, the rate of attacks went up. Every time.

The evidence is abundant that America's current get-tough policy will lead to an escalation of violence. But those who believe in violence-as-necessary won't see it.

We all know the analogy that you can't put out a fire by pouring gasoline on it. But, when we see a fire of terrorism, we start pouring the gasoline, hoping the fire will go out. We do this because we believe our only tool is gasoline and our only option is to pour it on the fire. We believe that the gasoline is actually water.

RUMORS OF PEACE

On the other hand, there have been instances of violence abating, of terrorist bombings declining or disappearing completely, of peace initiatives and activities increasing. What precedes these "outbreaks of peace"? Again, let's look at a few examples:

- Israel: Between Intifada One and the current Intifada Two, Israelis and Palestinians enjoyed a period of real freedom from violence. The reason: Both sides were talking instead of shooting.

- Sri Lanka: As of this writing, a robust cease-fire and unprecedented détente exists between the government and the Tamil Tigers, along with real freedom from violence. The reason: Both sides are talking instead of shooting.

- Northern Ireland: As of this writing, an unprecedented détente exists between the parties, along with a signed peace accord and real freedom from violence. The reason: Both sides are talking instead of shooting.

Talking has preceded every instance of decreased violence and increased peace. Every time. The British government talked to their "enemies," the IRA. The Israelis talked to their "enemies," the Palestinians. The Sri Lanka government talked with their "enemies," the Tamil Tigers.

No matter how much one hates "the enemy," the only way to peace is through dialogue. The only way. Violence is not a prerequisite to dialogue.

SEVEN STEPS TO A WORLD BEYOND TERROR

Neither side can win the war on terror. And, paradoxically, neither side can lose. More violence creates more killing, not resolution. The only way terrorism can end is by all sides talking to each other. Our security lies in building relationships, not prolonging animosities.

How do we build those relationships? How do we change consciousness—not just our own but the "other's"? What are the essential steps that will bring about an end to terrorism?

Below are the seven essential steps to a terror-free world:

1. Isolate the Perpetrators of Violence

We must make sure that the people who plan terrorist attacks are never, ever in a position to carry out their plans.

This means identifying and finding the real perpetrators and planners, apprehending them, and then trying them in competent courts with competent evidence. Perpetrators of state-sponsored terrorism must be removed from positions of power.

This does not mean creating witch-hunts or international lynch mobs. This does not mean declaring war on an unknown enemy. The response must not add to the problem.

2. Renounce Violence

The United States, directly and indirectly, supports violence throughout the world. Denying it won't make this truth go away. We seem unable to understand the anger of someone whose village was leveled by American cruise missiles, or whose family was killed by a U.S.-backed dictator. Believe me, they are angry, they feel powerless, and they blame us. Anger and powerlessness are the root of violence.

From the outset, we must rule out violence as a method of resolving our problems. Three of the twentieth century's most profound political/social shifts were led by people who, from the very beginning, renounced violence—Mahatma Gandhi, Martin Luther King Jr., and Vaclav Havel. Part of their power stemmed from the fact that violence was removed as an option for their struggle.

Asking the "other" to renounce violence means that we have to renounce violence—first. We must teach this to our children. We must renounce the use of violence as a means of achieving our personal goals and our domestic and foreign policies. This is actually easy, since there are no foreign nations that threaten the United States, now or in the foreseeable future. This is a perfect time to direct the resources of war and violence toward building a peaceful, secure, prosperous, and sustainable world.

3. Defuse the Next Wave

We must effectively defuse and demobilize any other suicide bombers and terrorists. Instead of an ineffective missile defense shield to defend us from nonexistent enemies, we need a terrorist defense shield.

The recent U.S. bombing in Afghanistan has aggravated the anger, frustration, and powerlessness that will fuel the next wave of terrorists. Instead of making bad matters worse, we must work in ways that will create less anger and more understanding and connection.

There is no way to stop determined, coordinated suicide bombers. No amount of technology, vigilance, or preparedness can prevent a terror attack. The only thing that can be done is to defuse the terrorists by taking away their cause. We must replace "a cause to die for" with "a reason to live for."

This is what happened to me. I was defused as an instrument of violence. There were people who, despite my anger, ugly words, and violent deeds, never gave up on me, never returned my hatred and violence in kind. These were people who ensured that I got the best education, people who exposed me to a world larger than my circle of pain. These friends and supporters saw the good behind the layer of anger, and always believed in my potential as a human being, not in my ideology born of suffering. Through their compassion, they turned me from being a vehicle of violence into an instrument of peace. They are the reason I can be an advocate for nonviolence and for a global society of the spirit.

4. Stop Creating the Monsters of the Future

The United States must end all practices, done in the name of the American people, that create, nurture, and support criminals, dictators, terrorists, and social monsters in the first place.

This means ending such shortsighted policies as those that funded or otherwise supported the Taliban, Osama bin Laden, Saddam Hussein, and many others, both domestically and internationally. In the recent Afghanistan war, the U.S. government has covertly funded a number of "liberation" groups, including the Northern Alliance. Until September 11, the U.S. government gave funds to the Taliban. Will we have to fight the Northern Alliance as "evil terrorists" ten years from now?

We can and should support all those who are in line with our deepest values and clearest principles. We should not support those who are not in line with those values, regardless of geopolitical expediency.

5. Learn How to Listen

Because the threat is human, our terrorist defense shield must be human also. The United States cannot rely on high-tech means to respond to low-tech threats. Once we penetrate the minds and hearts of the terrorists, we can then determine what it will take to deflect them from their chosen course and transform them from sociopaths to productive human beings, from enemies to friends.

This is much easier than it sounds. Suicide attackers feel driven to despair, precisely because they do not feel that they have been heard. So, the first step to defusing suicide attackers is to listen to what they are already saying.

How we listen is important. If we assume that they are crazy, evil fanatics, we cannot really hear what they are saying to us. In order to penetrate the mind of the terrorists, we have to be prepared to listen to them honestly, without preconception and without judgment.

6. Develop Citizen Wisdom

Knowledge is intelligence about things and events. Wisdom is intelligence about relationships. For example, knowledge is knowing how to make an atomic bomb; wisdom is knowing not to use it. In the United States, we mistakenly rely on the government to build and create relationships—relationships with other countries, relationships with our fellow citizens, sometimes even relationships with ourselves. We rely on commercial media (broadcast, print, and electronic) to express our relationships to each other. If the government, or the commercial media, doesn't recognize us, we feel unheard.

Citizen wisdom is the recognition that each of us is inextricably linked to all others. In our wisdom, we see that we are responsible for our relationships—not lawyers, not the media, not the government.

7. Catalyzing Leadership

It is increasingly obvious that the interests of people diverge from the interests of the governments that claim to represent them. We have all heard the saying "If the people lead, the leaders will follow." We must encourage the people to lead—locally, regionally, and globally.

We must create mechanisms and institutions where people can have meaningful and powerful dialogues. We must learn how to talk to the "other" before they become the "enemy." We must have powerful dialogues, more powerful than talk radio, opinion polls, and voting in predetermined beauty contests called elections. Dialogues of power will help encourage citizen involvement and will train the next wave of leaders. By talking to the people of the world (and the people of our neighborhood), we form bonds of community that can survive the stresses of our lives.

CONCLUSION

When I think back on my own life, I remember the words of the Christian hymn, "Amazing Grace":

> Amazing Grace!
> How sweet the sound
> That saved a wretch like me.
> I once was lost, but now am found,
> Was blind, but now I see.

It was the grace of God that saved me from the life of a terrorist. Blinded by my own pain, blinded by the violence being done to me, I believed that violence was the only possible response. Through the grace of God and the compassion of some special people, I now see a different world.

Is it possible for a terrorist to turn his or her life around? Is it possible for a terrorist to become an advocate of nonviolence and inclusivity? Is it possible for a terrorist to have a change of heart? Yes, if there are enough compassionate people in the world to catalyze that change of heart.

Violence, in all of its forms, cannot end by the consciousness that creates and maintains it. Violence will end only with a profound shift in consciousness. Our ultimate security lies in creating a world where no one gains from harming another. A world where there are no terrorist groups or terrorist governments. A world where violence is no longer a tool of domestic or foreign policy. A world no longer dominated by anger and violence. A world that works for all.

8

Understanding Suicidal Terror Through Humanistic and Existential Psychology

Nira Kfir

This chapter is written in memory of my patient Hanna, who was killed in a recent bomb attack on a bus in Tel Aviv. She was in her thirties, a mother of three. She had searched for identity and meaning all her life. Nothing seemed clear to her. That was how she lived; it was how she died.

No one claimed her. Her body could not be identified. The newspapers described her as an unknown person, perhaps a tourist. Due to a misunderstanding, her family thought she was away at a workshop. It was only after three days that they started to worry, and finally found her.

With her death, she obtained a definite identity. She was a terror victim.

Like you, Hanna, we all search.

INTRODUCTION

This chapter will discuss one psychological outlook on Islamic suicidal terror. There are three basic assumptions:

1. Suicidal terrorism is seen, from the viewpoints of such humanistic psychologists as Ernest Becker and Abraham Maslow, as heroism that mega-overcompensates for inferiority and as a search for fulfill-

ing peak experiences. Psychopathology is dismissed as a possible easy explanation for the behavior.

2. This heroism and sacrifice are aimed at a domestic audience. We suggest that although recent attacks have targeted Western countries, the real goal is the terrorists' own homeland, where groups of like-minded citizens are oppressed and bypassed. We will discuss the opinions of two Islamic thinkers: Fouad Ajami of Princeton University and Abdel Hamid El-Ansari of the University of Qatar.

3. The present wave of terror and destruction threatens to create chaos everywhere. We'll look at chaos through the eyes of Ilya Prigogine, the Nobel laureate for physics in 1977. He sees the rotation of order and chaos as an inevitable part of the universe. There have been chaotic upheavals in the past, but a new order has always prevailed before the chaos has ended in catastrophe.

In discussing the use of suicidal terrorism, we range from the individual living in an oppressive regime, struggling to achieve personal gratification, to a world that is indifferent to these struggles and prone by its very nature to cycles of order and chaos.

HUMANISTIC PSYCHOLOGY AND THE ELEVATED INDIVIDUAL

In his Pulitzer Prize-winning book *The Denial of Death*, Ernest Becker (1973)— one of the leading humanists—presents his ideas about the eternal despair of man. He believes that man is driven by two important forces: the prime motivator and the great anxiety.

Man has a God-like ambition, in an animal body, and man's potential for growth is endless. We know that we can invent and create, and refine our observations beyond imagination, but simultaneously we know that our fate is to die. We are aware of the great potential for change within us; nevertheless growth, in the end, is pointless. Great achievements and human enlightenment end and leave emptiness. To Becker, these two sensations—greatness and annihilation—compose the major struggle in life.

The sense of potential inspires a drive to excel, to actualize what we are, while anxiety about death, ever present although denied, inspires the illusion of eternalizing oneself. History has always encouraged heroism as a promise for eternal meaning.

Cosmic Specialness

Humanists express themselves in a grandiose manner, but also touch on sensations particular to individuals.

Cosmic specialness is an example of their grandiose terms. Becker relates it to the unique potential we each possess as our individual contribution. Failing to fulfill this potential prevents us from contributing, or even really belonging. Dissatisfaction and failure to actualize oneself is often related to a lack of the sense of fulfillment and cosmic specialness.

This gift of cosmic specialness is not part of average, normal development. One cannot rely on time to unveil this ability. It must be encouraged by others, or by life itself, even by pressure, crisis, or threat.

Whatever is special in us cannot be compared or measured, since it is unique. This holds true for individuals, and generally for cultures as well. Some cultures work to develop their potentials, others avoid even trying. Western civilization is rapidly changing its conventional systems of education in order to enable all children to learn and express themselves as individuals. From gifted children to those in special education, from music to physical education, all specialties are rated equally. Sports is as important as mathematics. Each is a potential gift.

The best example of this new focus is the attitude toward children with attention deficit disorder and attention deficit hyperactivity disorder. These hyperactive children, who cause endless turmoil in the classroom, are now recognized for their special abilities rather than their disability. Edward Hallowell and John Ratey (1994) open *Answers to Distraction* with a list of the great abilities that these children possess. Hallowell and Ratey teach us to discover better ways of restricting unruly behavior so that we can bring out these children's authentic ability.

Education presents a quiet revolution in the conventional hierarchy of underachieving and excellence. We now try to bring out a degree of excellence in every child.

At this time, however, these ideas are embraced only in parts of the world. When we discuss the Islamic countries later, we will touch on the inferiority of a great culture that cannot present any "cosmic specialness" because the individual has not yet been granted the right to his or her own happiness or self-actualization.

Becker claims that the other possible excellence is to express oneself through heroism. Heroism, for lack of any other choice, became the mode of excellence in today's Islam.

THE GOAL OF HEROISM

The sacrifice of oneself for a cause—any cause—is a type of paradox. On the one hand, we overcome the anxiety of death by controlling it; on the other hand, by dying in this way, we eternalize ourselves, thus "living" forever.

Heroism may be noble and altruistic, but as long as it carries within it the promise of an everlasting personal affirmation of our existence it can also be cruel and destructive. Every one of these themes can be seen in the recent Islamic suicidal attacks. It is almost as if, thirty years ago, Becker foresaw the current wave of terror.

Becker spoke about heroism as a value that represents man's capacity for devotion, for community, and for the impact that can only be achieved through the sacrifice of life. Real heroism is executing the deed and not having the satisfaction of seeing the goal achieved. The soldier who wins the battle will not survive to see the victory, as he dies in the process, believing in the promise.

Heroism can have various goals. The soldier is a hero who goes to war. But there are also everyday heroes. The instant hero, such as the fireman who saves a baby from a fire, is a problem-solving hero, who gets an immediate reward. In this category, we find the firemen and civilians who became heroes on September 11, 2001, or the one person out of fifty spectators who jumps into the water to save someone who is drowning. Even the man working on an assembly line to make a living for his family is a hero. Heroism stems from a need for survival, but when it becomes a way of life and a way of self-elevation, it starts to threaten the survival of others.

THE HEROISM OF SUICIDAL TERROR AND DESTRUCTION

Consider the sense of inferiority prevalent in the Islamic world today. Followers of Islam are both rich and poor, and make up one of the largest populations in the world. Culturally, Islam's accepted social code is hierarchic. Inferiority and superiority are clearly defined, but not by personal achievement. As long as such societies are closed, there is no danger to their social order. The social network enables satisfaction of personal significance, by religious devotion, obedience, and tribal values.

In the last decades of the twentieth century, however, the walls of their world fell. Millions of Muslims emigrated to the West and, although they still live within their own communities, the influence of a different way of life has become a real danger. Women and young people have lost their sense of purposeful obedience, and the result for them is simply oppression.

Inferiority, in its most cruel sense, hovers over the most important Islamic countries. Their way of life has not enabled them to contribute anything to the extraordinary progress of the past century. As the West has become more advanced—in ideas of democracy, freedom, civil rights, equality, communication, free information, and technology—Islamic countries' sense of danger and inferiority has grown.

In the midst of this amazing thrust forward in the West, Islam introduced the world to a new brand of fundamentalism. At the beginning of the twenty-first century, this step backward makes a mockery of all the great achievements of the present day.

Back to the burqa, the veil and mesh covering the eyes of women in a world of increasing gender equality. Back to an emphasis on prayer in a time of increasing self-reliance. Back to mullahs and ayatollahs in a time of free education and self-made men. The old way of life carries the promise of a new gospel—a superior way of life, of safety, and of reward in heaven.

Fundamentalism is the only cosmic specialness that Islam can offer. Extreme religion in this time is special in its spartanism, its demands on the devotees, and its parading of a new future. When it was at the point of losing significance in the world, Islam found a new significance in extremism. It gained meaning, in the sense that it cannot be overlooked any longer.

The modern world—the global village with television, Internet, easy travel, and international organizations—has made inroads in almost every country and group. Islam was bypassed. Brave Bedouin on horseback with scimitars in their hands remain the stuff of its movie screens. While Islam remained unchanged, the West developed democracy, civil rights, nationalized medicine, and the many other basic freedoms and privileges to which the young people of today are born. All this has one basic message—no one shall be inferior.

To be inferior as a group in this day and age can be devastating. The gap between the "winning" society and the "other" is growing in an irreversible way. This is where Islamic heroism emerges and teaches the world a lesson. It is not about destroying the West. It is not about converting the whole world to Islam. It is about impossible inferiority. It is about trading the most common and most precious commodity there is—life itself.

These people have nothing to trade in knowledge, technology, social ideas, or quality of life. But we are all equal in birth and death. Western superiority cannot be overtaken, so death is the great equalizer.

The heroism of these suicides is the equalizer: We cannot compete with you, but we can kill you. As existential philosopher Martin Buber said, one can die easily with the promise of everlasting impact. The young, intelligent, educated men who flew into the twin towers of the World Trade Center made exactly that—a quantum leap to equality.

In this way, destructive suicide is a dramatic heroism reminding us how equal we all are. Destructive heroism, as opposed to defensive heroism, touches on the fundamental need to live. Heroism is not a necessity in life, it is a choice. Defensive heroism stems from the need to survive, while destructive heroism elevates one from an inferior to a superior position.

Thirty years ago, Becker anticipated that the biggest change in contemporary life would be the decline of heroism. He observed that our modern life, with the individual's claim to "the right to the pursuit of happiness," is the beginning of life without heroism. The anti-hero becomes the hero.

But in the other half of the world, self-actualization is not the aim of life. Heroism is culturally ingrained as the way out of inferiority. This may be the conflict of our time, the conflict between one culture that reaches for the highest human potential and another that is left only with heroics.

THE HUMANISTS AND THE UNDERSTANDING OF THE HEROIC

After decades of theories of instincts, conditional behavior, and Skinnerian philosophy, the leaders of humanistic psychology used, in contrast, a rather poetic and prophetic terminology. At a time when empirical science and valid research findings were the only accepted "facts," they reminded us of possibilities and achievements that cannot be rated or empirically measured.

In the wake of the existentialists of the time (Jean-Paul Sartre, Martin Buber, Albert Camus, R. D. Laing, and Viktor Frankl), humanistic psychology related mainly to the higher and yet deeper cravings of men. These writers were wise enough to present general terms of experiencing that the layperson could understand.

While Becker's heroism was presented as a perpetual craving for meaning, Abraham Maslow (1964) presented its goal as other emotional rewards. A great humanist of the 1960s and 1970s, also known for his theories of self-actualization, Maslow introduced us to our "higher needs" by presenting his hierarchy of needs.

In *Religions, Values and Peak Experiences*, Maslow presented a new jargon. He wrote about enlightenment, in nonreligious, nonmystical terms. In this little book, he states that mental health draws from the ability to experience peaks. He reminds us that the word "enthusiasm" derives from the Greek, and means "the God in you." Thus, every peak experience is "religious" by definition. It may occur as a religious experience, but also as an experience in nature, love, sex, creativity, or simply in observing. A peak experience can occur in therapy, or in a single contact with a group or person. Life is inspired by these rare—but necessary—peak experiences.

IS SUICIDAL TERROR A PEAK EXPERIENCE?

The old world and the great religions understood the need for peak experiences and suggested rituals that provided these, such as prayer, meditation, devotion, fasts, pilgrimages, and so forth. One may question the relevance of these ideas to suicidal terror today. Nevertheless, we cannot avoid observing the heroic devotion of sacrificing one's life for a cause, the heroic recognition of a leader, and a peak experience that elevates an individual to the promise of heaven.

Islamic terror is inspired by religion. As Maslow says, religion may actually support evil. This occurs when heaven is too far away and progress in this life is too slow. Then the zealot may renounce this world and the lack of hope in it—and choose "heaven."

The existential philosophy of our time puts experience above understanding or legalism. A religious peak experience can become a model of illumination and instant conversion. The history of all religions is crowded with such stories. Being drawn to illumination, to experiencing a peak, to having a cause to die for—this often occurs when present life is too limited and meaningless. The process of preparation for a suicidal attack—the peak—is in itself a withdrawal from life and its legal structures.

Maslow believes that "religionizing" a cause in life involves secularizing all the rest. For the holy experience, new rules are valid: the isolating rules of religion as presented by the leader, guru, or ayatollah. The isolation of the individual from the rest of life results in prevention of all other natural peak experiences (such as love, nature, art, and so forth.). The only peak is religious.

A Palestinian terrorist captured on his way to blow himself up in the Natanya market was later interviewed on television. He appeared devastated that he was still alive. He was asked about his children and, with a frozen expression on his face, said he only regretted missing out on the "grand conversion" of life.

Suicidal terror reminds the world that heroism—even destructive heroism—is an equalizer. The basic drive of these people is overcoming the inferiority they feel at being bypassed by the ruling culture.

ISLAMIC SUICIDAL TERROR STRIKES GLOBALLY BUT AIMS LOCALLY

To begin understanding Arab countries as systems that produce suicide, consider a few theses pertaining to suicide and its provocation. Existential philosophies of the last century (as represented by Kierkegaard, Jaspers, Camus, Sartre, and Heidegger) saw the topic of suicide is the central problem of philosophy.

Suicide can be understood through theories of psychology, sociology, constitution, demography, global politics, and the supernatural.

In the earlier section, we presented altruistic suicide. To quote Emile Durkheim (1897), altruistic suicides are literally required by society. The rules and needs of the group demand suicide. This sort of demand can become a rule only in small societies or sub-societies. What Durkheim calls fatalistic suicide derives from excessive regulation. Both altruistic and fatalistic acts are expected from these small groups to create a social order and hierarchy of their own.

A Durkheim critic, Jack Douglas (1967), pointed out that the social meanings of suicide vary greatly. The more socially integrated a group is, the more it succeeds in disguising its demand for sacrifice. In small and persecuted sub-societies, the denial is open, direct, and not disguised.

Robert Litman (Peck, Farberour, & Litman, 1985) sheds light on the dynamics of small groups that demand sacrifices, by describing their feelings of abandonment, helplessness, and hopelessness.

The most important kind of suicide for everyone to comprehend is global suicide. It is not a new concern. In 1938, noted Harvard University psychologist Henry Murray stood at the dawning of the atomic age and termed it also the start of a "death haunted" time. Any danger that threatens people or groups—danger that will break their psychological connection, their sense of continuity and generativity—provokes fantasized immortality. Those fanatic, fantasized immortality suicides serve as a paradigm of global destruction.

ISLAMIC REGIMES AS CLOSED SYSTEMS

How are all the above theories validated in Islamic regimes?

I will first address the differences between open and closed systems.

I assume that terror on the part of individuals or small groups is directed psychologically to impress their own compatriots, in state and religion. It is activated outside their own countries, but it seeks recognition from their own governments. Small terror units, one may say, think locally and act globally.

Most of the Arab countries are trying to remain closed systems. Terror, as we'll see, rebels against its own system, but it gets out of the paradigm, to influence from the outside.

Consider the relevance of systems theory, founded by Bertalanffy (1973) in 1968. Any state is a system in itself, with interacting units that relate to each other. Any such system, therefore, has structure and function. A closed system has tight boundaries, and neither matter nor new energy nor new information can penetrate. Open systems allow a system within a system, multi-level systems, and access through which new information can penetrate. The arrival of new energy in a system encourages the process of change, which influences the structure and, with time, the function too.

Almost a century before Bertalanffy propounded this theory, Kierkegaard (Lowrie, 1962) proposed another possibility concerning systems. His thesis was that truth cannot be found in a system but rather in the human subject. He saw individuals as being superior to systems and argued that the freedom of the individual within the system was central. Kierkegaard's views posed a serious challenge to the view that rationalism was the only way to understand behavior.

How much freedom is allowed in a closed state? Islamic states are closed systems and terrorist groups create further closed systems within the Islamic states. These groups borrow from the state structure and function, but their goal is to dominate the mighty system, which is not allowed. Such a pattern has always been true of revolutionary groups, no matter in what ideological disguise, be it religion, communism, equality, or freedom.

THE ARAB PREDICAMENT

The belief that Muslim terror in the world is mainly aimed at its homeland can be clarified with a few points from Fouad Ajami's *The Arab Predicament*. Professor Ajami (2001) asks blatantly: What does this Islamic renaissance really represent? To what extent is this revival of fundamentalism an honest craving? And to what extent is it an ideological cover for a sense of inferiority toward the West, on which they find themselves totally dependent?

The Islamic world, in its present state, expresses its anxiety about inferiority via psychological tricks, pointing to its special nature and historic achievements. The more inferior and bypassed an Islamic state feels, the more it will demonstrate chauvinism and false pride. Much is made of the people's integrity. They revel in their stand against foreign temptations and influence.

Ajami identifies with the concept of freedom, which he describes as being foreign to Arab culture. The formal policy of traditional Arab states is to grant their citizens an observing role, while leaving the actual running of life in the hands of the leaders. Ajami claims that it does not matter to the disciples that their hero was a liar, an opportunist, a gambler, a brutal dictator, or a terrorist. The Arab soul will devote itself to turning the hero into a saint, immune to his crimes. This soul craves the heroic, to reverse political frustration, inferiority, and the inability to change. Ajami explains the urge to belong to a small fundamentalist active group as being the only way for young individuals to participate and practice freedom.

Far from Ajami, who is based at Princeton University, another Muslim intellectual and dean of the Faculty of Shariah Law and Islamic Studies at the University of Qatar, Abdel Hamid El-Ansari, said in a December 2001 speech at a symposium on American-Arab relations that the magic of heroes and heroism is built into the Arab soul. He cited as examples the charisma of Salah-A-Din, Gamal Abdel Nasser, and Saddam Hussein.

El-Ansari, like Ajami, understands the acting-out behavior of fundamentalist extremists not as a way to take over political power, but rather as a means to shatter the system. These two thinkers see psychological deprivation of meaning as the prime motivation for violence.

The Democratic Front for the Liberation of Palestine, led by Naif Hawatma, attributes the Palestinian defeat to the absence of a revolutionary theory. His argument is that before violence, anger, and fighting can win, one must be sure what one wants to achieve. Even self-sacrifice must have a superior motive. Thinkers in the Arab world had begun to question the goal long before September 11, 2001.

Such discussion must include an aside on the French anthropologist Claude Levi-Strauss. His analysis of Islam was that it is a great religion based not on any new truth, but rather on the *inability* to relate to the external world. Levi-Strauss argues that, unlike the friendly Buddhists, or Christians with their need for dialogue, Muslims cannot even tolerate the "other." Islam can only feel secure within its closed system and negation of others. Islam is the only religion, he claims, that preaches the destruction of other religions. This means that relations with non-Muslims create pressure. The provincial Islamic lifestyle can survive only as a closed system opposing other influences.

Thus, understanding the need to find an external enemy (Israel, America, globalization) may help us to focus closely not only on the extremist, but specifically on the suicidal terrorist.

A RUNNER WITHOUT A GOAL

Rebels have always fought for freedom, while Islamic extremists fight against freedom. Freedom at home, which is based on the penetration of Western ideals as well as Western commodities, is alarming to the Islamic way of life. The extremists cannot fight their own regimes that make alliances with international organizations that do not abide by Islamic law. Theirs is a rare case of a movement against a better quality of life.

Terrorists aim to tighten the gates of influence on women, on youth, and on the poor and illiterate. In this battle, the enemy is at home. Small *jihad* groups must create global chaos in order to gain power for their own closed Islamic system and way of life.

Prisons and torture have failed to stop the *jihad* movement over the years, as was proved in Egypt. These groups present themselves as the defenders of Islam, against regimes daring to open doors to foreign powers.

In this, Islamic terror is different from the French Revolution or the Russian Revolution. Those revolutions had an agenda for a new order, and they indeed went on to build a new order. Islam's revolution uses religion as a basis.

ORDER AND CHAOS IN HUMAN HISTORY

We can look at present-day disorder and the anxiety of millions of people on streets, in buses and airports, and even in the safety of their own homes, and translate this into an era of chaos slowly penetrating order. In normal times, our modern life functions like a machine with large systems serving individuals anonymously. These systems rely on order, in much the same way as road safety relies on drivers respecting the rules. In today's world, a small group or even a single individual can shatter a system and evoke chaos, by failing to respect these rules.

Since ideas are never totally new, but rather renewed or put together in another package, we may look for these two themes in earlier paradigms. Polarity is basic to all cultures. It is light and darkness, good and evil, Apollo and Dionysius, the sanguine and the phlegmatic, Freud's pleasure principle and death wish, Jung's anima and animo, war and peace. These two poles may rotate or even coexist in the world, and in each of us.

ORDER OUT OF CHAOS

The current danger of suicidal terror might be quantified through physics-based theories of order and chaos. Modern physics has revised old concepts of these two forces, coexisting or rotating throughout human history.

Existential philosophy sees human beings as ultimately responsible for their own fate. We take responsibility for the choice between goodness and destruction. Maslow, describing the characteristics of a peak experience, tells us that at this high moment we recognize evil as part of life and accept it.

Must we therefore accept evil in humans—chaos, mass murder, and possibly even the destruction of the planet itself—just because it exists? How do we recognize the wave of chaos for what it is? How do we minimize its impact, or even eliminate it, and move on to change?

In September 2001, the world was shattered by the awareness that a few people could heavily wound the West. But in other parts of the globe—the Middle and Far East—people have long experienced a similar anxiety.

Are we now at the beginning of the wave of chaos that cannot be stopped till it is exhausted?

Consider the theory of Ilya Prigogine, as described in a book he wrote with Isabelle Stengers, *Order Out of Chaos* (1984). He sees social systems acting in ways similar to modern physics. He describes the eruption of chaos in social systems by stating that, in nature and in human nature, certain aspects are in a state of continual change. If we divide societies into open systems (like the Western world of today) and closed systems (like the majority of Islamic states), we can assume that the open societies are tolerant of the ongoing flow of change described by Prigogine as an integral part of the system. But closed societies are alarmed by change, even if it is integral.

A closed society can be bound in by communism, religion, or dictators who use regime and religion as tools against change. In the Islamic world, a newly found *fatwa* in the Koran, based on a sentence long forgotten, has suddenly been highlighted as a revelation, inspiring millions of people. Old writings are disguised as change.

Islamic states such as Iran, Iraq, and Syria are closed systems that keep a tight grip on those small groups that oppose the regime. They imprison and execute instigators of change, whether that change looks to the future or to the past. The revolutions of the last two centuries—bringing equality, freedom, and fraternity, as well as the new "information revolution"—have been blocked by those closed societies. The age of information that is upon us now poses a great threat to a closed hierarchical system. In the fight against change, the worst enemy is new knowledge.

HOW DO SMALL GROUPS CREATE CHAOS?

As a physicist, Prigogine claims that there are nonlinear relationships in which small units can trigger massive consequences. Chaos occurs in a society when disorder, instability, and disequilibrium enter.

Small units are the agents of chaos. They have the potential to destroy, especially those states and societies that have been open enough to accept them. They include individuals who have chosen or been forced to leave their homelands, and have ended up in the caves of Afghanistan or the training camps of Lebanon.

ORDER AND CHAOS IN PERSONALITY

The danger to the Western world from Islamic terrorism also has parallels with psychological personality approaches addressing order and chaos. Freud named the inner chaos "id." This represents the instincts, passions, and animal needs. It uses Eros, and has a sort of drive that cannot be fought on its own ground by another passion. So the ego, which is cognitive, has a long-range goal and responsibilities and puts limits on the id. The super-ego contributes to the restraint of id forces by judgmental processes. Defense mechanisms and controls are recruited to keep the original id in its box. Freud recognized both this inner chaos and the inner need for order as fundamental to the personality. From Freud onward, personality theories and the understanding of behavior have always included these two dynamic forces—chaos and order.

Jean-Paul Sartre built his interpretation of human history around the concept of personal responsibility. "Response-ability" means that the person can potentially and actually produce a response to any new development. It implies that we are able to respond even to our own chaotic forces, forces with which we might not necessarily agree. Recognition of natural, inbuilt chaotic forces calls for restraint.

What can psychological personality theories teach us about the present global terror? Can psychology offer another possibility for dealing with these destructive id forces?

DEFENSE AND CONTAINMENT

The most likely reaction to a dramatic, dangerous invasion is using defense mechanisms:

1.   Denial (this is not a real danger)
2.   Repression (it is not directed at us)
3.   Rational solution (a few insane people cannot destroy us)

By definition, defense is a reaction that focuses on the attack and creates a response. Sophisticated societies build defenses against future attacks, as they can be anticipated or envisaged. The majority of people in a country that is in a defensive state do not need to take an active part in defending. Leaders try to contain, absorb, and draw strength from past victories, past resistance, and endurance.

Learning to contain and endure frustration is one of the basic characteristics of growing up. We teach parents to contain the anger of the child, so that with time the child will learn to contain himself or herself. Containing is a crucial element of interaction. This refers particularly to containing anger, impulsiveness, and demands. In the face of suicidal terror and prophecies of destruction, civilized society is behaving as a responsible parent should.

Western society contains the outburst of terror, with endurance, hoping that the chaos will burn itself out. At the same time, it holds on to order through civil institutions.

PARADOXICAL INTERVENTION

The U.S.-led invasion of Afghanistan in 2001 is the new order, with the courage to name countries like Iran and Iraq as part of a "Triad of Evil." This is unexpected. It is a paradoxical reaction. It is not another appeal to the United Nations.

Yet, is the invasion of Afghanistan an "ultra solution?" According to Watzlawick (Watzlawick, Weakland, & Fisch, 1974), the ultra solution not only solves the problem but also destroys everything around it. He says there are no ultra solutions.

So, paradoxical reaction is another possibility. The essence of paradoxical behavior is freedom, not being attached to former strategies, expectations, or anxiety. It takes courage and creativity. Paradoxical intervention may stop chaos, by creating more chaos, under control. The moral danger is that by taking steps such as invading Afghanistan we overrule our own rule.

CRISIS INTERVENTION

Consideration can also be given to my model of crisis intervention as it appears in *Crisis Intervention Verbatim* (Kfir, 1989). The Israeli Ministry of Defense accepted this model at the time of the Yom Kippur War in 1973. It was originally designed as a theoretical model for bereavement intervention at a time of national crisis. The basic rules, however, apply to any crisis situation, including terrorism and attempts to heal after terrorism.

First, let us define crisis. Attack or even destruction is not crisis. Crisis is defined as the actual or perceived collapse of a system. The system can be the self, the family, or the state. In crisis, it becomes nonfunctional. Even the possibility of collapse can create crisis.

Once one defines this process as critical, intervention may begin. Crisis reveals itself in courage or panic. Courage is the disintegration of conventional defense mechanisms and the realization of reality. Panic is the declaration of crisis and thus its creation.

The three phases of intervention are information, support, and new options.

Information

The ethos of our times does not affect all people in the same way. Knowing more morbid details can provoke paralyzing anxiety and yet calls for action. Many claim that a flood of information can, however, spread indifference. This may be correct, but if we are to act we cannot spare ourselves from recognizing reality. Information must instigate action. This is a first step out of crisis.

Support

Support in crisis is important, although not necessarily appreciated. Every person who has experienced crisis knows that one of the worst feelings is a sense of loneliness. It is always frustrating to family and friends when the person claims, "I am alone in this." We feel insulted. How can they say that when we are supporting them and living their crisis with them?

Loneliness and the sense of isolation accompany any situation of crisis. Members of the free world must support each other. The coalition spirit, the inclusiveness that brings together the most unlikely allies, is in itself an intervention. Like information, support is not a total answer, but it creates a new freedom to act— freedom by consensus.

New Options

New options are the creative parts of the intervention. "New" is not necessarily a panacea, a universal remedy that is suddenly discovered. When a person in crisis is guided toward a solution, this may not be a new idea as such, but it is a new option for the present moment. While waiting for an ultra-solution, the immediate options can be overlooked. Unlike therapy or even short-term therapy, crisis intervention is authoritative by nature. One intervenes when one feels another to be in crisis. Permission is not asked. What makes intervention possible is the temporary nature of the crisis. You intervene to help, and you retreat when the other can cope alone. Invading Afghanistan is an option for now, but not the beginning of the West taking over the world.

SUMMARY

This chapter has examined the theories of humanistic and existential psychology in an attempt to achieve a better understanding of suicidal terror.

Heroism, as a basic compensation for inferiority and as an old and disappearing ethos in the West is active and rising in Islamic countries.

Terror can be a peak experience, elevating the individual from meaninglessness to total involvement. I argue that what appears to be an attempt to destroy the West is, in reality, directed to and intended to overtake the terrorist's homeland.

Order and chaos coexist in a perpetual cycle. Now, we are experiencing a wave of chaos on the rise.

Psychology can help us to understand, and even to anticipate possible reactions. I have mentioned several modes of understanding and responding to this wave, but the paradoxical approach seems to be the most creative.

We are free to act, not just to react, because the free world is responsible, its systems are solid, and it does have a goal for the day after: more freedom, more responsibility, and more knowledge.

A Talmudic story presents the polarity of justice versus compassion as God's dilemma when creating the world. Finally God decided to mix them, a kind of rotation. Looking at his creation, he blessed it with the words "Halevai Sheyeamod" (Talmud, Midrash Raba), which means "Let it survive."

I cannot offer a better wish.

REFERENCES

Ajami, F. (2001). *The Arab predicament: Arab political thought and practice since 1967.* Cambridge, England: Cambridge University Press.

Becker, E. (1973). *The denial of death.* New York: Free Press.

Bertalanffy, L. von (1980). *General system theory: Foundations, development, application.* New York: Braziller. (Originally published in 1968)

Douglas, J. (1967). *The social meaning of suicide.* Princeton, NJ: Princeton University Press.

Durkheim, E. (1952). *Suicide: A study in sociology.* Glencoe, IL: Free Press. (Originally published in 1897)

Hallowell, E. M., & Ratey, J. J. (1994). *Answers to distraction.* New York: Pantheon Books.

Kfir, N. (1989). *Crisis intervention verbatim.* New York: Hemisphere.

Levi-Strauss, C. (1963). *Structural anthropology.* New York: Basic Books.

Lowrie, W. (1962). *Kierkegaard.* New York: Harper.

Maslow, A. H. (1964). *Religions, values, and peak-experiences.* New York: Bantam Books.

Murray, H. A. (1938). *Explorations in personality.* New York: Oxford University Press.

Peck, M. l., Farberow, N. C., & Litman, R. E. (Eds.) (1985). *Youth suicide.* New York: Springer.

Prigogine, I., & Stengers, I. (1984). *Order out of chaos: Man's new dialogue with nature.* New York: Bantam.

Watzlawick, P., Weakland, J., & Fisch, R. (1974). *Change.* New York: W. W. Norton.

9

Bioterrorism:
Separating Fact, Fiction, and Hysteria

William H. Reid

INTRODUCTION

Assault with biological and chemical agents occupies a very high priority in discussions about terrorism. Bioterrorism represents a substantial and worsening danger, possesses great potential for damage, and involves an insidiousness that creates special anxiety in even the nonaffected population. Some chemical-biological agents and strategies, such as the Aum Shinrikyo release of sarin (also called serin) nerve gas in a Tokyo subway during the late 1990s that killed twelve and injured thousands, are aimed directly at people. Others focus on sabotage of, for example, food and water supplies. All can be used to further the traditional terrorist goals of disruption, draining resources, deflecting purpose, attention, and profit.

Definition of Bioterrorism and Scope of This Chapter

Trying to understand or address terrorism without defining the type and form is a futile exercise. "Terrorism" has as many definitions as "stomach ache," and at least as many presentations, causes, treatments, and outcomes. For purposes of this chapter (and consistent with my definition elsewhere in this book), I will largely limit this discussion to the use of biologically active agents against groups, rather than against individuals (although particular events may have one physical victim).

"Biologically active" includes biological organisms (for example, bacteria, their spores, viruses, rickettsiae), nonliving biologically produced agents (such as botulinum toxin), and extraordinarily toxic chemical (such as Ricin and sarin) or radiological agents.

Unless otherwise noted, the principles considered will not allude to isolated incidents of violence spawned by delusion, paranoia, or simple antisocial behavior, but will instead refer to *patterns* of sudden violent or fear-inducing action against civilians, involving biological agents, that is not part of a military force in a declared war between nations. This definition omits the use of biological weapons against military targets in declared wars, and will avoid the pseudo-conundrum of so-called freedom fighters.

This chapter will focus on danger to communities and large populations. The application to smaller groups and isolated terrorist events will be mentioned, especially as they create fear and further some terrorist goals, but the reader should concentrate on "actual" danger and a realistic view of the biological hazard. From that, one can begin to predict, assess, and address the many other terrorist effects and damages discussed in this book (see below, and the chapter titled "Practicality and the Mental Disorder Perspective of Political Terrorism").

The chapter will not provide a detailed discussion of biological weapons, bioterrorist methods, or defenses against them. It will present principles, with examples, that should guide the reader to explore more detailed topics elsewhere in the literature.

The Purpose of Bioterrorism

Considering bioterrorism in the context of the terrorist's purpose helps one to understand some bioterrorist actions and how to prevent or prepare for them. In that regard, it is a mistake to picture terror-violence, especially transnational terrorism, as a way to overthrow stable governments or change the balance of international power. Professional terrorists, for whom terror-violence is a day-to-day campaign with carefully considered goals and objectives, rarely view their actions in such terms.

There are five often-overlapping purposes for almost all terrorist activity:

- Disruption of the target and its activities
- Deflection of the target's purpose
- Drain of the target's resources
- Bringing attention to the terrorist organization
- Profit for the terrorist organization

The usefulness of biologically active agents in reaching those goals is correlated with their likelihood of use. This means that the likelihood and patterns of bioterrorist activity are, for given target situations, different from those of other kinds of terror-violence. Put another way, one should not always expect bioterrorism to be used in the same situations, or for the same purposes, as, for example, hostage taking or bombings.

RISK VERSUS REALITY

It goes without saying that one's risk of death or serious injury from a bioterrorist event is very, very small. The relative risk of a biological assault versus something else is tiny, and the risk on any given day is minuscule. U.S. civilians, especially, are essentially certain to die from something else, even as they spend time and energy worrying about terrorism.

On the other hand, our minds know that many biologically active agents are extremely potent. Some are universally fatal. Most are virtually invisible. They can be transported fairly easily, and dispersal in small or contained areas is straightforward. The agents can penetrate homes, enter offices, and sneak into our bodies with relative impunity. Biological invasion and damage seem insidious, and many people flail about for ways to reduce perceived risk, and thus their anxiety.

Although the effect varies among different people, there is an enormous helplessness in confronting things one can't see, can't shoot at or physically fight off, and can't flee. When we are children, turning on the bedroom light drives away the bogeyman, but this new boogeyman is invisible, and creeps on a waft of air or hides in the heating vent or water pipe or mailbox. The image of death seeping under the door, permeating the air one breathes, dissolving mucous membranes, reproducing in one's body, and/or destroying vital organs is the stuff of nightmares. Anticipating the suffering or death of others, especially family members, is an added dread.

Perceived Danger

Much of this feeling of danger and dread is based in something other than actual risk, and much of what causes actual risk can be predicted, prevented, or contained. The boogeyman scenario relates to *perceived* danger. It may have little to do with the reality of biologically active substances. Nevertheless, perception of danger, whatever the source, increases terroristic potential. For many incidents, the greatest damage to the target stems from public perception.

Actual Risk

Bioterrorism may threaten death, or may focus on nonlethal disruption or group incapacitation (such as of combatants). Not all bioterrorism threatens immediate personal injury. Dispersed plant toxins, parasites, or tainted seed can wreak economic and social havoc without direct loss of life.

Direct Agent Damage

Inhalation anthrax, pneumonic plague, smallpox, and Ebola are examples of very dangerous infections with little effective treatment. Some, such as anthrax, are poorly transmitted from person to person; others, such as pneumonic plague, are highly contagious. Some other agents (such as the organism that causes epidemic typhus) are highly transmissible and often lethal without treatment, but they respond well to antimicrobial treatment.

Nonlethal agents are important as well, and may fit a terrorist's need to avoid offending constituent or supporting groups (see below). Brucellosis works primarily through its high infectivity, easy access, and dispersability to sabotage and disrupt the target population. Salmonella and staphylococcal enterotoxin B are cheap and easy to disperse in limited areas, and they create marked, if usually nonlethal, incapacitation for days or weeks.

Organisms and toxins may be chosen for a variety of reasons in addition to their lethality, including persistence and stability in the dispersal and resting medium (for example, water, soil, or food), availability and cost to the terrorist, availability of a particular dispersal medium (for example, untreated water supplies or closed environments such as subways or planes), and terroristic purpose (for example, to kill, incapacitate, disrupt, redirect resources, and/or frighten—with or without killing).

As a practical matter, most biological weapons do not destroy infrastructure. In combat situations (not the focus of this chapter, and ignoring ethics for the moment), once the chemical or biological attack has done its job of killing or incapacitating the enemy, and once the agent has dissipated or been neutralized, the structure and infrastructure of the target city or country can be easily occupied and used. If the agent is nonlethal, even civilians can be temporarily incapacitated and the target occupied with minimal loss of life (in contrast to the physical devastation of shelling or bombing, killing civilians, and rendering target cities useless and/or dangerous).

Broader Effects

We tend to personalize the concept of terrorism, to picture carnage or personal tragedy. Broader effects and costs, which are arguably far more important to entire populations and societies, should be considered, however. These effects include things like economic loss, disruption of work and productivity, and even small changes in daily life. Individual changes and behaviors that appear slight for each person may add up to billions of lost hours and dollars when large populations are affected. The overall social and psychological cost is an enormous multiple of countless individual inconveniences and anxieties (such as travel changes and delays, delays in mail delivery, new behaviors and mechanisms of vigilance, other small changes in daily physical and emotional life, and abridgments of privacy and freedom). The damage is anything but trivial, as shown in Figure 9.1.

FIGURE 9.1: VICTIM PYRAMID FOR SIGNIFICANT TERRORIST ACTS

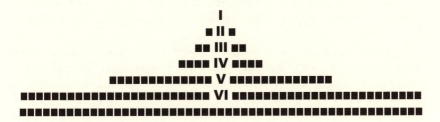

LEGEND:

I.   Persons physically attacked
II. Those with other direct loss (e.g., family)
III. Those with less acute loss (friends, rescue staff)
IV. Distant but particularly sensitive/vulnerable populations
V.   Those affected by lost commerce, decreased tourism, etc.
VI. Distant populations with minor concerns or behavioral changes

Individual Style and the Perception of Risk

Different people fear different things. Their choices and priorities of things to fear often have little to do with actual danger. This is particularly true of those whose impressions of reality are highly colored by unresolved external experience and/or internal conflict. Efforts to recognize and manage the public's emotional reactions to real or potential bioterrorism should take into account those who will view the risks maturely, those whose perceptions are skewed by psychological factors but amenable to correction, and those whose past experiences and internal conditions keep them from any semblance of accurate risk assessment and response.

Human Nature, Denial, and the Visibility of Risk

One way to manage risk is to deny it. Just as many people are overly sensitive to low levels of danger, others inappropriately remove it from their fields of vision. Denial does not, however, imply that they are unconcerned about the risk; just the opposite is the case. The risk so threatens the psyche (usually for internal reasons rather than because of actual danger) that it must be psychologically forced into submission. Thus those who seem not to be concerned at all may be as inaccurate in their view of actual risk as those who are paralyzed by it.

In spite of media overreporting and isolated group responses, at least one recent study suggests that most Americans overcame their new sense of national vulnerability to terrorism within a few months after the September 11, 2001, tragedies and the anthrax scares that followed (Glass & Schoch-Spana, 2002). The same paper suggests placing great faith in individual and community responses to terrorist threat, and recommends that government and military authorities trust individuals to be able to receive and process strategic information effectively, without exaggeration or panic.

Placing threat into proper perspective is important to recognizing actual danger and differentiating it from inaccurate perception, then managing all levels of that threat (direct and psychological) through prediction, prevention, interdiction, preparation, and damage management (see below). Denial of realistic danger, however, interferes with all of those basic principles. Denial by those in leadership and authority positions goes beyond individual failure to place whole communities and larger populations at risk.

The Media: Influence and Imbalance

The print and broadcast (and now Internet) media are significant sources of important information, misinformation, unnecessary public concern, and even terrorist support. Without addressing whether their statements are within our current vision of freedom of speech and the press, it is clear that the way print and broadcast news organizations choose, place, and present information is usually determined by their markets rather than by pure public interest. The media are uniquely positioned to bring accurate, important information to hundreds of millions of people very quickly. Public trust in the media, plus the media's talent for tapping into the public's wishes and fears, gives the media enormous influence over public perception and behavior. Exaggeration and misinformation are terrorist assets; the often-resulting public fear is a terrorist goal.

Public reaction to news coverage illustrates (but does not monopolize) the difference between relative risk and perceived risk. For example, the media were crucial in creating enormous, but scientifically unrealistic, public concern about silicone breast implants at huge and undeserved cost to industry as well as to the public. Media treatment of the risks associated with bioterrorism is similarly powerful, tapping primal and irrational fears, and often driven more by market forces than by interest in the public good. Small events with much less threat to society than, say, drunk driving or even lightning strikes are given attention far out of proportion to their threat, with interviews carefully calculated to "hook" the viewer/listener/reader with shock, fear, publicity-seeking interviewees, and the ever-useful interviewers' credo: "make 'em cry on camera."

It bears repeating: Exaggeration and misinformation are terrorist assets; public fear is a terrorist goal. Those who promote exaggeration and misinformation are working for the wrong side.

COMPONENTS OF THE BIOTERRORIST THREAT

The threat from chemical or biological weapons designed for mass destruction is substantial. Broad, accurate release of certain toxins or infectious agents would be devastating given our present state of knowledge and preparedness (even since the September 2001 attacks). Prevention of attacks *per se* is very difficult and rests largely on political/diplomatic, intelligence, and military factors rather than on medical or mental health expertise.

Fortunately, "successful" direct bioterrorism attacks on large populations (for example, entire cities) is not easy. Small groups lack the resources for a large-scale bioterrorist action. (The same Japanese cult that released sarin gas in a Tokyo subway had earlier attempted to release aerosolized botulinum toxin at several civilian and U.S. military sites in Japan, apparently failing because of mechanical and/or microbiological dispersant problems or "internal sabotage" [Arnon et al., 2001].) But small groups can fairly easily mount attacks on smaller, contained targets. Larger terrorist organizations that are supported by, or contract with, foreign governments or other well-funded sponsors often have access to highly sophisticated personnel and materials. Use of biological and biologically active materials by governments themselves, as weapons of war, is beyond the purview of this chapter, but such use is an enormous threat and, in some cases, already a reality. Stockpiles of dangerous bioactive agents, with local and ballistic delivery systems, exist in several countries, and evidence of some past deployment is unmistakable.

If individual effectiveness of the biologically active agent were all that is necessary for target devastation, bioterrorism by smaller groups (within the definition used in this chapter) would be an even greater threat, but agent-specific effectiveness is not the only component of terroristic potential, nor are specific acts the only consideration for damage prevention or reduction. Both the terrorist and the target victim must consider factors including availability, cost, handling safety, transportability, deliverability, ease and accuracy of dispersal, and suitability for the terrorist purpose.

Some biologically active agents, such as salmonella and enterotoxin B, are readily available to almost anyone and cost little. Others are very difficult to produce, obtain, "weaponize" (refine to a state in which they are useful weapons), and store. Anthrax spores, for example, are common in nature, but creating a broadly lethal combination of infectiousness and dispersability requires considerable technical skill. The smallpox virus was recently thought to be available in only two places in the world (a U.S. Centers for Disease Control and Prevention facility and the Russian "Vector" laboratory), and it is probably still very hard to obtain. For many agents, terrorists must either be sophisticated enough to produce their own or locate—and pay—a product source. This is not, however, an insurmountable task for larger and well-organized groups.

Once obtained, the material must be handled, stored, and transported to the target site. Substances that are highly infectious, contact-toxic, or radioactive require great care, and sometimes considerable technical skill and experience. The most dangerous and most frightening substances are extremely hazardous for the group to store and transport. "Suicide" assailants notwithstanding (see below), dead terrorists can't carry out their missions.

Transportability is nevertheless an advantage of potent biologically active weapons. The amount needed to create damage is often small, and discovery by defenders is not as straightforward as that for firearms, explosives, and large items. Concealment risk is thus relatively small.

Delivery and dispersal, on the other hand, are generally difficult, and become an even greater problem when targeting entire communities or populations. Choosing an effective dispersal point, breaching it, placing the material, releasing it properly, and accurately estimating broad dispersal usually require great skill, sophisticated information, and (often) blind luck. Although a mere gram of crystal botulinum toxin is enough to kill more than a million people if evenly distributed, getting it *into* a million people is almost impossible.

Airborne dispersal (for example, of dusts, spores, microdroplets, or gases) makes scary fodder for the movies, but is actually quite difficult and complex. After first refining the material into a form that will both disperse properly and be effective on victims, one then must develop a dispersal mechanism that spreads it. After that, there must be a way to get the material into the air.

Up to this point, one might think of crop-dusting technology and equipment, which has been well developed for spreading chemicals from the air. But crop dusting has a different kind of target, and takes place under different circumstances. The equipment is designed to spread relatively heavy droplets over a contained area. The point of crop dusting is for the material to sink quickly to the ground, not disperse widely. The "crop-duster" strategy for bioterrorist materials works for small areas, but it does not seem easily convertible for large populations.

One reason aerial dispersal is generally unsuitable for large populations is that distribution patterns are difficult to predict and even harder to control. Studies that try to predict maximally effective dispersal assume exactly the right particle weight and size, point of release, weather conditions, and wind speed and direction, then further assume that the target population is directly in the chosen dispersal path and that conditions remain consistent long enough for the material to reach the target. Under those conditions, and considering dilution effects (gases, especially, tend to reach dilutions measured in parts per quadrillion or less within a very short time), the potential damage from certain aerosolized substances is substantial; however, those ideal conditions, and the terrorist's ability to predict them and release the material at exactly the right place and time, are so rare that many analysts believe airborne dispersal toward large population areas of the United States is unlikely to be a direct-target initiative for ordinary terrorist groups (although it is feasible for ballistic [missile] delivery systems).

Strategists sometimes discuss the possibility of a living, perhaps human, vehicle for bioterrorism. Severe illnesses that are highly contagious, such as smallpox, would theoretically spread geometrically if "suicide" terrorists placed themselves in positions to transmit the disease to many others. The infectious agent would not have to be refined, contained, and dispersed; nature itself would do the work. There are a number of impediments to this scenario, such as the fact that many "ideal" diseases (including smallpox) do not become extremely contagious until the victim is quite sick and arguably unable to move about and infect many other people. Nevertheless, the prospect adds another frightening dimension to consider.

The bioterrorist assault must suit the terrorist's purpose(s) and priorities. Is number of immediate deaths the goal? Is lingering fear or realization of vulnerability more important to the terrorist group or its financing government than actual death and destruction? Is the action to be a demonstration of what might be accomplished in the future, or a "practice run"? Many terrorist activities are well funded by constituent (or contracting) governments or other very large organizations. Those groups may be able to finance complex biologically related programs; however, it seems to me that the majority of terrorist organizations working in this grisly field are relatively unstable, with transient goals and structures that are better served by short-term, relatively simple and inexpensive actions. Those that have the resources and opportunity to overcome issues of availability, cost, handling safety, transportability, deliverability, and ease and accuracy of dispersal discussed above are unlikely to be independently funded, even if one or two of the leaders is quite wealthy, and much more likely to be a tool of one or more national governments.

With the above paragraphs in mind, the relative feasibility, probability of success, and level of likely damage for bioterrorist assault can be evaluated and compared with other means of terrorism. Those in the "business" of terrorist activity understand this, and tend to plan their activities to take advantage of their available resources, skills, and opportunities. (Note that radicals and terrorists who are acting alone or are mentally unbalanced are less predictable and often plan less logically, making them a lower individual threat to target nations. Their collective damage may, however, be greater than that of an organized group, simply because there are more of them and their unpredictable attacks force broad social reactions and defenses [cf., abortion clinic bombers].) Weapon availability, target availability and proximity, constituent preference[1], and a number of other factors suggest that for most violent initiatives, explosives, firearms, sabotage, guided attack (such as missiles or car bombs), or personal assault (by combatants or "suicide" bombers, for example) accomplish more, at lower overall cost to the terrorist organization.

Local, and sometimes much broader, damage from biological threat (with little or no action) doesn't require such skill or financing, and can easily be generated through visibility, publicity, and/or hoaxes (see The Media: Influence and Imbalance, above). Hoaxes and simple mail or telephone threats, of course, are an inexpensive way to disrupt target activities and divert their resources. (Fake bombs and "anthrax letters" received by abortion clinics are good examples.)

WHAT DEFENSES DO WE HAVE?

Defense against specific bioterrorist actions involves five basic principles:

- Prediction
- Prevention
- Interdiction
- Preparation
- Damage management

Application of these principles, and their relative importance and effectiveness, varies with the situation.

Defense against the terrorist organizations themselves generally follows four broad guidelines:

- Target hardening
- Weakening or eliminating the terrorist
- Decreasing terrorist funding and sponsorship
- Making the terrorist goal too expensive to pursue

Target hardening includes predicting which targets are likely to be attacked, making them more difficult to reach or damage, and/or lowering their value to potential assailants.

Weakening or eliminating the terrorist is often difficult and expensive. In larger groups, eliminating one or more leaders may not stop terrorist behavior by the rest. (For example, "cutting off head of the viper," a commonly employed counterterrorist strategy, often fails due to the Hydra-like leadership of some established organizations, in which new leaders emerge quickly after old ones have fallen.) The "cell" structure of many organizations, in which small groups know little if anything about other cells, means the organization has few critical parts that are vulnerable to attack.

Decreasing terrorist funding and sponsorship is an effective large-scale approach for dealing with transnational terrorism. It includes interrupting cash flow and banking mechanisms, decreasing local and popular sponsorship (often through propaganda, education, and/or humanitarian aid), rewarding individuals and governments that engage in counterterrorism, and punishing those who support or shelter terrorists.

Making the terrorist goal too expensive to pursue is an effective strategy that may involve any of the above measures. It may also include increasing the chronic and incremental costs of operating the terrorist organization (for example, by interrupting funding, arresting members, causing sheltering countries to ostracize them, or artificially increasing the costs or otherwise decreasing the number of weapons and explosives). Western countries commonly purchase "black market" weapon systems at inflated prices, thus raising their cost and lowering their availability to terrorists and rogue nations.

ROLES FOR HEALTHCARE PROFESSIONALS AND SYSTEMS

The medical and mental health professions have roles in prevention, treatment, and damage amelioration of biological and chemical threats, often through military and other government resources. This book is not designed to discuss details of specific agents, transmission, infectivity, prodromal symptoms, treatment, and prognosis. One may, however, consult a number of reports in the emergency medicine, infectious disease, and disaster-preparedness literature (Benjamin, 2000; Carus, 1998; CDC Strategic Planning Workgroup, 2000; Fullerton & Ursano, 1990; Henderson, 1999; Kadivar & Adams, 1991; Leggiadro, 2000; Pellerin, 2000; Sharp et al., 1998; Wheelis, 2000). Psychological and psychiatric aspects of the bioterrorist threat, and roles for professionals, are featured less prominently but are also reviewed in the literature (DiGiovanni, 1999; Holloway, Norwood, Fullerton, Engel, & Ursano, 1997; and Reid & Stout, in press).

INDIVIDUAL PREPAREDNESS: HYSTERIA VERSUS COMMON SENSE

Gas Masks, Water Filters, Antibiotics, and Moving to the Country

Individuals naturally think about actions they can take to protect themselves and their families. For most people, such thoughts are little more than fantasies. In addition to law enforcement and simple vigilance, our primary protection comes from nationally and regionally coordinated defense.

Gas Masks and Sealants

Most consumer products for antibiological defense are virtually worthless. Military surplus gas masks based on filtration are not only ineffective for most biologically related agents, but are difficult to use without proper training. Most use surface-based media, such as activated charcoal, whose filtration ability is exhausted in a few hours (and sometimes, if not factory-sealed, even before they are purchased). In addition, airborne risk implies an unexpected, very sudden attack, for which one would have to avoid ambient air continuously to be safe. A few people have used certain masks, in what they apparently erroneously thought were contaminated settings, without removing factory-placed filter seals; they suffocated, perhaps dying even as they believed their shortness of breath was caused by some poisonous agent.

Some communications and pamphlets recommend sealing one's house against penetration by airborne agents. Sealing is designed for situations in which decreasing the amount of agent substantially dilutes risk. Unfortunately, the most dangerous airborne bioterrorist agents are of such high potency and infectivity that, in small spaces, a little is almost as dangerous as a lot. The level of sealing and filtration necessary to keep these agents out of ordinary homes and small offices, not to mention vehicles, is neither feasible nor safe.

Water Filters

Sales of home water purification systems reflect fears of waterborne toxins and pathogens. While some kinds of filters (notably reverse osmosis filters) and distillers are very effective in removing almost all harmful agents, their use and maintenance requires care. Small home units are fairly expensive, and while they can produce sufficient water for drinking and cooking, they do not address washing and bathing, both of which can cause significant exposure. Like airborne agents, waterborne toxins and microbes are likely to appear suddenly. Chronic, continuous filtration or distillation is impractical in most settings, and lack of need for months or years may make most people relax their vigilance.

Fortunately, central water treatment systems are effective for most externally introduced agents (barring sabotage). Private systems, such as small community water sources and individual wells, are unlikely to be affected unless an entire aquifer or water table is poisoned.

Stockpiles

The late-2001 series of small-scale anthrax episodes and hoaxes brought antimicrobial measures into the public eye. Since vaccination is impossible or not feasible for most agents, and since many agents are almost uniformly fatal, the focus is on post-exposure prevention. Large, chronic doses of certain antibiotics (notably ciprofloxacin [Cipro®], doxycycline, tetracycline, rifampin) are effective preventives for several dangerous bacterial and rickettsial agents (but certainly not for all biologically active substances).

In late 2001, physicians and consumers alike were asked not to stockpile supplies of those antibiotics. All were commonly available, but some (such as Cipro) were in danger of depletion if very large numbers of people were affected. Consumers could often obtain them (for example, on the Internet), but they (like many physicians) were not trained in diagnosis or recognition of the situations in which they might be useful. Some of the drugs can have severe adverse effects, and all have potential side effects.

Nevertheless, maintaining a supply of effective but relatively innocuous antibiotics (such as doxycycline and tetracycline), with instructions for emergency use if medical care is not available, is more logical than some other preparations. Such antibiotics are inexpensive, can be stored for months or years, may be effective for a few commonly anticipated bioterrorist events, and have few adverse effects.

Iodine supplements are an example of illogical stockpiling. Some time ago, it was noted that radiation poisoning targets the thyroid gland, and that iodine supplements may prevent resulting thyroid cancer. Some groups, encouraged by media coverage highlighting words like "cancer" and "children," now loudly demand that school districts stockpile supplies of iodine tablets against the possibility of nuclear sabotage or accident. The facts that iodine is not a proved preventive and that there are many other target organs (for which iodine is useless) do not seem to curtail their demands.

Changing Location

Are cities dangerous places, plump targets for terrorists and vulnerable to mass bioterrorist disaster? There is little question that changing location, although costly, can decrease one's risk of bioterrorist assault, and is something an individual can do without relying on government defenses; but there is little indication of a large-scale exodus from Manhattan, Houston, or Los Angeles. The balance may have tipped, however, for a few people already predisposed to moving to smaller communities or rural areas.

Government Information and Advice About Bioterrorism

Some pundits say the government "line" in this and other areas of risk is inaccurate or politically motivated, at the expense of the individual. "Official" information must seek compromise among accuracy and reassurance, individual advice and group interests, national interests and political expediency. The public, aided by the media, often notices apparent discrepancies in official statements (for example, "Everything is safe; go about life as usual" versus "We need an army of citizens alert for terrorist activity"). Generic measures do not always match individual needs and styles, and federal action often tends to be bulky and unfocused. Nevertheless, the government's resources and access to information about potential perpetrators, methods, vulnerabilities, and defenses are extremely valuable. The U.S. government, and our support of it, is our strongest defense against terrorism.

REFERENCES

Arnon, S. S., Schechter R., Inglesby, T. V., Henderson, D. A., Bartlett, J. G., Ascher, M. S., et al. (2001). Botulinum toxin as a biological weapon: Medical and public health management. *Journal of the American Medical Association, 285*, 1059–1070.

Benjamin, G. C. (2000). Chemical and biological terrorism: planning for the worst. *Physician Executive, 26*, 80–82.

Carus, W. S. (1998). Biological warfare threats in perspective. *Critical Reviews in Microbiology, 24*, 149–155.

CDC Strategic Planning Workgroup (2000). Biological and chemical terrorism: Strategic plan for preparedness and response. Recommendations of the CDC Strategic Planning Workgroup. *Morbidity and Mortality Weekly Report, 49*, 1–14.

DiGiovanni, C., Jr. (1999). Domestic terrorism with chemical or biological agents: Psychiatric aspects. *American Journal of Psychiatry, 156*, 1500–1505.

Fullerton, C. S., & Ursano, R. J. (1990). Behavioral and psychological responses to chemical and biological warfare. *Military Medicine, 155,* 54–59.

Glass, T. A., & Schoch-Spana, M. (2002). Bioterrorism and the people: How to vaccinate a city against panic. *Clinical Infectious Diseases, 34,* 217–223.

Henderson, D. A. (1999). The looming threat of bioterrorism. *Science, 283,* 1279–1282.

Holloway, H. C., Norwood, A. E., Fullerton, C. S., Engel, C. C., Jr., & Ursano, R. J. (1997). The threat of biological weapons: Prophylaxis and mitigation of psychological and social consequences. *Journal of the American Medical Association, 278,* 425–427.

Kadivar, H., & Adams, S. C. (1991). Treatment of chemical and biological warfare injuries: Insights derived from the 1984 Iraqi attack on Majnoon Island. *Military Medicine, 156,* 171–177.

Leggiadro, R. J. (2000). The threat of biological terrorism: A public health and infection control reality. *Infection Control and Hospital Epidemiology, 21,* 53–56.

Pellerin, C. (2000). The next target of bioterrorism: Your food. *Environmental Health Perspectives, 108,* A126–129.

Reid, W. H., & Stout, C. E. (in press). Terrorism and forensic psychiatry. In R. R. Rosner (Ed.), *Principles and Practice of Forensic Psychiatry.* New York: Chapman & Hall.

Sharp, T. W., Brennan, R. J., Keim, M., Williams, R. J., Eitzen, E., & Lillibridge, S. (1998). Medical preparedness for a terrorist incident involving chemical or biological agents during the 1996 Atlanta Olympic Games. *Annals of Emergency Medicine, 32,* 214–223.

Wheelis, M. (2000). Investigating disease outbreaks under a protocol to the Biological and Toxin Weapons Convention. *Emerging Infectious Diseases, 6,* 595–600.

NOTE

1. The ability of the terrorist group to retain approval by, support from, and/or credibility with those generally aligned with their cause or view (cf., so-called "Earth First" radicals who need at least some level of support and approval by nonviolent environmental activists, without which they would be further ostracized and the group would shrink in size and stature).

10 _____

Looking Beyond Terrorism: Transcending the Mind of Enmity

John E. Mack

CAUSATION AND UNDERSTANDING

It seems difficult in these heady times of action to seek beyond evil to its roots, much less to the sources of the very idea of evil in the way that human beings seem programmed to think. But seek we must; otherwise a world we have trouble understanding may, finally, explode around us, bringing us all down with the rubble of the twin towers.

The words of wise leaders have cautioned us about the need for a fundamental shift in thinking and perception. Czech President Vaclav Havel and Albert Einstein are two such figures. Havel, in his February 1990 address to the U.S. Congress, spoke of the "antiquated straitjacket of the bipolar view of the world," and stressed that "without a global revolution in the sphere of human consciousness, nothing will change for the better in the sphere of our being as humans." Einstein warned repeatedly that without a fundamental change in human thinking our species would drift toward ultimate catastrophe.

The search for the understanding, knowledge, and insight that such wisdom demands may seem "soft" in a time of radical patriotism, polarization, and simplification. But it may be that only a profound shift in how we perceive the world, in consciousness itself, can, in the end, create a secure and just civilization in which opportunity is available for all and no one is left out.

The distinguished political scientist Michael Walzer (2001) concluded his article "Excusing Terror: The Politics of Ideological Apology" with words that I look upon as a kind of backhanded invitation. "Maybe psychologists have something to say on behalf of understanding," Walzer wrote, "but the only political response to ideological fanatics and suicidal holy warriors is implacable opposition."

The article itself, as the title implies, sets up a row of explanatory straw men, distorted representations of efforts to understand the events of September 11, and then proceeds to mow them down as ideological "excuses." Walzer is far from unique in equating understanding with excusing; he just states this position more baldly. Even a thoughtful scholar like Boston University professor Hillel Levine (2001) can write, "Those who call for the 'examination of the underlying issues' at this moment attribute rationality, cause and effect, that lends legitimacy to the most horrific madness." Walzer's article is also useful as a starting place for these thoughts because of his dualistic thinking, the separation of politics from psychology. For "implacable opposition" may be Walzer's political stance of choice, but this in itself surely reflects a psychological position or point of view.

As a "psychologist"—in this context, I feel certain that a psychiatrist would qualify as one of those—I would like to take up Walzer's challenge to say something "on behalf of understanding" (not excusing or lending any legitimacy whatsoever to aggression), however dismissively his words are intended. The "psychology" that I am suggesting is linked to spirituality. It is more a psychology of transcendence and connection than of separation, pathology, or mechanism.

On the radio program "Me and Mario," former New York governor Mario Cuomo (2001) said, "This may get me into trouble" [indicating his awareness of how unpopular any effort to understand seemed to be in the jingoistic climate of that moment], "but the only way to solve the terrorist problem is to change the minds of those who practice terrorism." Cuomo is on the right track, I think, but it is not likely that the minds of the terrorists themselves will change, nor is it only terrorists whose thinking is problematic. The need to change "minds" must apply to all of us who would prefer to avoid trying to face the fact that terrorism does not arise in a vacuum, or from some inchoate reservoir of evil out of which particular bad people may spontaneously emerge at certain times in history.

The proper place to begin our effort to understand (not to excuse), it seems to me, is with the question of causation. For no matter how loathsome we may find the acts of "fanatics," without understanding what breeds them and drives them to do what they do in a particular time and place, we have little chance of preventing further such actions, let alone of "eradicating terrorism."

We can think of three levels of causation, each calling for solutions or responses appropriate to its own level. These might be called 1) immediate causes, in this case the purposive actions of men who are willing to die as they destroy other lives in the process; 2) proximate causes, the human pain and socioeconomic breeding ground of such desperate behavior; and 3) deeper causes, deriving from the nature of mind, of consciousness itself.

Immediate Causes

At the most immediate level, the cause of the recent events is obviously the actions of men governed by implacable hatred who are willing to sacrifice their own lives in the process of killing others, without regard for those they destroy. The natural, perhaps inevitable, response to such actions is to find out who did it, stop others like them, and punish their supporters. This involves gathering of intelligence and a military campaign. Military action may produce real successes, but focusing exclusively on this level of the problem, while ignoring or giving too little attention to the deeper levels, may result mainly in provoking still greater antagonism, spawning more terrorism, and, in the long run, bringing about a widening war, without doing anything about what gave rise to the hatred and aggression in the first place.

Proximate Causes

Listening to the pronouncements of President Bush and other American leaders in the weeks after the events of September 11, one could get the impression that the rage that leads to the planning and execution of terrorist acts arises from a kind of void, unconnected with history, without causation other than pure evil fueled by jealousy. Yet it is not difficult to discover that the present conflict has complex historical and economic roots. It has grown out of the affliction of countless millions of people in the Middle East and elsewhere who perceive themselves as victims of the policies of a superpower and its allies that have little concern for their lives, needs, or suffering, and of the actions of multinational corporations that, in the words of an Indian writer, "are taking over the air we breathe, the ground we stand on, the water we drink, the thoughts we think" (Roy, 2001). For these millions, a figure like Osama bin Laden, who we see only as the mass murderer that he is, can become a hero for moving beyond helplessness to action against the seemingly indifferent and invincible oppressor.

It is inconceivable that terrorism can be checked, much less eradicated, if these causes are not addressed. This would require at the very least a reexamination of U.S. government policies that one-sidedly favor Israel in relation to the Palestinians (not to mention U.S. support of Saddam Hussein against Iran, before he started a conflict a few years later that continues to take the lives of tens of thousands of innocent Iraqi men, women, and children). It would require further help with the growing refugee problem and a turning of our attention to the toll that poverty and disease are taking in the Middle East and other parts of the globe. These may not be the difficult conditions under which the terrorist leaders themselves have lived, but they create the reservoir of misery, hurt, helplessness, and rage from which the foot soldiers of terrorism can be recruited.

The role of the United States in creating these conditions can be debated. But there can be little doubt that, as a superpower that consumes a major portion of the earth's resources, we are not only seen in many parts of the world as responsible for these conditions; we are also looked to, along with other privileged Western nations, for much more help in their solution.

Certainly there is more that could be and has been said about what I call the proximate causes of terrorism, but the principle focus of this essay is different. I am concerned here with what might be thought of as more fundamental causes, the roots of terrorism that derive from mind, from consciousness itself, and from the institutions that express its purposes and intentions.

Deeper Causes

Worldviews

Political psychology, or the application of psychological understanding to political phenomena, should begin with a consideration of worldviews. A worldview is an organizing principle or philosophy, a fixed way of thinking or habit of mind. Worldviews are similar to ideologies, but broader in scope. Ideologies derive from worldviews, but are more specific, having to do usually with particular social, political, and economic systems. A worldview might be thought of as a kind of mental template into which we try to fit events. Without some sort of worldview, which can also be thought of as a lens through which to see the world, we would feel even more helpless, unable to orient ourselves in a world that has become increasingly complex and unsettling. Worldviews tend to be rather rigidly structured, and are able to withstand a huge amount of information that is difficult, if not impossible, to fit into them. When faced with data that might appear to challenge a worldview, or reveal it to be dysfunctional, most of us, most of the time, will construe a situation or reconstrue the facts rather than modify the worldview.

Dualistic Thinking

In relation to the events of September 11 and the terrorist threat that they represent, we have a chance to observe two largely contradictory worldviews. One might be thought of as the dualistic, dichotomizing, or polarizing habit of mind, Vaclav Havel's "bipolar view." The dualistic mind divides the world into conflicting polarities—good and evil, God and the Devil, for or against, friend and enemy, deserving or undeserving (this polarity is particularly important in providing the assumptive underpinning for perpetuating racial and socioeconomic differences). The dualistic mind fragments, seeing separation and difference more easily than unity and connection. The polarizing mind is not incapable of love, but that love is restricted in its application to one side, leaving the lover free to hate a designated enemy.

Dualistic thinking might be illustrated by the response of a former U.S. national security adviser to an acquaintance who had written to him after he had appeared on a television news program. She had suggested possible solutions to the terrorism problem beyond retaliative violence, and that the attacks had something to do with poverty and policies related to the Middle East. He replied that there are some people who "must be rooted out and killed," that he did not believe American support for Israel "has anything to do with the WTC attacks," nor that poverty "plays any role in the situation," since he had lived in Africa with very poor people who were kindhearted and not "barbarians." The main point here is not his disagreement with her proposals, but the linear, straitjacketed thinking that divides people categorically into good and evil ones, and that cannot see, or chooses not to see, the interconnections among various conditions and events.

The second worldview holds tightly to the ideal of universal love and oneness. This worldview has its own rigidities, and can be inappropriate when applied uncritically to a situation that defies its precepts.

But I will focus here on the first worldview. For it is expressions of dualistic thinking in the form of blindness to diversity, obliviousness to the effects of inequalities of resources, and a lack of concern for the vast suffering that prevails on this planet, that have given rise to the present dangerous crisis. The polarizing mind will always be with us; it is the mind of instinct and survival. But it is also the mind of revenge and war that must be transcended if we are to survive as a species. In the months following September 11, the proponents of dualistic thinking ("This is a war of good against the evildoers," or "We must destroy America, the great Satan") on both sides have had a lock on public discourse, as committed patriots have heaped scorn upon those who do not fall into line, while cheerleaders of terrorism exhort their followers to commit further acts of violence.

Augmenting Dualistic Thinking

Nationalism

Political and religious institutions have a powerful role in shaping and perpetuating dualistic thinking. Nationalism, the emotional attachment to the idea of one's own country or nation, is a particularly powerful augmenter of dualistic thinking. For the nation state has usually carved out its boundaries at the cost of other peoples' lives ("natives," "aboriginals"), and nationalistic supporters stay in denial of unsavory elements of the nation's history while glorifying the conquests that brought the country into being. As the eminent British historian Sir Isaiah Berlin (1979) wrote more than two decades ago, the values "of *my* group—for the nationalist, of *my* nation; these thoughts, feelings, this course of action, are good or right, and I shall achieve fulfillment or happiness by identifying myself with them . . ." (p. 346).

Although nationalists tend to resist looking at the harmful actions in their nation's history, they may nevertheless fear unconsciously that retribution for the crimes of the past lies just across the next border. Patriotism is the emotional partner of nationalism, brought forth most intensely when the country or nation is threatened. Patriotism tends to be dualistic, for it is usually mobilized by political leaders to counter a real or perceived threat. But it does not have to be so narrow. Patriotism can be wedded to generosity, courage, loyalty, and love of country, although it can also give way to extreme divisiveness, blindness to complexity, and hatred of the "other."

Religion

Religion, as theologian Paul Tillich and others have noted, deals with spiritual or ultimate human concerns, such as the source of life and death, our highest values and selves, the roots of evil, the existence of God, the nature of divinity and goodness, whether there is some sort of life after the body has died, the idea of the infinite and the eternal, defining the boundaries of reality itself, and the possibility of a human community governed by universal love. Religious assumptions (atheism and agnosticism are themselves forms of religious belief) shape our minds from childhood, and for this reason religious systems and institutions have had, and continue to have, extraordinary power to affect the course of human history. If anyone ever questioned this power, the present crisis should put such doubts to rest. On each side the faithful have been rallied by religious slogans and exhorted to destroy the evil enemy. The language of crusading and religious warfare is all about us.

There have been efforts recently to "let religion off the hook." Jesus, it is said, preached of love, and Islam opposes the killing of innocents. But it is not that simple. For as former Paulist priest James Carroll (2001) has written, dualistic language is readily found in religious texts. Messages of universal love and peace coexist in the Bible and the Koran with contrasting statements. "Our noblest impulses," he writes, "come inevitably intertwined with opposite inclinations." Messages of universal love or division and exclusion, of lasting peace or holy war can all be found in the Bible and the Koran. It is a matter of selection and interpretation. Religion and religious institutions can serve to polarize and stimulate violence, or to unite and transcend it. Religious leaders bear a huge responsibility in the present crisis, and can play a critical role in moving beyond it.

Religious historian Elaine Pagels (2001) has shown how, in the time of the emergence of Christianity from Judaism after the death of Jesus, factional rivalries contributed to the dualistic elements in both Christianity and Islam, which in many ways still reflect these rivalries. Written in the first century, the Synoptic Gospels were a kind of wartime literature, one of whose purposes was to protect the followers of Jesus from the fate he met at the hands of the Roman occupiers of Palestine. Militant Jews were warring against the Romans at the time. By blaming Jewish groups other than themselves for Jesus' death, his early followers hoped to be safe from similar persecution. Pagels has shown that, beginning with Mark, other (non-Christian) Jews were increasingly demonized; by the time the Gospel of John was written, the Roman procurator of Judea, Pontius Pilate (in reality a bloodthirsty administrator), had become a hapless fellow who tried to negotiate Jesus' release, while Jesus himself is quoted as calling Jewish groups "sons of Satan."

Pagels notes that the gospels that were suppressed by the creators of the New Testament, many of which were written by women (including Mary Magdalene), tended to be more universal in their message than the official ones. The gospels of John (official) and Thomas (suppressed) contain an argument about what "the good news" is really about. The Gospel of Thomas is a mystical text, and interprets Jesus in the language of the Jewish Cabala. Thomas sees all human beings as created by God in the image of light. Jesus comes from the light, but so do all people, although for some who do not recognize the light, all is darkness. In contrast, for John, who writes in a polemical tone, the people of Israel (the Jews) did not grasp the light until Jesus came shining out of the glory of God. Thomas says, "I am the one from the undivided," and preaches a universal message of community for the persecuted. John's message on the other hand is exclusivist (dualistic), asserting that Jesus taught that no one comes to the light except through him.

In this divisiveness and factionalism of the first century, politically motivated as it is now, we find the beginnings of the demonizing tendency of Christianity, which was carried further in Islam, and also, of course, the early development of anti-Semitism within Christianity.

WHAT IS TO BE DONE? COMING TO TERMS WITH THE DUALISTIC MIND

After the Bombers

I state the task before us with such blunt words because, at this turning point in history, probably nothing less than a radical reorientation of mind, an authentic mastery of the psychology of violence, can offer any hope for the human future on this planet. The accumulated hurts are so deep, the consequent rage so intense, the ignorance of the roots of these hurts and rage so prevailing, and the technological means of destruction so sophisticated and readily available that, as President Bush stated in his December 11, 2001, address to the Citadel (a military academy in South Carolina), a relatively few determined killers can now plan and execute projects of annihilation that can end life as we know it. There is no guarantee that a profound psychospiritual sea change, a transformation of mind and heart, can prevent this, at least in time. But I cannot see how anything short of this offers the possibility of survival for our species.

The bombers have had their say, because in a time of extreme pain and rage the mind of survival and retributive justice tends to overwhelm reason, insight, and other possibilities. But then, if and when the larger "war against terrorism" goes badly, or it becomes unavoidably clear that making "war" cannot end terrorism,[1] questions will and must be asked.

Then the voices that ask whether hatred and violence can be successfully met with more violence—the voices expressing viewpoints and offering analyses that until now have been ignored, condemned, and swept aside as unpatriotic, leftist, or excusing terrorism—will have their time. Then it may be possible to see that violence and hatred are not a monopoly of terrorists, but a property of mind and heart that we all share—perpetrators, retaliators, and bystanders (Staub, 1989). Then, as these questions are asked, we will turn our attention to constructive ways to respond to the afflictions that generate violence. When that happens, we will no longer dismiss or attack the wise people around us who look to understanding, knowledge of other peoples, justice, love, compassion, and the redressing of grievances and the healing of wounds as the only way out of the crisis that now confronts the human species.

Addressing the Proximate Causes

The transformation I write of here must start with attention to what I have called proximate causes. These include the unconscionable inequalities in the distribution of resources, the unmet material needs of much of the world's population, and the continuing political affliction of the weak by the strong who will, in their desperation, turn inevitably to terrorists and dictators, if not for justice and relief at least for an outlet for their rage and frustration. There are those better qualified than myself to address how these needs may be met. My focus is different. But it is hard to resist pausing to ask one or two burning questions. Each of us has his or her most powerful statistic of injustice. For me, the most compelling question is whether it is right for the United States to consume nearly a third of the world's resources when we compose only 4 percent of the world's population (Loy, 1999). And coupled with this concern, is it not at least embarrassing that, as we fight a "war" that grows, at least in part, out of these injustices, we are asked by our leaders not to sacrifice in service to humankind, but mainly to do more shopping so that the great maw of American consumerism (the "American way of life") can be filled?

Italian diplomat Roberto Toscano (2001), who has participated in international efforts to find a workable post-Taliban government in Afghanistan, argues that the terrorist leaders themselves may be so committed to their missions of violence that nothing can change their minds or chosen courses of action. But they can only succeed when they find groups of people who are susceptible to their recruitment and projects. If the minimal material needs of the populations of the earth can be met, Toscano maintains, terrorists become in effect isolated and defused, with no soldiers to command and no masses of people to support them.

The Relevance of Political Psychology

The quest for understanding that can lead us out of our present catastrophic morass begins with the recognition that knowledge of the ways of the mind in the arenas of political conflict is relevant and useful. Political psychology is a relatively new field, but one to which academic psychologists and social scientists are being increasingly drawn, as are diplomats and other political professionals (Hermann, 1986; also see the journal of the International Society of Political Psychology, *Political Psychology*).

The dualistic mind, the focus of these considerations, is not, by nature, self-reflective. Inasmuch as it attributes good to its own motives and actions, it will find the opposite of good in the other. Negative or aggressive ideas and feelings that are not consistent with this positive self-regard must be pushed away, or projected outward, and attributed to the enemy. A vulnerable and frightened public can be all too easily enrolled in this dangerous way of thinking. Psychologists, social scientists, spiritual leaders, political professionals, and government and other institutional leaders who understand this basic truth have a responsibility to do whatever they can in their speaking and writing to change the public conversation so that the role of one's own group in the creation of political conflict can be acknowledged and examined, and new possibilities brought forth to create a genuine global community.

Transcending the Dualistic Mind

Once we begin to look at the private aggressor or terrorist in ourselves, and at our contribution as a nation to creating the hostility of which we find ourselves to be the object, other kinds of knowing become possible. Then we can begin to look at how the mind deals with differences and is prone to the creation of enemies, especially when our very existence appears to be threatened. Then we can begin to look beyond mere tolerance to true knowing of the other. Only the mind that has recognized and integrated or transcended its primitive dualistic habits can begin to identify with the suffering and rage of geographically distant peoples. Only then can we see the aggression and ignorance that underlies our dominance and neglect, and perceive our own role in the creation of victims far from our own shores.

A transformation of human consciousness that has a global reach is not a new idea. Its possibility is inherent in the religions of the world. Great religious leaders have all possessed a vision of universal brotherhood and love. But this vision founders when the dualistic elements in religion come to predominate—as expressed in crusades, holy wars, and other kinds of extremism, or in blind literalism and fundamentalism, which occurs when unscrupulous men invoke the language of a particular religion and use it to justify their own violent purposes.

Emerging Possibilities and Opportunities

Even as we face unprecedented peril from the forces that divide us, possibilities are emerging in science, religion, psychology, and technology that may bring us back from destruction. Certainly the Internet and other information systems offer the possibility of worldwide interconnection, although these systems have yet to realize their potential for transcending duality and enmity. But, more fundamentally, we are now witnessing a coming together of science, psychology, and spirituality after centuries of ideological and disciplinary fragmentation. Modern physics and depth psychology are both revealing to us a universe in which mind is not separate from matter, the very notion of separation is a kind of illusion, and all that we can perceive around us is connected by resonances, both physical and nonphysical (non-local), that make the possibility of universal justice, truth, and love more than a utopian fantasy.

At the heart of this possibility lies what in the Western secular world is called "non ordinary" states of consciousness, but in the world's great religious traditions (Nasr, 1989, 1993; Smith, 1992) are variously called primary religious feeling, mystical oneness, connection with the ground of being (Huxley, 1970; Tarnas, 1991), or universal love. For a person in this state of consciousness, neglect of the needs of others, the toleration of great suffering, killing of innocents ("collateral damage"), the making of war itself, or the desecration of the earth's environment are virtually unthinkable. At the heart of these states of consciousness or being is a potential extension of the self beyond its usual boundaries. Thus, these states make possible the identification with other beings or objects, wherever they are located, and with the earth itself.

The Buddhist monk Thich Nhat Hanh calls this quality of conscious interconnectedness "interbeing." It is what two of his followers (Brussat & Brussat, 2001) had in mind when, after the events of September 11, they adapted his poem "Please Call Me by My True Names" to read "I am a loyal American who feels violated and vows to stand behind any military action it takes to wipe terrorists off the face of the earth," and "I am a boy in a faraway country rejoicing in the streets of my village because someone has hurt the hated Americans," and "I am a doctor in a hospital treating patients burned from head to toe who knows that these horrible images will remain in my mind forever," and "I am a stone in the graveyard of Trinity Church covered with soot from the buildings that once stood proudly above me, death meeting death." The sequence is long, taking in all beings, including the terrorists themselves.

Toward a Consciousness of Interconnectedness

It is no longer just Buddhist monks or other holy men and religious leaders who are undertaking the practices that create a consciousness of interconnection. A great shift in consciousness is in fact taking place, even as the threat of annihilation grows around us. In the United States and throughout the world there is occurring a vast and growing movement to return to ancient traditions, or to create new forms of psychospiritual practice that can bring about the extension of empathy and the possibilities of knowledge beyond ourselves of which Thich Nhat Hanh and his students write.

This is taking place in several ways, which include

- The revitalization of established religions, enabling them to be more relevant to the challenges of our time

- The recognition that strong intuitive powers, sometimes crudely called "psychic" abilities, are, at root, not psychopathological as they have sometimes been regarded in the mental health professions, but, if used appropriately, shortened avenues to transformation, understanding, and love

- The increasing commitment of millions of people to various forms of individual and group spiritual practice

- The proliferation of large and small group experiential modalities that open consciousness and break down the barriers to connection and love

- Increasing recognition of the power of extraordinary experiences (such as spontaneous spiritual epiphanies, unanticipated traumas that lead to personal transformation, near-death experiences and so-called extraterrestrial encounters) to shatter the boundaries of the ego, expand identity, and open us to empathy, love, and relationship

- The emergence of new sociopolitical forms and institutions (such as the nongovernmental organizations at the United Nations) and the emerging power of citizen diplomacy, which enable a wider range of professionals and ordinary citizens to take part in the processes and practices of international relations and relationships

The United States is in a particularly strong position to take a leadership role in this transformation of consciousness. We are a pluralistic society, with a long experience of living with diversity. The relative security that our privileged isolation has provided has given us the luxury of freedom, even though it has left us unprepared for such a terrible assault upon our nation as occurred in September 2001. Yet this very safety and freedom has allowed us to become strong and creative in developing a practical understanding of the human psyche (Erikson, 1987; Grof, 1988; Taylor, 1999). Although we are jittery in the face of our new vulnerability, especially as we seem to receive alternating messages to beware of new attacks, but to go on living as if all were normal. But as we have been pioneers in creating a new political form—a democracy that inspires the world in its discovery of the power that resides in diversity, and a unity that can transcend differences—we can also lead the world in developing the transformation of consciousness that can lead the human species away from the edge of disaster.

CONCLUSION

Humanity seems to be at a turning point. We are experiencing a kind of race to the future between the forces of destruction and creation. The preservation of our lives and possibilities will not come from the strategies of terrorists or the bombs of the righteous. This can happen only through a great awakening, a worldwide shift of consciousness that transcends the habits of dualism and separation and enables the citizens of the earth to become a genuine family of people and peoples-a family in which each of us comes to feel a responsibility for the welfare of all others. As Gandhi once said, "We must be the change."

REFERENCES

Berlin, I. (1979). Nationalism: Past neglect and present power. *Partisan Review, 46,* 337–358.

Brussat, F., & Brussat, M. A. (2001, September). Rest in peace.

Bush, G. W. (2001, December 11). U.S. President George W. Bush addresses the corps of cadets, The Citadel, McAlister Field House, Charleston, SC.

Carroll, J. (2001, October 9). Religion: Problem or solution? *Boston Globe*, p. A11.

Cuomo, M. (2001, October 21). *Me and Mario* (Radio broadcast). Albany, NY: National Productions, WAMC.

Erikson, E. (1969). *Gandhi's truth: On the origins of militant nonviolence*. New York: W. W. Norton.

Erikson, E. (1987). *A way of looking at things: Selected papers 1930 to 1980* (S. Sclein, Ed.). New York: W. W. Norton.

Grof, S. (1988). *The adventure of self-discovery: Dimensions of consciousness and new perspectives in psychotherapy and inner exploration*. New York: State University of New York Press.

Havel, V. (1990, February 22). Address of the president of the Czechoslovak Republic to a joint session of the United States Congress. *New York Times*, p. A14.

Hermann, M. G. (Ed.) (1986). *Political psychology*. San Francisco: Jossey-Bass.

Huxley, A. (1970). *The perennial philosophy*. New York: Harper & Row.

Levine, H. (2001, October). Personal communication.

Loy, Frank (1999, October 12). Six billion world citizens: Choosing our global future. State Department Forum, Washington, DC.

Nasr, S. H. (1989). *Knowledge and the sacred*. New York: State University of New York Press.

Nasr, S. H. (1993). *The need for a sacred science*. New York: State University of New York Press.

Pagels, E. (2001, October 14). The origin of Satan. Wellfleet Group Lecture Series, Wellfleet, MA.

Roy, A. (2001, September 29). The algebra of infinite justice. *Guardian*, Saturday Review section, pp. 2–3.

Smith, H. (1992). *Huston Smith: Essays on world religions* (M. D. Bryant, Ed.). New York: Paragon House.

Staub, I. (1989). *The roots of evil: The origins of genocide and other group violence*. Cambridge: Cambridge University Press.

Tarnas, R. (1991). *Passion of the Western mind*. New York: Ballantine.

Taylor, E. (1999). *Shadow culture: Psychology and spirituality in America*. Washington, DC: Counterpoint.

Toscano, R. (2001, October). Personal communication.

Walzer, M. (2001, October 22) Excusing terror. *The American Prospect, 12* (18).

NOTE

1. Indian writer Arundhati Roy (2001) observes that "it's absurd for the U.S. government to even toy with the notion that it can stamp out terrorism with more violence and oppression."

11

From Terror to Triumph: The Path to Resilience

Edith Henderson Grotberg

Terror paralyzes. Terror intimidates. Terror makes you lose your sense of safety and security. That is its intent. It wants you to be fearful, to withdraw, to submit, to give up your dreams, your hopes, your self-confidence, and your confidence in others. Terror wants you to suffer. It certainly does not want you to become resilient, because terror fears independence, initiative, trusting relationships, self-determination.

You may well respond to terror in all the intended ways. You have had little experience, except through the unending news about terror around the world, and the inexhaustible supply of films focused on terror. You are stunned that acts of terror can happen so close. You have no background to put the terror experienced in the United States on September 11, 2001, into any kind of perspective. And having perspective is important as you begin to take the path to resilience. Resilience is a human capacity that everyone can develop to face the inevitable adversities of life and to overcome them. You can become stronger as you deal with adversities and sometimes even be transformed by them, becoming a more caring, compassionate person.

If you want perspective, turn to older people, especially resilient older people. They are the ones who can tell you how they faced, overcame, were strengthened and even transformed by experiences of terror in America. They have perspective.

In the 1940s, after the bombing of Pearl Harbor, the fear of an invasion on the mainland was so intense that it created a sense of terror everywhere. And the early failures and losses Americans experienced in the war added to the fear.

In the 1950s there was intense fear of atomic bombs being dropped on the United States by Russia. Children practiced getting under their desks at the sound of an alarm, and families were urged to dig bomb shelters in their yards, or someplace safe. Also during the 1950s, the fear of polio created an atmosphere of terror across the country.

And the 1950s saw Sputnik, a phenomenon that terrified America and began a race for similar achievements and protections.

In 1963, the fear of missiles coming from Cuba put America in a state of terror requiring drastic preventive actions on the part of the American government.

In the 1980s and 1990s, mail bombs were the source of terror, as were bombings of American embassies in different parts of the world.

In 1993, the first bombing of the World Trade Center, quickly seen as a terrorist attack, sent fear throughout the nation. In 1995, the Oklahoma City bombing, at first thought to be a foreign terrorist attack, revealed that Americans also were capable of heinous crimes. Again, fear took over.

From the perspective of resilient older people, you learn that fear is important to keep you on the alert, to encourage you to take whatever steps you can to protect yourself, your loved ones, and, in some cases, your country. Fear triggers the flow of energy you need to take the necessary steps—to do a lot of thinking about what is going on, and what more you should be doing. Anger is good, too. It is the emotion that tells you something needs to be changed, and also gets the energy flowing in the resolve to make those changes.

What resilient older people can also tell you is that while fear is good for generating energy, continuing in a state of fear will get you nowhere. It will accomplish what the terrorists intended. You are paralyzed. You will do nothing. You will submit. You are an easy victim. On to the next victim!

The perspective of older people is acquired through years of experiencing events that generated reactions of intense fear and uncertainty. They learned that they would get through each one, would learn from each event, and be stronger as a result. They know that looking for and expecting guarantees of safety is futile. No one can guarantee that an engine won't fall off an airplane, as happened in New York just two months after the tragedy of the World Trade Center. No one expected that disaster either. Life involves risk. What is more risky than driving your car every morning to join the rush hour traffic, or trying to cross a street where cars notoriously ignore stop signs and red lights? Minimize risk, yes. Totally eliminate it, no.

Does perspective diminish the tragedy we are experiencing, the loss of loved ones, the uncertainty of the future? Absolutely not! The losses are permanent. The sadness is continuous. The physical and mental damage takes its toll. But dealing with loss, sadness, and damage is the role of resilience. Resilience provides the tools and the behaviors to deal with these tragedies, these losses. It can enrich life by bringing new insight, new understanding, and new commitments to life. Transformation is the greatest result of resilience, and it inevitably involves having more empathy and compassion—not pity—for others. It results in actions to help others. Life has meaning again. One gains a deeper sense of fulfillment and comfort.

WHAT DO WE KNOW ABOUT RESILIENCE?

It took time for the concept of resilience to be accepted as important in dealing with adversities. As a matter of fact, the word, as it relates to human behavior, is new to many languages. Spanish, for example, used the phrase, *la lucha contra la adversidad* (the fight against adversity) for many years before adopting *resiliencia* as the accepted word.

A major reason for this delay was the limits of our thinking. The dominant conceptual framework for studying human behavior was the medical model, a deficit, disease model, requiring studies of diagnosis and treatment. This important medical model led to attempts to diagnose "behavioral diseases" and find effective treatments. The public health model, an epidemiological model, was one variation of the medical model, counting the number of instances of a particular illness, and then supporting programs to reduce the unacceptable numbers, a kind of inoculation model. The epidemiological model, like the medical model, was applied to behavior problems. How many cases of drug-related problems? How many incidents of violence? How many teenage pregnancies? How many cases of abuse and abandonment? Have they reached epidemic numbers? The numbers determined public policy for funding of research, program, and service development, to bring the numbers down and stop the epidemic. The Centers for Disease Control keeps track of the numbers, but recently recognized that more was needed.

In 1999, the Centers added the words "and Prevention" to its title. The purpose was to bring attention and support to efforts that prevent a condition or dangerous and unacceptable behavior from happening in the first place, with the implicit interest in promoting behaviors that enhance life. The new emphasis included the promotion of resilience.

Another important shift in thinking came from redefining the ecological model of human behavior. The ecological model examines individual behavior within the context of the family and the community. However, it, too, had been used within a deficit model. The shift in thinking raised new questions: What can the community do to help families and children deal with adversities? What can the family do to help children deal with adversity? What can the individual do to deal with adversity? What are the separate and interrelated roles each plays in the promotion of resilience? The redefined ecological model provides the theoretical setting for promoting resilience in individuals, families, and communities. How we think about resilience continues to grow as new findings emerge and as new perspectives are considered (Grotberg, 2001a).

Most of the research in the 1970s used the deficit model in studying children and families. The environment of the family was believed to be the dominant influence in the development and behavior of the children. Thus, if the family was dysfunctional, impacted by mental health problems, abuse, drugs, and poverty, the assumption was that the children would be negatively affected, even adopting some of the undesired behaviors. The pioneer researchers of what became known as resilience, were, in fact, studying the impact on children living in dysfunctional families. Norman Garmezy (1974), Emily Werner (1982), and Michael Rutter

(1979), all were examining how children were negatively affected by the family environment.

The findings were unanticipated, even shocking. About one-third of the children were doing very well. They were happy, had friends, were doing OK in school, and were looking forward to the future. This was not only inconsistent with expectations, but forced a reexamination of their hypothesis. What was going on that prevented these children from being negatively influenced by the home environment? Had the family been misdiagnosed? Were the data incorrect?

To the credit of these researchers, they began to identify what differentiated these healthy, happy children from their siblings who, indeed, were negatively affected by the dysfunctional families. They found that these healthy, happy children reached out to neighbors, relatives, teachers, or other adults, to find help. These adults became mentors and role models for the children. The children were likable, happy to help others, and optimistic and confident that their lives would be good. They could express their thoughts and feelings, manage their own behavior, and solve problems they faced. In short, the researchers identified what are accepted today as the resilience factors. How the resilience factors were promoted, and in what dynamic interaction they were used, was not yet addressed. But identifying the factors provided the basis for future research on resilience. Grotberg (1995) organized the factors generally agreed on by the field into three categories: I HAVE, I AM, I CAN.

I HAVE are the external supports provided:

- Trusting and loving relationships within and outside the family
- Structure and rules at home and in the school (stable environment)
- Role models of behavior
- Encouragement to be independent
- Access to health, education, welfare, and social and security services

I AM are the inner strengths that are developed:

- Likable, with an appealing temperament
- Empathetic, feeling compassion for others
- Respectful of self and others
- Autonomous and responsible
- Optimistic, having faith and hope

I CAN are the interpersonal and problem-solving skills that are acquired:

- Share thoughts and feelings, and communicate
- Solve problems in school and in life
- Gauge the temperament of others
- Manage feelings and impulses
- Reach out for help

(Humor and creativity are often referred to, but have not been included in the research.)

Some studies included average and above-average intelligence and socioeconomic status as resilience factors (Masten & Coatsworth, 1998), but other studies found that resilience behavior did not rely on intelligence or socioeconomic status (Grotberg, 2000; Grotberg, 2001b; Vaillant & Davis, 2000).

THE INTERNATIONAL RESILIENCE RESEARCH PROJECT

The International Resilience Research Project (IRRP) (Grotberg, 2000) began in 1993 and continues. The IRRP conducted research in twenty-two countries at twenty-seven sites around the world, and asked two questions: How do children become resilient? What is the role of culture in the promotion of resilience? As a result of further data analysis and related research relevant to the current focus on terror, two more questions could be addressed: What is the role of the family in promoting resilience? What is the role of the community in promoting resilience?

The findings, briefly, are these:

- About one-third of the people studied are promoting resilience.
- The promotion of resilience is tied to the growth and development of each person (his or her life-trajectory).
- Resilience involves a process of behavior.
- Children are able to promote their own resilience by about the age of nine.
- Socioeconomic status and intelligence are not critical to becoming resilient.
- Boys and girls are equally resilient but with different ways of dealing with adversities.
- Cultural differences exist, but do not prevent the promotion of resilience.

These findings are addressed and integrated as they relate to the overall goal of promoting resilience. Culture plays the initial role in the promotion of resilience, and so cultural differences are examined first, to determine the impact of these differences on the promotion of resilience in children.

The Role of Culture

Culture is introduced as part of child rearing, and cultural differences are apparent from the beginning of a child's life. The differences, however, do not prevent the promotion of resilience; rather, they reflect the values of a culture that shape the styles of child rearing, as well as the promotion of resilience. The following eight differences have been noted.

1. *Pushing the rate of development versus letting it progress naturally.* The speed with which development can be advanced is important in some cultures. This push for faster development is particularly common with regard to girls. Often, they are toilet trained early, taught to become dexterous in handling food and household utensils, and trained to look after siblings. The girls are needed by their mothers to help around the house. Their brothers are not so burdened and have more time for their own pace of development.

2. *Democratic versus authoritarian family.* In an authoritarian family, children have little to say about decisions directly affecting them, and the same is usually true for their mothers. This lack of democracy is usually countered by a great concern on the part of their parents for the safety and well-being of their children.

3. *Dependence versus independence.* Probably the most notable cultural difference in families is the degree to which family members are dependent on or independent of other members. At what point can children make their own decisions? When can a family member decide on his or her own to take a certain job, or go to a certain place, or solve a problem independently? Often, girls were found to be kept dependent longer than boys, except for household chores and responsibilities.

4. *Strict versus permissive.* Setting limits for what a child can or cannot do and where a child can or cannot go varies among cultures. Sometimes, limits are set only when it appears a child will injure himself or herself, or someone else. When strict limits of behavior are set, they provide security for children but they also rob them of an opportunity to explore new places and activities. When there are no limits—permissiveness is the rule—a child who is adventurous does not know when to stop and is very likely to get into dangerous situations. On the other hand, a shy child can be so intimidated by freedom that he or she may well go off into a corner and stay alone. These extremes appeared repeatedly in the international study. Clearly, resilience is not independent of the personality and temperament of the child.

5. *Gender differences.* Cultures differ in the role of the father in the family. Major cultural differences include the amount of time spent with the children, what kinds of activities they engage in, the degree of risk they encourage their children to take, and the differential treatment of the sons and daughters.

   An important gender difference that cuts across cultures, however, involves the different ways men and women, boys and girls, deal with adversities. Girls and women tend to use empathy, faith, interpersonal relationships, and family supports to deal with adversities.

Boys and men tend to be more pragmatic. They size up the adversity, make some decisions about consequences of specific actions they might take, and then act. They may or may not involve others. Violence is more acceptable to boys and men in resolving problems than to girls and women. The most basic difference between the genders may well be that girls and women cherish life while boys and men challenge death. Prepubescent boys in some cultures are taught to fight and kill, joining the military part of the society.

6. *Cooperative versus competitive.* Cultures differ in whether they tend to emphasize cooperation or competition. In other words, does the individual who is competitive, wanting to do better than someone else, violate the cultural norm of the society? A number of countries attribute their lack of creativity to the need to be part of the group and not do things independently. Their children are discouraged from acts of competition.

7. *Physical versus verbal punishment.* Discipline styles differ from culture to culture, with both physical and verbal punishments practiced. Disobeying a parent or lying to a parent (the worst offense in many cultures) often brings physical punishment. Other cultures place more emphasis on discipline through conversation (that is, helping the child understand limits of behavior). When discipline is severe, the child tends to be fearful of bodily harm, and may well become submissive or resort to lying. When discipline is verbal, there is the opportunity to talk about what happened, why it happened, and what needs to be done to make things right again. Fear is not involved, so the child can learn how to be responsible without unnecessary anxiety. Fear, as terrorists clearly know, is a powerful weapon to control people, but little growth occurs for the individual or group so controlled.

8. *Free versus utilitarian use of time.* There are cultural differences in how parents view their children's use of time. Some cultures stress the importance of play and freedom of action for their children, while others stress the importance of time being directed to "useful" activities, such as family chores or learning something related to future jobs and responsibilities. Children in the latter case are seen more as apprentices than free spirits, and they miss out on exploring their environment and enjoying the fantasy and creativity that go along with that freedom.

These cultural differences in child rearing do not prevent the promotion of resilience. About one-third of the people in each culture were promoting resilience in their children, and engaging in resilience behavior in their families. Resilience was not compromised; instead, different resilience factors were emphasized and used in dealing with adversities.

Resilience and the Life-Trajectory

Another major IRRP finding was the relationship between a person's stage of development on the life-trajectory and what resilience factors can be expected to develop at each stage. The major developmental stages are trust, autonomy, initiative, industry, identity, intimacy, generativity, and integrity (Erikson, 1985). It is important to recognize the stage of development an individual has reached in order to determine what can be expected, and what cannot, in terms of dealing with adversities. For example, young children cannot be expected to deal with such adversities as terrorist bombings. Young children do not have the ability to manage or even label their emotions. They do not have the ability to analyze the intent of the perpetrators, other than to know that the perpetrators want to harm them. They do not know what to do and they often regress to an earlier stage of development. They rely on adults, particularly their parents, to help them deal with extreme situations of adversity. Parents are especially important in helping children deal with extreme situations of adversity, and in helping them become more resilient as a result (Baruch, Stutman, & Grotberg, 1995).

THE BUILDING BLOCKS OF RESILIENCE

The developmental stages of life are, indeed, the building blocks of resilience (Grotberg, 1999a). One developmental stage leads to another, while resilience factors are being built, consistent with each stage. However, there are often gaps that prevent children, youth, and adults from completing a stage of development and, concomitantly, from becoming resilient. The first five building blocks are the ones most critical to the promotion of resilience.

1. *Trust.* Trust is defined as believing in and relying on another person or thing, and believing in and relying on oneself. The trust we develop in our lives begins at birth. As babies, we had no choice but to trust others to love us, feed us, comfort us, and protect us. Our very survival was at stake. Then we began to trust ourselves to work out a rhythm of feeding, calming, and managing our bodies. This trust was tied to special people to whom we felt emotionally attached. We loved them; we were bonded with them. And, as we grew up, we learned to trust others—not necessarily to love them, but to have good feelings about them. We learned to trust ourselves—our ability to do things, have friends, and develop a career or a hobby. We even learned to trust the world. All of this trust was not blind—it was an informed trust, a selective trust.

    People who do not trust others may develop certain ways of dealing with the world. Three rather common methods are the following:

- Control others. If you feel you cannot trust anyone to be loving or helpful, you may have come to see everyone as dangerous and potentially hostile. You may feel that to keep them
  from harming you, you need to control them. If you can
  control them, they cannot harm you, and trust, then, is irrelevant.

- Withdraw from human interaction. The reason for this reaction is to feel safer and less threatened by a world that cannot
  be trusted. You may have become self-reliant and avoided
  getting involved emotionally, rejecting efforts of others to
  develop any meaningful relationship with you.

- Become dependent. If you feel that you cannot trust yourself
  to achieve, then you may try to protect yourself from what
  you see as inevitable failure. You may let others do things for
  you. You may allow yourself to be manipulated because you
  feel certain that others are better than you are, know more,
  and are the most likely to protect you.

Trust is needed to promote related resilience factors. When a
child trusts a parent or other adult, the child is more willing to
accept limits of behavior, and imitate role models (I HAVE); be likable, empathic and caring, optimistic and hopeful (I AM); and
increasingly be able to express thoughts and feelings, solve problems, and reach out for help (I CAN).

2. *Autonomy.* Autonomy is defined as independence and freedom—
    the ability to make your own decisions. Your autonomy began to
    develop when you were about two years old, and it is critical
    throughout your life. You first began to be autonomous when you
    recognized that you were separate from those around you and that
    you had some power over others. Saying "No!" was perhaps your
    first use of power. This autonomy brought a sense of independence
    and freedom, but it also brought new responsibilities, especially for
    your own behavior. You began to develop some idea of right and
    wrong, and to feel a sense of guilt if you did something considered
    wrong, like harming someone, or breaking something. You made
    many mistakes as you tried to become more independent. And the
    way adults around you—especially your parents—reacted to your
    mistakes determined how autonomous and independent you would
    become.

    Autonomy is needed to promote related resilience factors. As a
    child becomes autonomous, accepting limits of behavior is rein-
    forced (I HAVE); respect for oneself and others is promoted, empa-
    thy and caring are reinforced, and responsibility for one's own
    behavior is promoted (I AM); and managing feelings and impulses

is promoted (I CAN).

To promote resilience in children around the first two building blocks, it is effective to use a dynamic interaction of resilience factors such as these:

- Balance freedom to explore with safe supports
- Offer explanations and reconciliation along with rules and discipline
- Give the child comfort and encouragement in stressful situations
- Provide a stable environment for the very young child, but some novelty for the two- and three-year-old—new experiences, people, places and changes in routine
- Change and modify the mix of freedom and safety, explanations and discipline, help and independence, etc., as the child's reactions suggest.

3. *Initiative.* Initiative is the ability and willingness to take action. Your initiative began to develop around the ages of four and five, when you started to think and do things on your own. At this age, you may have started all kinds of projects or activities that you did not or could not finish. But whether you succeeded was not important. It was the willingness to try that was important to building initiative. Creative ideas in art and science, new inventions, and problem solving in every area of life require initiative. When you face adversity in your life, you are in a stronger position to deal with it if you are able to take the initiative for finding creative responses.

Sometimes things interfere with the development of initiative. If you were stopped or criticized too many times when you started a project or activity, you felt guilty for bothering people or bad for making a mess of things. If you experienced too much rejection from those you wanted to help, you felt unworthy. Eventually, you stopped wanting or trying to take the initiative in anything. Initiative is needed to promote related resilience factors. When initiative is developed in children, it reinforces trusting relationships, recognizing limits of behavior, and accepting encouragement to be autonomous (I HAVE); it reinforces empathy, caring, responsibility, optimism (I AM); and it contributes further to expressing thoughts and feelings, solving problems, managing feelings and behavior, and reaching out for help (I CAN).

To promote resilience in children, it is useful to draw on different resilience factors, using them in dynamic interaction. Here are some suggestions:

- Balance providing help with encouraging independence
- Offer explanations and reconciliation along with rules and discipline
- Accept errors and failures while providing guidance toward improvement
- Give the child comfort and encouragement in stressful situations
- Encourage and model flexibility in selecting different resilience factors as an adverse situation changes (for example, seek help instead of continuing alone in a very difficult situation; show empathy instead of continuing with anger or fear; share feelings with a friend instead of continuing to suffer alone)

4. *Industry.* Industry is defined as working diligently at a task. Most people develop industry during their school years, and the process may well be continuous throughout life. During the school years, your attention is focused on mastering skills, both academic and social. These skills are critical to promoting your resilience so that you have the tools to deal more effectively with experiences of adversity. It is also during the years of this developmental stage that you become able to promote your own resilience. By the age of nine, many children can promote their own resilience at the same rate as their parents; however, they reach out for help more frequently. But, if you were unable to succeed in mastering academic and social skills, you may have felt inferior and become extremely sensitive about your limitations.

5. *Identity.* The fifth building block of resilience, identity, corresponds to development during the teen years. The major questions usually on your mind at this age are:

- Who am I?
- How do I compare to other teens?
- What are my new relationships with my parents (and other authority figures)?
- What have I accomplished?
- Where do I go from here?

When you answer these questions to your satisfaction, you show skills in monitoring your own behavior, comparing your behavior with accepted standards, being helpful and supportive of others, using your fantasy to make dreams come true, and recognizing the role of idealism in thinking and planning. If you are not able to do these things, you may become self-doubting and unsure of who you really are. You may feel that no one understands you, including yourself. You may be totally confused about how to behave and about your role in life. These insecurities can lead to feelings of inferiority, frustration, and anger.

The following strategies work to promote resilience in older children during the development of industry and identity:

- Balance autonomy with available, but not imposed, help
- Modulate consequences for mistakes with love and empathy so that the person can fail without feeling too much stress or fear of loss of approval and love
- Communicate about and negotiate some limits to growing independence; discuss new expectations and new challenges
- Encourage the person to accept responsibility for consequences of his or her behavior, while communicating confidence and optimism about the desired outcome
- Encourage and model flexibility in selecting different resilience factors as an adverse situation changes (for example, seek help instead of continuing alone in a very difficult situation, show empathy instead of continuing with anger and fear, share feelings with a friend instead of continuing to suffer alone)

RESILIENCE IS A PROCESS OF BEHAVIOR

Another important finding from the research is that engaging in resilience behavior involves a process. The first step in the process is to identify the problem, the adversity. Often a person or group is not certain what the adversity is and there is need to clarify what is causing the problem, the risk, the adversity. The more threatening the adversity, the more difficult it is to assess it and react effectively. The second step is to determine who will be affected or who is already affected. The third step is to identify the obstacles that will need to be overcome to deal with the adversity. The fourth step is to determine who can provide help. And the fifth step is to identify the inner strengths people have and the interpersonal and problem-solving skills they have to deal with the adversity. The process takes some time, some thinking, and making changes in resilience factors used as the situation changes. People who are already resilient tend to go through this process almost intuitively and act quickly when adversity strikes.

It is important to select an appropriate level and kind of response. For children, a limited exposure to the adversity will build resilience behavior, whereas a total exposure may be overpowering or traumatic. Another kind of response is a planned one, which assumes there is time to plan for dealing with the adversity. This approach would apply in the case of planned surgery, moving, divorce, changing school, and so forth. Still another kind of response is a practiced one, which involves talking out or acting out what will be done. This approach might be used in the case of a fire drill, or a meeting with someone who has authority to make decisions affecting the person or group, or when practicing how to deal with problems such as bullying. Finally, an immediate response requires immediate reactions. This would be the case in an explosion, an accident, or an attack by terrorists.

All the resilience factors should be promoted and practiced by the end of the first five developmental stages. There are more stages, including intimacy (the need to develop sexual identity and intimate relationships); generativity (the need to provide leadership and model behavior); and integrity (the need to demonstrate values and ethics). However, the first five stages are when the resilience factors are developing and resilience behavior is practiced. Later stages strengthen the factors for increasingly mature, caring behavior in more complex situations of adversity. Practice doesn't make perfect, but it certainly helps in knowing how to respond to adversities. If you have been there, done that, you are more confident and probably more effective.

TERRORISTS AND RESILIENCE

There is no reason to believe that terrorists would countenance resilience in the people they need to keep in a state of fear and vulnerability. The very building blocks of resilience challenge their power. Trust, the first building block, is most at risk. Terrorists cannot trust the people they are terrorizing. They cannot expect to receive trust from the terrorized. This impasse creates a climate of fear and hatred on both sides.

This lack of trust forces the terrorists to be in a constant state of alert, adding law after law to assure their own safety. You drive at night from the airport to your place of residence and are stopped ten times by armed patrols who check your identification papers, ask where you are going, and decide if they will let you continue to the next armed patrol. Constant vigilance is needed if you don't trust the people you are oppressing, are "governing." The oppressed, in turn, do not trust their oppressors. Distrust, even hatred, become dominant emotions. Whatever trust children develop is restricted to the family, perhaps the extended family.

Terrorists have reason to fear autonomy in the people they are oppressing. They do not want independence of thought and behavior. The oppressors will dictate what can and cannot be done, will provide the rules and punishments. Terrorists must control the people they do not trust. So autonomy, that second building block of resilience and human development, must be restricted, even crushed.

No one takes the initiative in a terrorist state. There is no room for original ideas; they might threaten the oppressors. So that third building block of resilience, initiative, is not promoted for the benefit of society.

Industry is more easily accepted, provided the terrorists control what is learned, what jobs and tasks are acceptable, and who can learn what. So, industry, that fourth building block of resilience and human development, is permitted within predetermined boundaries.

But identity is also likely to be a threat. To have a strong sense of self, to identify with anything other than the agenda of the oppressors, is to invite retaliation, even death. So the fifth building block of resilience and human development is hostage to the limits set by the oppressors, the terrorists. The punishments are severe, even fatal.

THE RESILIENT FAMILY AND COMMUNITY

The emphasis of this chapter has been on the individual. That is because it is the individual who must learn to draw on I HAVE factors of resilience increasingly over the years; it is the individual who must develop the inner strengths from the I AM factors; it is the individual who must master skills to interact with people and to solve problems and adversities of life, the I CAN resilience factors. It is the individual who must learn how to draw on these factors, use them in dynamic interaction for resilience behavior to deal with the adversities. This emphasis on the individual, however, does not imply that the individual is alone and must become resilient independent of the family or of the community. Clearly the family and the community are essential parts of an individual becoming resilient.

The Family

The family provides the setting, both physical and emotional, for resilience to be developed. Trust is not only the first building block of resilience, it is also the first factor of resilience. And that trust begins in the family. The intimacy of the family allows free expression of thoughts and emotions, with little fear of damaging consequences. It is the laboratory of life, where actions can take place, ideas can be tested, and behaviors can be experimented with. The family is the place where socialization occurs at an intimate level. There is freedom to say and do things that cannot be said or done outside the family. There is the opportunity to test social behavior with siblings and parents without the risk of social isolation. There is opportunity to experiment with such different behaviors as how and when to compete and when to cooperate. A member may be teased or ridiculed, but usually remains a valued member of the family. The family is, of course, the predominant place where culture is learned.

Role modeling is probably the most important factor in promoting resilience in children. What family members do, what they say, and how they prepare for or respond to adversities are models of behavior that influence the promotion of resilience in the children. The most powerful example of the impact of role modeling on children came from a study in Peru conducted by Giselle Silva (1999). Her study, using the resilience paradigm I HAVE, I AM, I CAN, examined the role of parents in helping their children deal with the effects of political violence, and the role of resilience in that effort. She examined the reaction of parents to the trauma, and the impact of parents as role models on the resilience of their children. Many parents became poor as they escaped the violence, moving from the countryside and the mountains to the city and lower lands. They were required to make a new life in the new setting and raise their children there. Two major reactions to the trauma distinguished families who were modeling and promoting resilience in their children from those who were not.

Some of the families focused their attention on the trauma of the violence and the necessary escape to a new environment. The focus of these families was on the violent events the family had experienced; the orientation was toward the past; close relationships in the family were negatively affected; the social relationships were affected by lack of confidence and feelings of fear and isolation; there was no adaptation to the new setting, with fantasies about returning to the former home; and deep feelings of nostalgia were experienced, with a major focus on memories.

Most children of these families did not become resilient, and, in fact, many developed severe social and psychological problems, adopting many of their parents' behaviors. In addition, the children showed lack of confidence in others, changed in negative ways their relationships with their parents, experienced frequent feelings of sorrow over the losses from the violence, frequently engaged in games repeating the trauma, and had difficulty in communicating with others.

In contrast, other families focused their attention on the new environment, sought out opportunities in the new setting (jobs, education, friends), refused to allow the trauma to affect family relationships, focused on the here and now and the future, were receptive to new relationships with neighbors, adapted and adjusted to the new setting, and remembered sad experiences of the past but used them to encourage progress. These parents were role models of resilience for their children.

The children of these families were optimistic about the future made plans for the future, attended school for the first time, learned Spanish for the first time, helped out in the family during vacations, and talked through their experiences of violence. They sometimes showed fear and uncertainty, but they could recover. These were resilient children.

The Community

The community is in the I HAVE part of the resilience paradigm. People expect the community to protect them from harm. This involves police and fire departments and emergency services. Further, the community is expected to provide social services, health services, and education opportunities. In many countries, however, these services and protections are not available and people turn to their families and neighbors for such help. The IRRP study found fewer external supports than needed in many countries, but also found that substitutes were usually available.

The community provides for the promotion of the inner strengths in the I AM part of the resilience paradigm, especially through the church. There are few communities in the world without a church, mosque, synagogue, or other form of religious center to promote the inner strengths of people—primarily faith, hope, and confidence. The moral aspects of living are stressed in all religions.

Schools play a critical role in the promotion of the interpersonal and problem-solving skills in the I CAN part of the resilience paradigm. Teachers, administrators, and related personnel not only provide the settings for acquiring knowledge and skills of learning and performing; they also provide settings for social development. Social skills are learned and the broader social setting of the schools provides opportunities to acquire and practice them. The way you behave, the way you talk, and the way you approach people are all acquired skills. The home may be so informal that an outsider would feel uncomfortable. Some educators may feel that students should be left to socialize on their own terms as they see fit. The result, too often, is children who suffer from a lack of social skills and who have difficulty using such skills to deal with adversities. This is a particularly troubling problem for minority groups, especially immigrant groups, who face bullying, isolation, rejection, and discrimination by other children in the schools. Educators often feel they do not have the time or facilities to deal with these problems and the problems are too frequently ignored. The neglected children cannot look to the school to promote resilience, unless they find a teacher or other students to help them.

The major study of resilient communities was done by Nestor Suarez-Ojeda (2001), a former official at the Pan American Health Organization (PAHO), in Washington, D.C., a participant in the IRRP, and now head of the International Center of Information and the Study of Resilience (CIER) in Argentina. As a result of analyzing communities that recovered quickly from disaster and those that did not, he learned what differentiated them.

Four major factors characterize resilient communities:

1. *Collective self-esteem.* The community is proud of itself in terms of cleanliness, provision of services, and caring for its citizens. It also cares about how it looks, what cultural experiences it provides, and what it is noted for.

2. *Cultural identity.* The members of the community identify themselves with the community even through changes. New companies may move in, new schools are built, new families appear, but the sense of cultural identity remains strong and can integrate the new companies and people, adding new benefits, ideas, and even problems.

3. *Social humor.* The community does not take itself too seriously and is able to engage in jokes to show its ability to recognize the humor in their lives. One community, for example, was competitive with

another community, and both of them were hiding their limitations. So, a man in one community said, "Let's just keep up with them; don't try to pass them, because they might see the holes in our pants!"

4. *Collective honesty.* The community demands that all of its institutions be honest. This goal often means cleaning out corruption and voting for people who have integrity and who will not tolerate dishonesty, nepotism, or other behaviors that damage a community.

Suarez-Ojeda described nonresilient communities he studied as having these qualities:

1. *Lack of cultural identity.* Many people do not identify with their community; rather they continue to identify with the community they came from or with some concept of a foreign community. This distancing oneself or one's family from the community weakens the community, and can be especially dangerous when adversities strike.

2. *Fatalism.* When people believe they can do nothing about what happens to them, that all is predetermined, they become passive and are easy targets for those who wish to dominate and control. This leaves no room for resilience, and submission takes its place.

3. *Authoritarianism.* When there is a vacuum of cultural identity combined with fatalism, it is inevitable that authoritarian governments will take over. These communities are easy pickings—there will be no resistance. There will be no resilience.

4. *Corruption.* When no one cares about the community; when one's sense of identity exists elsewhere, or when there is passive acceptance of conditions, the community will be taken over by the corrupt, the greedy, the unsavory. You can bet your life on that. Resilience cannot be promoted in such an atmosphere.

Here are recent examples of resilient communities. One is a community after a hurricane: In 1998, Hurricane Mitch settled over Honduras and Nicaragua for days, killing countless people and creating a range of problems and tragedies for the survivors. Yet reports from the region pointed out how quickly the people began helping themselves. Because of the delays in receiving outside help, family members from other parts of the country brought supplies and food to their stricken relatives, many by walking. Teenagers got involved in the relief effort, too, carrying jugs of water on their heads.

This shows the deep pride found in many people that makes them unwilling to see themselves as victims. They want to believe they are capable of dealing with the most severe conditions and experiences, and believing it makes it true. There's no need for pity. They are strong people who will survive. They are resilient. They come from resilient families and resilient communities.

A second example is of a resilient city after the bombing of the World Trade Center: Mary McGrory (2001), a favorite columnist with the *Washington Post*, assessed New Yorkers in their response to the September 11, 2001, tragedy. She said that while New Yorkers don't want to be seen as "nice guys," that is their reputation now. She went on to say that New Yorkers overwhelmed the country with their valor and their human kindness when some 3,000 people lost their lives in the attack on the World Trade Center. She wrote about their exemplary conduct after the fall of the twin towers—especially that of the valorous policemen and fire fighters. Fellow citizens responded with heartbreaking generosity and solicitude, bringing the public servants coffee and sandwiches and socks, and hanging around Ground Zero at all hours to applaud as they came off their shifts. She wrote that New Yorkers have had their famous self-esteem ratified. They feel, with reason, they helped give one in the eye to Osama bin Laden, who did not anticipate their extraordinary resilience and resourcefulness.

RESILIENCE CANNOT BE STOPPED

No one, no group, however oppressive, can kill resilience. In one occupied country where there was no trust and where there was great fear and hatred of the occupiers, groups met in special rooms late at night to share thoughts and feelings, gloat over some undetected trouble they caused the oppressors, and enjoy the moment. Here are some examples of resilient behavior.

A woman met by the writer in an airport described how she and her friends function in a war-torn country. Each morning they telephone each other and check on their safety. Then they decide where they will meet for lunch or to plan some activity. If an area where they plan to meet has been attacked the night before, they change their place of meeting, and continue with the plans. In fact, they accommodate to the situation, while keeping their relationships intact and caring for each other. The woman's greatest concern was not being home to safeguard her children while she was on this necessary trip.

More than 1,100 high school students were to attend a career fair at another school on the morning of September 11, 2001, when the news of the terrorist attacks was first reported. As the students were to arrive by bus any minute, there was no possibility of canceling the fair. The concern of the teachers was for the students. What should they be told? Should the schedule be shortened or changed? Vicky Foote, reporting this event to the writer, indicated that she wanted to go home to her family and that she was frightened. But she was also responsible for the 1,100 students. She knew her demeanor would be very important to lessen the fear she was sure the students would be feeling. She was transfixed by what she saw as the students came in.

These were not the chattering, smiling sophomores from the year before who acted more like 10-year-olds than 15-year-olds, giddy with excitement about having a morning off from school. These students were somber, and painfully thoughtful. They talked in low voices, almost whispers. As I welcomed them and handed them career brochures, several leaned forward and in a hushed voice asked, "Have you heard what happened?" That was all they knew to say.

In the exhibit hall, the television booth, where students were to learn information about careers in communications, quickly became a magnet as students drew close and stared at the screen. Young eyes stared, young foreheads wrinkled, young minds trying to grasp the situation, struggling to understand.

Slowly, some began to ask questions: Will we go to war? Where? Against who? They began to express concern for relatives living near the disaster areas, and for loved ones in the military. Then, amazingly, without any answers to their questions, they moved on to other career booths and began to ask questions about job opportunities in health care, in law enforcement, in teaching, in firefighting. They were students again, trying to gain information to help them make wise career decisions. They were focusing on the future, considering, more than usual, careers in services. I could not help thinking. How brave they are. How totally resilient. I admired them. They were great role models for resilience.

Other examples of the power of resilience include two that the writer has witnessed. First, several women living in a country controlling their lives, even how they must dress, are dropped off at the hotel of the visitor, go to her room, shed the veils and go down to the restaurant, free to express themselves. No one recognizes them because they have always been seen covered. Second, women in airplanes head for the lavatory as soon after takeoff as permitted, remove their veils, and come back in the regular clothes worn beneath. They now begin to talk with passengers, both men and women. The process is reversed when they return.

Resilience shows up even in families or children alone and under constant surveillance in detention camps, far from their war-torn homes. The writer (1999b) analyzed findings from a study by Margaret McCallin (1993). McCallin, of the International Catholic Child Bureau in Geneva, Switzerland, reported on the psychosocial well-being of Vietnamese children in Hong Kong detention centers. Through observations and a series of interviews, she found the worst and the best in the ways those in detention dealt with their situations.

The interviews were conducted with children and youth. McCallin identified six areas that were most damaging to the children and that did not promote or sustain resilience.

- *A pervasive sense of loneliness.* This quality was particularly true of children, regardless of their age, who had no relative with them. These children craved affection, guidance, and help.

- *A deep sense of loss and abandonment.* Much of this resulted from the loss of a parent through death or remarriage.

- *Depression.* This was characterized by a profound lack of initiative and a sense of hopelessness. It was further demonstrated by passivity, and a strong sense of powerlessness. A depressive inertia seemed to grip many of the children. This quality was adaptive in the situation of powerlessness and dependency these children faced, but it did not contribute positively in the long run.

- *Fear for personal safety.* Girls feared sexual assault and harassment. Boys feared bullying by older, more powerful males. Many children reported a strategy of invisibility, withdrawing into reading or studying or neutralizing their appearance through dress, posture, and behavior to appear younger. This way they hoped to avoid being noticed and therefore attacked by predatory elements within the camps.

- *Current stressors.* The main stressor was the separation from their families and the constant worrying about them. A stressor of almost equal intensity was their fear of violence. They were also affected by other daily concerns, such as confinement within the detention center, lack of clothing, and monotonous and unappetizing food. Of greater concern, however, were those who reported no problems in the center at all, despite acknowledging their awareness of the existence of fights, riots, and violence against women in the camps.

- *Delays in screening.* The process for screening to determine if the detainees will be accepted to stay in Hong Kong or be sent back to Vietnam takes years. A constant finding was that this time lag has the most negative impact on the children and youth. Length of time at the center and age of the child combine to heighten the negative impact of the experience. The longer the children are detained and the older they are, the more they lose interest in life.

Evidence of Resilience

How can there be anything positive in such an experience? Surprisingly, many resilience factors were found that helped the children and youth deal with the adverse situation. For example:

- *Hope.* Even though some of the children felt the future seemed hopeless, more than 90 percent had hopes of leading a normal life. The strength of the children, in spite of their experiences, is consistent with the human capacity for resilience.

- *Planning for the future.* Access to education is consistent with planning for the future. Not only was education available at the center, it was used. The unexpected finding was that girls took advantage of the opportunity more than boys. These girls earned higher scores than girls and boys in Hong Kong, scoring two years above Hong Kong students in mean level of education. Such preparation for the future is consistent with hope and confidence. Why the boys were less interested in the opportunity was not clear. They reported spending more time in physical activities with other boys.

- *Feeling in control.* This quality completely contradicts the reality of the situation, and yet 78 percent of the children and youth said that others did not control their lives. This suggests that many of the children made adjustments in their thinking and believing in order to feel in control. They must have had certain small areas of behavior and experiences that allowed them to maintain a sense of control even when they described all the things that made them depressed and afraid. Perhaps the children maintained a sense of their own identity in spite of all that happened. This is not unlike the examples of the women living in the war-torn country or the women shedding their veils.

RESILIENCE TRIUMPHS

As discussed, time was needed to recognize the importance of resilience in dealing with the adversities of life. Research was primarily focused on a deficit, disease model, relying on diagnosis and treatment of identified problems. This model, basically a medical model, was enlarged by the public health model, concerned with the overall health of the nation. The public health model, an epidemiological model, involves counting the number of instances of a particular illness and then supporting research and program development to reduce the unacceptable numbers—a kind of inoculation model.

A new way of thinking was required to shift the focus of attention from disease and vulnerability to well-being and strengths. Resilience became part of the new way of thinking. But even at the beginning, it was difficult to convince groups, such as those involved in mental health, to see resilience as something needed to deal with the inevitable adversities of life. A chief of a mental health department in a government agency was certain that people in good mental health could deal with any adversity. He changed his view when he was told of a boy who was brilliant, who helped his fellow first-graders with their reading, but who could not throw or catch a ball. He was teased and embarrassed and he finally banged his head against a brick wall. He might have been saying that his brains were no good; his successes did not help him now. No one had told him he wouldn't be successful in everything. His mental health from successes and his self-confidence were no match for the adversity of failure and teasing.

The early research on resilience provided the resilience factors, and subsequent research attempted to determine how resilience is promoted and used to deal with the adversities of life. Studies of differences in culture, gender, and age of children indicated that all cultures promote resilience, but with use of different resilience factors; gender differences are mainly important in the manner of dealing with adversities; and the developmental stage of a person determines what resilience factors can be promoted at each stage. Families and the community have special roles in helping children deal with adversities, and they play an especially important role when an adversity comes from acts of terror.

Resilient people can deal with acts of terror. They become stronger as they refuse to succumb to the tragedies perpetrated by terrorists. They can be transformed as they decide to help others who have experienced similar losses. Children become resilient as the resilience factors are promoted at each developmental stage, and as they model the resilient behavior of their parents and other adults. Their resilience is enhanced as they recognize the support of the community, and indeed, the nation, in overcoming the destructive aspects of terrorism. Terrorists have good reason to fear resilient people. Resilience triumphs over terror.

REFERENCES

Baruch, R., Stutman, S., & Grotberg, E. (1995). *What do you tell the children? How to help children deal with disasters.* Washington, DC: Institute for Mental Health Initiatives.

Erikson, E. H. (1985). *Childhood and society.* New York: Norton.

Garmezy, N. (1974). The study of competence in children at risk for severe psychopathology. In E. J. Anthony & C. Koupernick (Eds.), *The child in his family: Children at psychiatric risk* (Vol. 3, pp. 77–97). New York: Wiley.

Grotberg, E. H. (1995). *A guide to promoting resilience in children.* The Hague, Netherlands: Bernard van Leer Foundation: www.resilnet.uiuc.edu (Also available in Spanish and in Polish.)

Grotberg, E. H. (1999a). Countering depression with the five building blocks of resilience. *Reaching Today's Youth, 4,* 66–72.

Grotberg, E. H. (1999b). *Tapping your inner strength.* Oakland, CA: New Harbinger Publications.

Grotberg, E. H. (2000). International resilience research project. In A. L. Comunian & U. Gielen (Eds.), *International perspectives on human development* (pp. 379–399). Vienna, Austria: Pabst Science Publishers.

Grotberg, E. H. (2001a). *Introduccion, nuevas tendencias en resiliencia* (What's new in resilience?). In A. Melillo & N. Suarez-Ojeda (Eds.), *Resiliencia: Discubriendo las proprias fortalezas* (Resilience: Discovering your inner strengths) (pp. 19–30). Buenos Aires, Argentina: Paidos.

Grotberg, E. H. (2001b). Resilience programs for children in disaster. *Ambulatory Child Health, 7,* 75–83.

Grotberg, E. H. (2001c, Spring). Resilience and culture. *International Psychology Reporter*, 13–14.

Masten, A. S., & Coatsworth, J. D. (1998). The development of competence in favorable and unfavorable environments: Lessons from research on successful children. *American Psychologist, 53*, 205–220.

McCallin, M. (1993). *Living in detention*. Geneva, Switzerland: International Catholic Child Bureau.

McGrory, M. (2001, November 25). A nice change in New York. *New York Times*, p. B1.

Rutter, M. (1979). Protective factors in children's responses to stress and disadvantage. *Annals of the Academy of Medicine, Singapore, 8*, 324–338.

Silva, G. (1999). *Resiliencia y violencia politica en ninos* (Resilience in children dealing with political violence). Lanus, Argentina: Universidad Nacional de Lanus.

Suarez-Ojeda, N. (2001). Una concepcion latinoamericana: La resiliencia comunitaria (A Latin American concept: The resilient community). In A. Melillo & N. Suarez-Ojeda (Eds.), *Resiliencia: Discubriendo las proprias fortalezas* (Resilience: Discovering your inner strengths) (pp. 67–82). Buenos Aires, Argentina: Paidos.

Vaillant, G., & Davis, T. (2000). Social/emotional intelligence in mid-life resilience in school boys with low-testing intelligence. *American Journal of Orthopsychiatry, 70*, 215–222.

Werner, E., & Smith, R. S. (1982). *Vulnerable but invincible: A study of resilient children*. New York: McGraw-Hill.

Afterword

Harvey Langholtz
Series Editor
Psychological Dimensions to War and Peace

In the four edited volumes of the *Psychology of Terrorism,* Dr. Chris Stout and forty-three contributing authors have explored terrorism from the perspectives of psychological theory, therapy, history, sociology, political science, international relations, religion, anthropology, and other disciplines. These authors have brought differing viewpoints and they offer different views. In some cases the reader might even wonder if these authors have been addressing different subjects and different realities.

But this is the fundamental anomaly in the study of terrorism. On the one hand, it is easy to oversimplify and explain terrorism. On the other hand, recent events show us how difficult it is truly to understand terrorism, much less to know how to deal with it both reasonably and effectively. There is no universally agreed-upon definition of terrorism. Views on terrorism are often politically driven and it seems to be easier to cloud the discussion than to agree on an understanding. The issue urgently demands immediate solutions but these solutions appear to be a long way off.

As we look back over the ten years that preceded September 11, 2001, it seems we all missed the signals—the bombing of the Khobar Towers in Saudi Arabia, the U.S. embassies in Kenya and Tanzania, the USS *Cole,* and the federal building in Oklahoma City; the gas attack on the Tokyo subway; and of course the 1993 attack on the World Trade Center itself. Did our world actually change on that one day or were we only coming to realize as we watched the events in helpless disbelief that our understanding of the world had been wrong?

In the long view of history, September 11 will be remembered as a day when we were forced in fear and pain to reexamine some of our fundamental assumptions. And in this long view scholars will look to see what the serious and well-considered reactions were in the months following the event as psychologists and others took the time to reflect on the events of the day. That is what the contributing authors to these four volumes have sought to do in the immediate aftermath of the event: To consider terrorism, the causes of terrorism, people's reactions to terrorist acts, interventions to prevent or contain terrorism, and the possible role psychologists can play in understanding, explaining, and limiting terrorism and its effects.

Index

Needs theory: asymmetrical warfare in, 33; and perverse empathy, 30

Nichols, James, 101

Nobel Peace Prize winners, terrorists as, 52

Non-state terrorism, forms of, 132

Oklahoma City bombing, and terrorist's motivations and effect, 77

Order Out of Chaos (Prigogine & Stengers), 153

"Other, the," 113–28; and collectively-held distortions, 118; constructed as enemy, 55–58; defining, 135; dehumanization of, through trauma, 20; and denial, 118; destructive use of, 118–21; fear-based and distorted conceptions of, 115–16, 118, 127; and justification and denial of wrongdoing, 118–19; and justified violence, 126–27; and manipulation/ exploitation dynamics, 120–21; positive conceptualization of, cultivation of, 122–24; and projective identification, 22; psychological process construction of, 113–116, 118; as reference for self-definition, 121–22; situational pliability of, 116–18; stereotyping of, 121, 122, 123; and universal standards of behavior, 124–27; and victim identity, 119–20, 121; and Western commercial influence, 123

Palestinian people: collective trauma of, 22; Western media characterization of, 53

Palestinian-Israeli conflict: escalation of retaliation in, 34; and failure of Oslo accords, 22; mythmaking and construction of the enemy in, 58; Palestinian motive in, 151; suicide bombings in, 32

Paradise Lost (Milton), 27

Patriotism, political mobilization of, 177

Peace initiatives: loss of credibility of, 37–38; in Sri Lanka, 131, 137; and talking with the enemy, 137

Pearl, Daniel, 27

People's Republic of China, murderous regimes of, 51

Persian Gulf War, 62

Personality theory, chaos and order in, 153–54

Pierce, William, 49, 50, 52, 88*n*2

Political assassinations, and procedural justice requirements, 77

Political evolution: and concept of redemption, 40; and reduction of violence, 36–37

Political psychology: and contradictory worldviews, 176; and dualistic/polarizing thinking, 174, 176–79, 181; in service of understanding terrorism, 176, 180–81

Political strategists, terrorists as, 99, 109

Political violence: moral justification for, 59; in social theory, 9, 50, 54–79. *See also* Religio- and ethnopolitical violence; Violence

Positive feedback spiral: asymmetrical warfare and, 33–34, 37; de-escalation of violence and, 34; retaliation and, 19; in systems theory, 33–34

Prabhakaran, Velupillai, 100, 104

Prigogne, Ilya, 153

Primitive Edge of Experience, The (Ogden), 24

Projective identification: terrorism and, 19, 22; traumatic reenactment, 29–30

Psychological models of terrorist motivations, 2–3

Psychological mutation: and malevolent transformation, 23–25; as response to trauma, 19

Psychological pathology, and terrorist acts, 101–3, 108

Psychology of peace, as framework for terrorist studies, 9

Psychology of terrorism/terrorists: behavioral perspective on, 9–14; Hacker's categorization of, 2; limited utility of models of, 2–3

Psychospiritual practice, transcending terrorism through, 182–83

Punishment: of child, physical versus verbal, 191; and susceptibility to authority, 22

Rabin, Yitzhak: murder of, 64; and procedural justice requirements, 77

Radical right, U.S.: and constitutional rights issues, 62; delegitimating discover-

About the Editor and Advisory Board

CHRIS E. STOUT is a clinical psychologist who holds a joint government and academic appointment in the Northwestern University Medical School, and serves as the first Chief of Psychological Services of the state of Illinois. He served as an NGO Special Representative to the United Nations, was appointed by the U.S. Department of Commerce as a Baldrige Examiner, and served as an advisor to the White House for both political parties. He was appointed to the World Economic Forum's Global Leaders of Tomorrow. He has published or presented more than three hundred papers and twenty-two books. His works have been translated into five languages. He has lectured across the nation and in sixteen countries and has visited more than fifty nations. He has been on missions around the world and has reached the top of three of the world's Seven Summits. He was Distinguished Alumni of the Year from Purdue University and Distinguished Psychologist of the Year, in addition to receiving more than thirty other postdoctoral awards. He is past President of the Illinois Psychological Association and is a member of the National Academy of Practice. He has been widely interviewed by the media, including CNBC, CNN, Oprah, *Time*, the *Chicago Tribune*, and the *Wall Street Journal*, and was noted as "one of the most frequently cited psychologists in the scientific literature" by Hartwick College. A distinct honor was his award as one of ten Volunteers of the Year in Illinois, and both the Senate and House have recognized his work by proclamation of "Dr. Chris E. Stout Week."

DANA ROYCE BAERGER is a practicing clinical and forensic psychologist in Chicago. She specializes in issues related to children, families, mental health, and the legal system. She is on the clinical faculty of the Department of Psychiatry and Behavioral Sciences at Northwestern University Medical School, and is also a staff member of the Children and Family Justice Center at Northwestern University Law School. In her private practice she provides psychotherapy services to individuals, couples, and groups; consults with attorneys regarding clinical and forensic practice standards; and consults with mental health professionals regarding ethical and risk management issues.

TERRENCE J. KOLLER is a practicing clinical psychologist in Chicago. He also serves as Executive Director and Legislative Liaison of the Illinois Psychological Association. He is Clinical Assistant Professor of Psychology in the Department of Psychiatry at the University of Illinois Medical School in Chicago. His areas of expertise include attachment and loss, parent-child interaction, and ethical and legal issues relating to the practice of psychology. He was the 1990 recipient of the Illinois Psychological Association's Distinguished Psychologist Award, and received an honorary doctor of humane letters degree from the Chicago School of Professional Psychology in 1995.

STEVEN P. KOURIS is associate chairman of the Department of Psychiatry at the University of Illinois College of Medicine in Rockford and medical director of the Jack Mabley Developmental Center in Dixon, Illinois. A medical graduate of Des Moines University, he interned at the Mayo Clinic and served clinical residencies at the University of Michigan and Detroit Medical Centers. He also completed an epidemiology research fellowship at the Minnesota Department of Health, and earned degrees in environmental health from the University of Minnesota and in preventive medicine from the University of Wisconsin. An accomplished clinician, teacher, and researcher, he is certified in multiple areas of psychiatry and medicine, and specializes in pediatric and developmental neuropsychiatry.

RONALD F. LEVANT is Dean and professor of psychology at the Center for Psychological Studies at Nova Southeastern University. He chairs the American Psychological Association (APA) Committee on Psychology's Response to Terrorism, and is a Fellow of APA Divisions 1, 12, 17, 27, 29, 31, 39, 42, 43, and 51. He has served on the faculties of Boston University, Harvard Medical School, and Rutgers University. He has authored or edited thirteen books and more than one hundred refereed journal articles and book chapters. He has served as Editor of the *Journal of Family Psychology*, is an Associate Editor of *Professional Psychology: Research and Practice*, and is an advisory editor or consulting editor to the following journals: *American Journal of Family Therapy, Journal of Marriage and Family Therapy, Men and Masculinities, Psychology of Men and Masculinity, Journal of African American Men, Journal of Trauma Practice, In Session: Psychotherapy in Practice*, and *Clinical Psychology: Science and Practice*.

MALINI PATEL is clinical associate professor of psychiatry and behavioral sciences at Finch University of Health Sciences/Chicago Medical School, and Acting Medical Director at a state psychiatric facility. She is board certified with added qualifications in addiction psychiatry. She is actively involved in resident and medical student training programs and has received awards for her teaching and contributions to psychiatric education. She also practices in a community mental health clinic where she sees patients in the Dual Diagnosis and Assertive Community Treatment Programs. She has published and presented on topics related to court-ordered treatment, administrative psychiatry, and substance abuse.

About the Contributors

SHARIF ABDULLAH is an adjunct faculty member at Marylhurst University and Portland State University. An author, proponent, and catalyst for inclusive social, cultural, and spiritual transformation, his work as a humanistic globalist has taken him to more than two dozen countries and to every continent. He received a B.A. in psychology from Clark University and a J.D. from Boston University. He has appeared on several international globalization forums. His writings include *The Power of One: Authentic Leadership in Turbulent Times*. He is founder and president of Commonway Institute in Portland, Oregon.

RUBÉN ARDILA is Professor of Psychology at the National University of Colombia (Bogota, Colombia). He has published twenty-three books and more than one hundred and fifty scientific papers in different languages, mainly Spanish and English. He founded the *Latin American Journal of Psychology* and has been the editor of this journal for several years. His main areas of research are the experimental analysis of behavior, social issues, peace psychology, and international psychology. He has been a visiting professor in the United States, Germany, Spain, Argentina, and Puerto Rico. He is a member of the executive committee of the International Union of Psychological Science.

BENJAMIN BEIT-HALLAHMI received his Ph.D. in clinical psychology from Michigan State University in 1970. Since then he has held clinical, research, and teaching positions in the United States, Europe, and Israel. He is the author, coauthor, editor, or coeditor of seventeen books and monographs on the psychology of religion, social identity, and personality development. In addition, he has a special interest in questions of ethics and ideology in psychological research and practice. In 1993, he was the recipient of the William James Award for his contributions to the psychology of religion.

FRED BEMAK is currently a Professor and the Program Coordinator for the Counseling and Development Program at the Graduate School of Education at George Mason University. He has done extensive work in the area of refugee and immigrant psychosocial adjustment and mental health. He has given seminars and lectures and conducted research throughout the United States and in more than thirty countries in the areas of cross-cultural psychology and the psychosocial adjustment of refugees and immigrants. He is a former Fulbright Scholar, a Kellogg International Fellow, and a recipient of the International Exchange of Experts and Research Fellowship through the World Rehabilitation Fund. He has been working nationally and internationally in the area of refugee adjustment and acculturation for the past twenty years as a researcher, clinician, and clinical consultant and has numerous publications in the area. He has recently written a book in collaboration with Rita Chi-Ying Chung and Paul Pedersen, *Counseling Refugees: A Psychosocial Approach to Innovative Multicultural Interventions*, published by Greenwood Publishing.

BRENDA ANN BOSCH is Clinical and Research Coordinator, Senior Clinical Psychologist, and Lecturer in the Department of Medically Applied Psychology, Nelson R. Mandela School of Medicine, University of Natal, Durban, South Africa. She is a member of several scientific organizations and professional societies. She is a consultant in clinical neuropsychology/disability, dissociative disorders in forensic psychology, traumatic stress, and peer supervision. Her current research and publication thrusts include the relationship between stress and neuropsychological deficits, stress and psycho-oncology, the intensive care unit, and mortuaries/law enforcement.

HENRY BREED has worked more than a decade in the United Nations, having been a Humanitarian Affairs Officer, Assistant to the Under-Secretary-General for Peacekeeping, and Assistant to the Special Representative of the Secretary-General to the former Yugoslavia and to the North Atlantic Treaty Organization. He is currently Political Affairs Officer in the Office of the Iraq Programmed. In past posts, he has been called upon to go to Mozambique, Rwanda, and the former Yugoslavia. In his current post, he has been closely involved in a broad range of international activities within Iraq. He has worked as a consulting editor for UNESCO on issues including education, development, and cultural preservation, and he has been actively involved in a range of environmental activities related to the Earth Summit. Born in Norway and raised in New York, he received undergraduate degrees in music and fine arts from Indiana University in Bloomington. He also holds a master's degree in public administration from Harvard University, a diplôme in international history and politics from the Graduate Institute of International Studies in Geneva, and a master's in international affairs from Columbia University. A member of the Council on Foreign Relations and of the International Institute of Strategic Studies, he was awarded the Beale Fellowship at Harvard and was admitted to the academic fraternity Pi Kappa Lambda at Indiana University. He is also a Fulbright Scholar, a "boursier de la Confédération Suisse," and a Regents Scholar. He lives in New York.

GIOVANNI CARACCI is a Clinical Associate Professor of Psychiatry at the Mount Sinai School of Medicine and Director of Residency Training and Medical Student Education at the Mount Sinai School of Medicine (Cabrini) Program. He is the Chair of the World Psychiatric Association on Urban Mental Health and a member of the Commission on Global Psychiatry of the American Psychiatric Association. He represents the World Psychiatric Association at the United Nations in New York, where he is Chair of the Non Governmental Organizations Executive Committee on Mental Health and Treasurer of the NGO Executive Committee of HABITAT (Center for Human Settlement). His main fields of expertise are international mental health, education, and cultural issues in mental health.

RITA CHI-YING CHUNG received her Ph.D. in psychology at Victoria University in Wellington, New Zealand. She is currently an Associate Professor in the Counseling and Development Program in the Graduate School of Education at George Mason University. She was awarded a Medical Research Council (MRC) Fellowship for postdoctoral work in the United States. Following the MRC fellowship, she remained as a Project Director for the National Research Center on Asian American Mental Health at the University of California, Los Angeles. In addition, she has been a visiting professor at the Federal University of Rio Grande do Sul in Brazil, Johns Hopkins University, and George Washington University, and a consultant for the World Bank. She has conducted research and written extensively on Asian immigrants and refugee mental health and has worked in the Pacific Rim, Asia, Europe, and Latin America. She has recently written a book in collaboration with Fred Bemak and Paul Pedersen, *Counseling Refugees: A Psychosocial Approach to Innovative Multicultural Interventions*, published by Greenwood Publishing.

JOHN M. DAVIS is Professor of Psychology at Southwest Texas State University. He completed advanced work at two German universities and received his Ph.D. in experimental/social psychology from the University of Oklahoma. He has lived and worked as a psychologist in Germany, China, England, and the United States. He has researched and published in the areas of interpersonal relations, refugee stress/adaptation, health psychology, and international psychology. Recent publications include a book chapter (1999) on health psychology in international perspective and an invited article (2000) on international psychology in the prestigious *Encyclopedia of Psychology* (APA/Oxford University Press). His current research interests include international terrorism from the perspectives of social and international psychology, and the influences of ethnic self-identity and attitude similarity on interpersonal and intergroup attraction.

ARTHUR A. DOLE is Professor Emeritus at the University of Pennsylvania Graduate School of Education, and former Chair of the Psychology in Education Division. He is a member of the Board of Directors of AFF, a nonprofit organization that encourages education and research about abusive groups, and a consulting editor of the *Cultic Studies Journal.* His research has focused on the harmfulness of cultic groups.

BORIS DROZDEK is a psychiatrist working at the GGZ Den Bosch/Outpatient and Daytreatment Centre for Refugees, the Netherlands. He is researching, publishing, and teaching in the field of psychotrauma and forced migration.

JONATHAN T. DRUMMOND is a doctoral student in social psychology at Princeton University. Prior to beginning doctoral work, he taught at the United States Air Force (USAF) Academy in the Department of Behavioral Sciences and Leadership as a major in the USAF. His research interests include psychological construction and attributions of legitimacy about political and judicial institutions in the United States and South Asia, retaliatory violence, white separatism, and divergent Aryan identity narratives (present and historical) in Indian Hindutva, Sinhalese Buddhism, and Euro-American Wotanism.

SOLVIG EKBLAD, a clinical psychologist, is Adjunct Associate Professor in Transcultural Psychology at the Karolinska Institutet, Department of Neurotec, Section of Psychiatry, Stockholm, Sweden. She is also Head of the Unit for Immigrant Environment and Health at the National Institute of Psychosocial Factors and Health, Solna, Sweden. She is in charge of the research group "Transcultural Psychology" and supervises Ph.D. and master's level students. At present, she has research grants from the National Swedish Integration Office, the European Refugee Fund, and the Stockholm County Council. She is collaborating with several foreign and local research teams. She is Co-Chair for the International Committee of Refugees and Other Migrants (ICROM), World Federation for Mental Health. She has written many articles and book chapters and has presented papers at international and national conferences in the field of migration and mental health.

SALMAN ELBEDOUR received his Ph.D. in school psychology from the University of Minnesota. After working at Ben-Gurion University, Israel, for six years, and at Bir Zeit University in the Palestinian Authority, he joined the School of Education at Howard University. He is currently an Associate Professor and the Coordinator of the School Psychology Program. His research and clinical interests are focused on psychopathology, maltreatment, child abuse, and neglect. He has published in the areas of cross-cultural and developmental studies of young children and adolescents placed at risk, specifically children exposed to political unrest, family conflict, and school violence. He has published extensively on the impact of the Israeli-Arab conflict on the development and socialization of children in the region. His Ph.D. thesis, "Psychology of Children of War," investigated the traumatic risk, resilience, and social and moral development of Palestinian children of the uprising, or *intifada.*

J. HAROLD ELLENS is a retired Professor of Philosophy, Theology, and Psychology, as well as the author, coauthor, and/or editor of 68 books and 148 professional journal articles. He spent his professional life on the issues involved in the interface of psychology and theology, served for fifteen years as Executive Director of the Christian Association for Psychological Studies, and as Founding Editor and Editor-in-Chief of the *Journal of Psychology and Christianity*. He holds a Ph.D. from Wayne State University in the psychology of human communication, a Ph.D. from the University of Michigan in Biblical and Near Eastern Studies, and master's degrees from Calvin Theological Seminary, Princeton Theological Seminary, and the University of Michigan. His publications include *God's Grace and Human Health* and *Psychotheology: Key Issues*, as well as chapters in *Moral Obligation and the Military, Baker Encyclopedia of Psychology, Abingdon Dictionary of Pastoral Care*, and *Humanistic Psychology*. He is currently a research scholar at the University of Michigan, Department of Near Eastern Studies. He is also a retired Presbyterian theologian and minister, and a retired U.S. Army Colonel.

TERI L. ELLIOTT is a clinical psychologist in New York City, specializing in children and adolescents. She is an Assistant Professor at the Disaster Mental Health Institute (DMHI), where she focuses on children and violence, bullying interventions, disaster response and preparedness, and psychological responses to weapons of mass destruction. She teaches and consults nationally and internationally on topics including children and trauma, crisis intervention, psychological support, and refugee mental health.

STEPHEN D. FABICK is a consulting and clinical psychologist in Birmingham, Michigan. He is past President of Psychologists for Social Responsibility (PsySR), past Chair of the PsySR Enemy Images program, and current Chair of its Conflict Resolution Action Committee. He is also Chair of the Conflict Resolution Working Group of the Society for the Study of Peace, Conflict and Violence (Division 48 of the American Psychological Association). His interest has been in conflict transformation and prejudice reduction. He authored *US & THEM: The Challenge of Diversity*, a Workshop Presenter's Manual. The program was included in President Clinton's Initiative on Race Relations and selected by the Center for Living Democracy as a model program in their book *Bridging the Racial Divide*. The program focuses on transforming group prejudice and conflict.

DON J. FEENEY, JR., is a clinical psychologist and Executive Director of Consulting Psychological Services in Chicago. In practice for more than twenty-five years, he has authored books including *Entrancing Relationships* (Praeger, 1999) and *Motifs: The Transformative Creation of Self* (Praeger, 2001).

RONA M. FIELDS is a clinical psychologist and Senior Associate at Associates in Community Health and Development and Associates in Community Psychology, in Washington, D.C. She has been an Assistant Professor at California State University, a Professor at the California School of Professional Psychology, and an Adjunct Professor at George Mason University and the American School of Professional Psychology. Her research includes studies of terrorism, violence and prejudice, peace-keeping operations and hostage negotiations, and treating victims of torture.

TIMOTHY GALLIMORE is a certified mediator, facilitator, and third-party neutral in conflict resolution. He researches and writes on trauma healing and reconciliation and on violence prevention. He earned a Ph.D. in mass communication from Indiana University in 1992. He was a consultant to the United Nations Development Program for Women and on the USAID Rwanda Rule of Law project to institute a community restorative justice system for trying genocide suspects.

TED G. GOERTZEL is Professor of Sociology at Rutgers University in Camden, New Jersey. His books include *Turncoats and True Believers, Linus Pauling: A Life in Science and Medicine,* and *Fernando Henrique Cardoso: Reinventing Democracy in Brazil.* His articles include "The Ethics of Terrorism and Revolution" and "Myths of Murder and Multiple Regression," and can be found on his Web site at http://goertzel.org/ted.

EDITH HENDERSON GROTBERG, a developmental psychologist, works for the Civitan International Research Center at the University of Alabama, Birmingham, and with the Institute for Mental Health Initiatives, George Washington University, Washington, D.C. Through the International Resilience Research Project (IRRP), she found many answers to the role of resilience in understanding and enhancing human health and behavior. Her articles have been published in *Ambulatory Child Health* and *The Community of Caring,* and some of her books on resilience have been translated into other languages.

RAYMOND H. HAMDEN is a clinical psychologist and Director of Psychology Services at the Comprehensive Medical Center in Dubai, United Arab Emirates. Born in the United States, he was a 1986 Visiting Fellow at the University of Maryland, College Park, Center for International Development and Conflict Management. His research and consultations focused on the psychology of the terrorist and hostage situations. He earned a Ph.D. at Heed University, Department of Psychology, and continued postgraduate study in psychoanalysis at the Philadelphia School of Modern Psychoanalysis. In 1990, he moved to the United Arab Emirates and established his own practice. He holds adjunct faculty positions at institutions including the University of Indianapolis, and has taught at the American Universities in Dubai and Sharjah. He holds Diplomate and Fellow status at the American College of Forensic Examiners and the American Academy of Sexologists. He is licensed by the Dubai Department of Health and Medical Services, as well as by the Board of Psychology Examiners in Washington, D.C. He is also a member of the International Society for Political Psychology and the International Council of Psychologists. He is an ACFE Diplomate, American Board of Psychological Specialties.

FADEL ABU HEIN is a community and clinical psychologist on the faculty of Al Aksa University in Gaza. He was for many years the senior psychologist at the Gaza Community Health Center, where he developed the research program and also instituted a broad outreach service for a traumatized population that had no other mental health resource. He has more recently established his own clinical practice in Gaza in conjunction with his teaching responsibilities at Al Aksa University.

CRAIG HIGSON-SMITH is a research psychologist employed in the Child, Youth and Family unit of the Human Sciences Research Council of South Africa. He is a specialist researcher in the fields of violence and traumatic stress. Previously, he cofounded and managed the KwaZulu-Natal Programme for Survivors of Violence, a nongovernment organization dedicated to supporting communities ravaged by civil conflict in Southern Africa. More recently, he cofounded the South African Institute for Traumatic Stress.

J. E. (HANS) HOVENS is a clinical psychologist and psychiatrist. He has published extensively on the subject of post-traumatic stress disorder. Currently, he is a lecturer on psychiatry at the Delta Psychiatric Teaching Hospital in Poortugaal, the Netherlands.

NIRA KFIR is a clinical psychologist who received her Ph.D. in social psychiatry at the Université de Paris, Sorbonne, Center for Social Psychiatry. She is the Director of Maagalim-Institute of Psychotherapy and Counseling in Tel Aviv. In 1973, she developed a Crisis Intervention program adopted by the Israeli Ministry of Defense, and it is still in use for group work with bereaved families. She developed the psychotherapeutic diagnostic system of Personality Impasse/Priority Therapy.

OLUFEMI A. LAWAL is a Ph.D. candidate at the University of Lagos, Akoka-Yaba, Lagos, Nigeria. He has been a teacher and coordinator at St. Finbarr's College in Lagos, and is now an instructor at Quantum Educational Services, Ilupeju, Ibadan, Oyo.

JOHN E. LeCAPITAINE is Professor and former Chair of the Department of Counseling and School Psychology, University of Wisconsin, River Falls. He has a doctorate in counseling psychology (Boston University), a doctorate in metaphysics, a master of science in school psychology, and a bachelor of science in mathematics. He is a Diplomate Forensic Psychologist and a member of the International Council of Psychologists, the American Psychological Association, the American College of Forensic Examiners, the Institute of Noetic Sciences, the National Association of School Psychologists, and *Who's Who in the World*. He has written a number of articles, receiving the Special Merit award from *Education* for *Schools as Developmental Clinics: Overcoming the Shadow's Three Faces*.

JOHN E. MACK is a Pulitzer Prize–winning author and Professor of Psychiatry at Harvard Medical School who has explored how cultural worldviews may obscure solutions to social, ecological, and spiritual crises. He is the founder of the Center for Psychology and Social Change. He also founded the Department of Psychiatry at the Cambridge Hospital in 1969. In 1983 he testified before Congress on the psychological impact of the nuclear arms race on children. He is the author or coauthor of ten books, including *A Prince of Our Disorder*, a Pulitzer Prize–winning biography of T. E. Lawrence, and, most recently, *Passport to the Cosmos.*

SHERRI McCARTHY is an Associate Professor of Educational Psychology at Northern Arizona University's Yuma campus. She has published research in international journals on a variety of topics, including developing critical thinking skills, anger management training, substance abuse counseling, and the role of psychology in improving society. She has also written books in the areas of special education and grief and bereavement issues. She is active in the International Council of Psychologists' Psychology and Law interest group. She is also active in the American Psychological Association, serving as the Division 2 Teaching of Psychology liaison to the Council on International Relations in Psychology and as the leader of the P3 Global Psychology Project.

CLARK McCAULEY is a Professor of Psychology at Bryn Mawr College and serves as a faculty member and Co-Director of the Solomon Asch Center for Study of Ethnopolitical Conflict at the University of Pennsylvania. He received his Ph.D. in social psychology from the University of Pennsylvania in 1970. His research interests include stereotypes and the psychology of group identification, group dynamics and intergroup conflict, and the psychological foundations of ethnic conflict and genocide. His recent work includes a new measure of intergroup contact, "the exposure index."

STEVE S. OLWEEAN is a psychotherapist with a degree in clinical psychology from Western Michigan University. He is President of the Association for Humanistic Psychology (AHP), and Founding Director of Common Bond Institute. Since 1990, he has served as AHP International Liaison and Coordinator of International Programs. His principal treatment area is trauma and abuse recovery and reframing negative belief systems. His primary international focus is conflict transformation, forgiveness, reconciliation, and humanitarian recovery efforts. He cofounded and each year coordinates the Annual International Conference on Conflict Resolution held in St. Petersburg, Russia. He also developed an integrated Catastrophic Trauma Recovery (CTR) treatment model for treating large populations experiencing trauma due to war, violence, and catastrophe.

DIANE PERLMAN is a clinical psychologist in Pennsylvania, with a special interest in political psychology. She is Co-Chair of the American Psychological Association Committee on Global Violence and Security within Division 48, the Society for the Study of Peace, Conflict, and Violence. She is also a research associate with the Citizens Panel on Ultimate Weapons at the Center on Violence and Human

Survival. She is Vice President of the Philadelphia Project for Global Security, and Liaison to the psychology community for the Global Nonviolent Peace Force. She is also Founding Member of and a research associate for the Transcending Trauma Project, studying adaptation of Holocaust survivors and their children. She is a Fellow of the Solomon Asch Center for Study of Ethnopolitical Conflict at the University of Pennsylvania and was a speaker for two decades for Physicians for Social Responsibility.

MARC PILISUK is a clinical and social psychologist. He is Professor Emeritus of the University of California and a Professor at the Saybrook Graduate School and Research Center in San Francisco. He is a past President of APA Division 48, the Society for the Study of Peace, Conflict, and Violence; a member of the steering committee of Psychologists for Social Responsibility; and one of the founders of the first teach-in.

JERRY S. PIVEN is a Professor of Psychology at New School University and New York University, where his courses focus on the psychology of religion, death, and sexuality. He is a member of the National Psychological Association for Psychoanalysis and author of *Death and Delusion: A Freudian Analysis of Mortal Terror*. He is editor of the series Psychological Undercurrents of History and is presently working on a psychoanalytic exploration of the madness and perversion of Yukio Mishima.

WILLIAM H. REID is a Clinical and Adjunct Professor of Psychiatry at the University of Texas Health Science Center, Texas A&M College of Medicine, and Texas Tech University Medical Center. He is past President of the American Academy of Psychiatry and the Law. He is a fellow of the Royal College of Physicians, American College of Psychiatrists, and American Psychiatric Association. He is also past Chair of the National Council of State Medical Directors, and a U.S. Observer for the Board of Presidents of the Socialist Countries' Psychiatric Associations, Sofia, Bulgaria. He was U.S. Representative, Ver Heyden de Lancey Conference on Psychiatry, Law, and Public Policy at Trinity College, Cambridge University, as well as visiting lecturer, Hunan Medical College, Changsha, Hunan.

LOURENS SCHLEBUSCH is Professor and Head of the Department of Medically Applied Psychology, Nelson R. Mandela School of Medicine, University of Natal, Durban, South Africa. He is a suicidologist, stress management and medico-legal/disability consultant, Chief Clinical Psychologist for the Hospital Services of the KwaZulu-Natal Provincial Administration, and Chief Consultant in Behavioural Medicine at various hospitals in Durban, South Africa. He is a member of many scientific editorial boards, organizations, and societies, and is a reviewer of scientific publications both nationally and internationally. He has many professional listings, honors, and awards. He has made many significant research contributions to his field and has published widely. He is currently researching various aspects of traumatic stress and suicide prevention.

KLAUS SCHWAB is Founder and President of the World Economic Forum, an organization committed to improving the state of the world, and based in Geneva, Switzerland. He has worked in several high-level roles with the United Nations and is now a Professor at the University of Geneva. He studied at the Swiss Federal Institute of Technology, the University of Fribourg, and the John F. Kennedy School at Harvard University.

KATHY SEXTON-RADEK is Professor of Psychology at Elmhurst College and Director of Psychological Services, Hinsdale Hospital/Suburban Pulmonary and Sleep Associates. She has designed conflict resolution and stress management curriculums for elementary and secondary school children and has implemented these programs with inner-city students at risk for violence and substance abuse. She has also constructed and taught anti-violence workshops for teachers. She is the author of more than thirty peer-reviewed articles in the areas of behavioral medicine, applied cognitive behavior theory in school settings, and psychology pedagogy. She is an elected member of her local school board, and a member of the American Psychological Association, Sigma Xi, and the Sleep Research Society.

ERVIN STAUB is Professor of Psychology at the University of Massachusetts at Amherst. He has published many articles and book chapters and several books about the influences that lead to caring, helping, and altruism, and their development in children. His upcoming book is *A Brighter Future: Raising Caring and Nonviolent Children.* He has also done extensive research into and writing about the roots and prevention of genocide and other group violence, including his book *The Roots of Evil: The Origins of Genocide and Other Group Violence.* Since 1999, he has been conducting, with collaborators, a project in Rwanda on healing, reconciliation, and other avenues to the prevention of renewed violence. His awards include the Otto Klineberg International and Intercultural Relations Prize of the Society for the Psychological Study of Social Issues. He has been President of the Society for the Study of Peace, Conflict, and Violence (Division 48 of the American Psychological Association) and of the International Society for Political Psychology.

MICHAEL J. STEVENS is a Professor of Psychology at Illinois State University in Normal. He is a Fellow of the American Psychological Association, serving as Chair of the Committee for International Liaisons of the Division of International Psychology. He is also a member of the Advisory Board of the Middle East Psychological Network. He is an honorary professor at the Lucian Blaga University of Sibiu, Romania, where he completed Fulbright and IREX grants. In 2000, he received the Recognition Award from the American Psychological Association for his work in international psychology.

TREVOR STOKES is Professor of Child and Family Studies, Professor of Psychology, Professor of Psychological and Social Foundations of Education, and Professor of Special Education at the University of South Florida, Tampa. He received his bachelor's degree with first-class honors in psychology at the University of Western

Australia, a Ph.D. in developmental and child psychology from the University of Kansas, and Ph.D. Clinical Psychology Augmentation at West Virginia University. His research, teaching, and clinical activities involve the behavior analysis and developmental assessment of aggression within families, with a focus on techniques for interception of violent repertoires by children.

TIMOTHY H. WARNEKA treats adolescents and children in a community mental health center near Cleveland, Ohio. He specializes in working with sexually aggressive and/or aggressive juveniles. He has studied the martial art of aikido for more than twelve years and incorporates aikido principles into his psychotherapeutic work. He is President of Cleveland Therapists, Ltd. (www.clevelandtherapists. com), a referral site for mental health professionals. He is President of Psyche & Soma Consulting, Ltd., an organization that offers training and consultation on a variety of mental health subjects.

MICHAEL WESSELLS is Professor of Psychology at Randolph-Macon College and Senior Technical Advisor for the Christian Children's Fund. He has served as President of the Division of Peace Psychology of the American Psychological Association and of Psychologists for Social Responsibility. His research examines psychology of terrorism, psychosocial assistance in emergencies, post-conflict reconstruction, and reintegration of former child soldiers. In countries such as Angola, Sierra Leone, East Timor, Kosovo, and Afghanistan, he helps to develop community-based, culturally grounded programs that assist children, families, and communities affected by armed conflict.

ANGELA WONG is a University of California student in sociology and social welfare. She is a research assistant and an intern providing assistance at homeless shelters.